Religion and Inequality in Africa

Bloomsbury Studies in Black Religion and Cultures

Series Editors: Anthony B. Pinn and Monica R. Miller

Bloomsbury Studies in Black Religion and Cultures advances innovative scholarship that reimagines and animates the global study of black religions, culture, and identity across space and time. The series publishes scholarship that addresses the mutually constitutive nature of race and religion and the social, cultural, intellectual, and material effects of religio-racial formations and identities. The series welcomes projects that address and foreground the intersectional and constitutive nature of black religions and cultures and privileges work that is inter/transdisciplinary and methodologically intersectional in nature.

African Spirituality, Politics and Knowledge Systems
Toyin Falola

Black Transhuman Liberation Theology
Philip Butler

Innovation and Competition in Zimbabwean Pentecostalism
Edited by Ezra Chitando

Religion and Inequality in Africa

Edited by
Ezra Chitando, Loreen Maseno and Joram Tarusarira

BLOOMSBURY ACADEMIC
LONDON • NEW YORK • OXFORD • NEW DELHI • SYDNEY

BLOOMSBURY ACADEMIC
Bloomsbury Publishing Plc
50 Bedford Square, London, WC1B 3DP, UK
1385 Broadway, New York, NY 10018, USA
29 Earlsfort Terrace, Dublin 2, Ireland

BLOOMSBURY, BLOOMSBURY ACADEMIC and the Diana logo
are trademarks of Bloomsbury Publishing Plc

First published in Great Britain 2023
This paperback edition published 2024

Series design: Maria Rajka
Cover image: Traditional Imigongo art on display in Rwanda
© Stuart Forster / Alamy Stock Photo

A catalogue record for this book is available from the British Library.

Library of Congress Control Number: 2022942273

ISBN: HB: 978-1-3503-0737-7
          PB: 978-1-3503-0741-4
          ePDF: 978-1-3503-0738-4
          eBook: 978-1-3503-0739-1

Series: Bloomsbury Studies in Black Religion and Cultures

Typeset by Integra Software Services Pvt. Ltd.

Contents

Contributors

Kudzai Biri is Associate Professor in the Department of Philosophy, Religion and Ethics at the University of Zimbabwe. She specializes in African Indigenous Religions and Christianity with a focus on religion and gender and religion and politics. Her recent publication is *The Wounded Beast? Pentecostalism, Tradition and Single Good in Zimbabwe.*

Mário Jorge Carlos is a postgraduate in rural sociology and development management, Faculty of Arts and Social Sciences, University Eduardo Mondlane, and a postgraduate in education and development, Technical University of Mozambique. Currently, he works in a non-governmental organization, ADPP-Mozambique, as a senior grant administrator. His research interests include civil society and development. His recent publications include Carlos, M. J. 2022. 'The Role of the Council of Religions and Peace in Mozambique (COREM) in Peace and Reconciliation, 2012–2019,' in E. Chitando and I. S. Gusha, eds, *Interfaith Networks and Development. Sustainable Development Goals Series.* Palgrave Macmillan, Cham. https://doi.org/10.1007/978-3-030-89807-6_12

Sinenhlanhla Sithulisiwe Chisale is Research Associate at the University of Pretoria, Department of Practical Theology and Mission Studies. Her research interests include practical theology/pastoral care and Ubuntu, disability, sexuality, HIV and AIDS, migration, gender, children and youth, sexual and gender-based violence, development and other themes. She has researched and published widely on these themes.

Ezra Chitando serves as Professor of Religious Studies at the University of Zimbabwe and Theology Consultant on HIV for the World Council of Churches. He is also an extraordinary professor at the Desmond Tutu Centre for Religion and Social Justice. He has diverse research and publication interests.

Nadine Bowers Du Toit is Associate Professor in 'Theology and Development' at the Faculty of Theology, University of Stellenbosch. Her research focuses on the intersections between religion, poverty and inequality with a special focus on the role of faith communities in the South African context. Nadine currently serves as the Vice President of the International Academy of Practical Theology.

Dion Forster is Professor and Chair of the Department of Systematic Theology and Ecclesiology at SU, where he is also Director of the Beyers Naudé Centre for Public Theology. His research focuses on issues related to ethics and public theologies.

Simbarashe Gukurume is Social Scientist working at the intersections of sociology and social anthropology and lectures at Sol Plaatje in the Department of Social Sciences (Sociology). He is also Research Associate in the Department of Anthropology and Development Studies at the University of Johannesburg. Simbarashe is interested in questions around youth, Pentecostalism, informality, livelihoods, displacement, money and other forms of youth everyday life.

Sokfa F. John is Postdoctoral Research Fellow at the SARChI in Sustainable Local Livelihoods, University of KwaZulu-Natal. He is also an associate of the Center for Mediation in Africa, University of Pretoria. His research interests are in ethnoreligious conflicts, peacebuilding and mediation, digital conflicts and digital cultures.

Mookgo Solomon Kgatle is Professor of Missiology at the University of South Africa (UNISA). Kgatle is a National Research Foundation (NRF) Y-Rated researcher (2019–24) in the area of African Pentecostalism. Kgatle has published several peer-reviewed articles in various high-impact journals and books in the same field.

Elisabet le Roux, a Sociologist, is Research Director of the Unit for Religion and Development Research in the Faculty of Theology at SU. As a faith and development expert, she conducts mainly qualitative empirical research for international faith-based organizations such as Tearfund and World Vision.

Júlio Machele is Researcher and Assistant Lecturer, History Department, University of Eduardo Mondlane, Mozambique. His research interests include religion, development, inequalities, health and diseases, music and migration.

Tshenolo Jennifer Madigele serves as Lecturer in the Department of Theology and Religious Studies at the University of Botswana. Her research interests include human sexuality, gerontology, Botho philosophy, religion and health, pastoral care and counselling and others. She has also published on other themes.

Alexander Makulilo is Professor of Political Science at the University of Dar es Salaam. He has researched and published widely on democracy, gender, conflicts, development and constitutionalism. Makulilo serves as Chief Editor of the *African Review: A Journal of African Politics, Development and International Affairs*, which is published by Brill.

Loreen Maseno (PhD) is Senior Lecturer, Department of Religion, Theology and Philosophy, Maseno University, Kenya and Research Fellow, Department of Biblical and Ancient Studies, University of South Africa. She has a solid research portfolio and has published extensively.

Jones Hamburu Mawerenga is Lecturer in Systematic Theology and Christian Ethics at the University of Malawi. He is the author of *The Homosexuality Debate in Malawi* (2018) and *Systematic Theology* (2019). His research interests include religion and: sexuality, albinism and abortion.

Mukerrem Miftah is Senior Lecturer at the Ethiopian Civil Service University (ECSU) in Addis Ababa, Ethiopia. Before joining ECSU, he had served as Assistant Professor of African Studies at the Social Sciences University of Ankara (ASBU) in Turkey. He has consulted Ethiopia's House of Federation on the role of elites in nation building in Ethiopia. His publications and research interest focus on policy studies, identity politics in the Horn of Africa, and Islam and Muslims in Ethiopia.

Rahina Muazu is a scholar of Islam. She is currently Visiting Lecturer at the Harvard Divinity School. Her areas of interest include Muslim women in West Africa, Islam, the Qur'an and Gender.

Nicholas Nyachega is a doctoral candidate in African History at the University of Minnesota. His research examines the local quotidian experiences of borderlanders living along the Zimbabwe-Mozambique border. He explores how borderlanders' everyday life goals and desires have changed over time and space, working sometimes in harmony or defiance to nation-state apparatuses of control.

Sonene Nyawo is Senior Lecturer in the Department of Theology and Religious Studies at the University of Eswatini. Her research interests include new religious movements in Africa, women's fertility, climate change, religion and gender, women and peacebuilding.

Kesiwe Phuthi is Administrator and Lecturer at the National University of Science and Technology, (Zimbabwe) Medical School in the Department of Social and Behavioral Sciences. Her research and specialization areas are HIV and AIDS, sexuality, health communication, child marriage and other themes. She has researched and published journal papers around those areas.

Nomatter Sande holds a PhD in religion and social transformation from the University of KwaZulu Natal (South Africa). Nomatter is an African Practical Theologian and Research Fellow at the Research Institute for Theology and Religion (RITR), University of South Africa (UNISA). His research interests include theology, disability studies, missiology and gender issues.

Joram Tarusarira is Assistant Professor of Religion, Conflict and Peacebuilding and former Director of the Centre for Religion, Conflict and Globalization at the University of Groningen. He is the author of *Reconciliation and Religio-political Non-conformism in Zimbabwe* (2016) and co-editor (with E. Chitando) of *Religion and Human Security in Africa* (2019) and *Themes in Religion and Human Security in Africa*, London: Routledge (2020).

Shantelle Weber is Associate Professor in the Faculty of Theology at SU. Her research interests include youth ministry, youth work and development; faith formation; cultural and interreligious studies; religious education and youth, family, ecclesial and societal relationships. She is the current president of the International Association for the Study of Youth Ministry.

Introduction

Religion and inequality in Africa

Ezra Chitando, Loreen Maseno and Joram Tarusarira

The Covid-19 pandemic, whose full effects sent shock waves across most parts of the globe in the first half of 2020, but whose impact will continue to linger for much longer, brought out the inequality that characterizes the world in a very eloquent way. Covid-19 was declared a public health concern by the World Health Organization on 11 March 2020. Who lived, who died and who died-while-living was very much an outcome of inequality. For example, the death rate among African-Americans was almost three times higher than that for other racial groups in the United States (*The Guardian* 20 May 2020). This was replicated in the UK, where six out of ten of the medical staff who died from Covid-19 were of ethnic minority backgrounds (*The Guardian* 25 May 2020). Although some members of royal families and senior politicians from across Europe and North America tested positive, for example, none of them died. This was not due to some divine intervention, but is a vivid demonstration of the reality of inequality. On the other hand, those who are marginalized, including women and girls, the elderly, people with disabilities, those with compromised immune systems, informal sector employees, migrants and others, were more vulnerable. UNAIDS (2020) bluntly referred to the 'extreme inequality that is hardwired into our global economy'. As we have learnt from our engagement with HIV, it is mostly the poor, the marginalized and those on the margins of society who cannot breathe in a world that privileges the rich, the powerful and the advantaged.

Tracing the diverse effects and responses to the pandemic across the continent, including the religious, socio-cultural and public health fraternities, a lot of questions remain unanswered. It is clear that the pandemic has affected people differently and has been responded to in various ways in the Global South. It is also clear that Covid-19 has exacerbated inequalities in many regions of Africa. Ethnicity, race, gender, age and education played a role in exposing the vulnerability to Covid-19 infection. Indeed, far beyond morbidity and mortality, the temporary shutdown of economies sent shock waves through communities. This made families have weakened economic resiliency and reinforced disadvantage, especially among groups that have historically been excluded. Families across Africa experienced pandemic precarity, risks, material and financial insecurity and inequalities even more. The chapters in this book consider inequalities in their various forms.

Inequality matters. It decides who lives and who dies. Unfortunately, as the World Social Report 2020, 'Inequality in a Rapidly Changing World' (UN 2020), highlights, inequality remains pervasive. This threatens the success of achieving the sustainable development goals (SDGs). For example, SDG 10 seeks to achieve 'Reduced Inequality'. However, there is a growing realization that inequality in the world is growing at a worrying pace. *The World Inequality Report* (2018) highlights that economic inequality is increasing globally. Similarly, organizations such as Oxfam have invested a lot in exposing inequality in different parts of world. The Oxfam report, 'Public Good or Private Wealth' (2019), underscores the urgency of addressing global inequality. Globally, indigenous peoples tend to experience inequality in diverse settings (Eversole, McNeish and Cimadamore 2005). Equally telling is the book *Divided: The Perils of Our Growing Inequality* (Johnston 2014), which x-rays the inequality that assaults and haunts the United States. The *South African Journal of Economics* devoted a special issue (2019) on 'inequalities in the least developed countries – some lessons from Africa'.

It is critical to observe that in as much as there is inequality within nations, there is also inequality across nations and regions. Thus, for example, Africa tends to be marginalized in the global economic system. Africa often comes as an after-thought in global affairs. This has resulted in Africa continuing to wallow in poverty, even as there are efforts to change the narrative. There is, therefore, an urgent need for governments, non-governmental organizations, faith-based organizations, the private sector and others to invest in reducing inequality in the world. In order for the movement against inequality to succeed, it needs to undertake an in-depth analysis of how religion both promotes and challenges inequality in various parts of the world. The book *A World of Inequalities: Christian and Muslim Perspectives* (Mosher 2021) is a valuable contribution in this regard. It provides reflections by Christians and Muslims on inequality in our world today. Similarly, the article 'Income Inequality and

Religion Globally, 1970–2050' (Navarro and Skirbekk 2018) underscores the importance of understanding the interface between inequality and religion.

This volume contributes to such an undertaking by focusing on religion and inequality in Africa, dating from the 1950s to the beginning of 2019. As Appau and Mabefam (2020: 262) rightly argue, 'In the fight against extreme poverty in Africa, there is certainly more to be gained by including religious agents and institutions than overlooking them. In Africa, no one can escape the African God.' Religion remains a significant factor of life in Africa and deserves attention from various angles. Addressing inequality in Africa and the world today is not a luxury that a few rich countries or global institutions have. No. It is an imperative. Inequality is an affront to human dignity. It is an egregious evil that demands urgent redress. Religious ideologies, problematic ethical and economic theories and questionable political philosophies have sought to justify inequality. However, all these need to be exposed for their failure (and refusal) to acknowledge the devastation wrought by inequality. We cite one scholar activist at length below to highlight the impact of inequality. Thus,

> inequality is a violation of human dignity; it is a denial of the possibility for everybody's human capabilities to develop. It takes many forms, and it has many effects: premature death, ill-health, humiliation, subjection, discrimination, exclusion from knowledge or from mainstream social life, poverty, powerlessness, stress, insecurity, anxiety, lack of self-confidence and of pride in oneself, and exclusion from opportunities and life-chances. Inequality, then, is not just about the size of wallets. It is a socio-cultural order, which (for most of us) reduces our capabilities to function as human beings, our health, our self-respect, our sense of self, as well as our resources to act and participate in this world.
>
> (Therbon 2013: 1)

Religion and inequality: Shining a light on a significant theme

How can one understand the extreme marginalization and systematic exclusion of the Dalits in India outside the religio-cultural caste system in India (Massey 1995; Rajkumar 2010)? Is it possible to take stock of the low position of women globally without appreciating the power of religious ideologies in the various contexts (Sharma and Young 2007)? Rastafari identity is often a marker of marginality and protest in different parts of the world. These examples confirm the extent to which religion contributes to, or is implicated in, inequality in different contexts.

Critically, but not pursued at length in the current volume, religion simultaneously serves as a resource for resisting inequality. For example, Rastafari is a movement against marginalization and exploitation (Murrell, Spencer and McFarlane 1998). Similarly, women have utilized religion to fight for a place at the table, while the Dalits have sought liberation from within the religions of Hinduism and Christianity. Thus, religion is critical for appreciating and resolving inequality.

Although religion is a factor in understanding inequality, it does not feature in most studies on inequality. For example, the voluminous *Inequality Reader* (Grusky and Szelényi 2018) does not focus on religion. While the *Reader* addresses the variables of race, class and gender, it is important to recognize that religion is equally implicated in inequality and that religion also has a bearing on race, class and gender. Similarly, the *Histories of Global Inequality* (Christiansen and Jensen 2019) glosses over the role of religion in causing, explaining or justifying inequality. Thus, although '[r]eligion plays a central role in creating and maintaining social and economic inequality' (Keister and Eagle 2014: 142), and there are very few scholarly reflections on the interface between religion and inequality, there is some growing interest in the theme.

The situation is even more acute in the context of Africa: only very few studies address the theme of religion and inequality in African settings. For example, Nel (2021) has provocatively argued that religious belief leads to what he regards as the Africans' tolerance of income inequality. Basedau (2017) and Basedau and Schaefer-Kehnert (2019) examine the impact of religious discrimination on violent conflict in Africa. With Christian missionaries having contributed immensely to education in sub-Saharan Africa, it is not surprising that Muslims and adherents of African Traditional Religions tend to lag behind in terms of accessing education (Alesina et al. 2020). Yet education is critical for sustainable development. The following conclusion highlights the extent to which religion is implicated in inequality in Africa. Thus,

> the differences in primary schooling among Christians versus others continue to be so great in some contexts that some perceive formal schooling as an institution made by and for Christians. Although we know that, along other dimensions, religious activity and membership appear to have politically integrative effects…, when it comes to education, religion is, at the very least, a marker – and potentially a driver – of inequality in the region.
>
> (Manglos-Weber 2017: 320)

This volume seeks to fill the *lacuna* in scholarship by focusing on the extent to which religion is implicated in discourses on inequality in Africa. While the interface between religion and gender inequality has received, and continues to receive, attention, especially through the efforts of the Circle of Concerned African Women Theologians (see, for example, Oduyoye 2019), the impact of religion on other forms of inequality remains under-researched and under-theorized. Thus, for example, the relationship between religion and other forms of inequality such as *income inequality, sexuality inequality, political inequality, (dis)ability inequality, age inequality and others* requires serious interrogation in different African contexts. Critically, inequality prevents many members of society from realizing their capability. Thus,

> inequality is a historical social construction which allocates the possibilities of realizing human capacity unequally. It is a historical social construction; it is not something which is given by nature or by God. There are differences which are given, but the important thing about inequality is the unequal allocation of possibilities to realize your human capability.
>
> (Álvarez 2016: 118)

This volume seeks to contribute to the discourses on the SDGs in Africa (see, for example, Ramutsindela and Mickler 2020), as well as religion and development by interrogating religion and inequality in Africa more intently and intensely. Contributors to the volume engage with the interface between religion and various forms of inequality in different African contexts. They highlight the extent to which religion causes, justifies, explains, addresses and counters inequality in its various forms in Africa. The volume, therefore, approaches the discourse on religion and development in Africa through the lens of inequality. As Ogbonnaya (2012) rightly observes, religion is key to the achievement of sustainable development in Africa. For example, SDG 5 seeks to 'achieve gender equality and empower all women and girls'. However, the cooperation of religion is critical since religious ideologies contribute significantly to gender inequality. In a refreshing development where an African male theologian takes the gender debate seriously, Orobator (2018: 141) recognizes the capacity of religion in Africa to contribute towards ending gender inequality.

Religion, therefore, is the proverbial double-edged sword in relation to inequality (as it is in relation to human security, for example): on the one hand, it is implicated in causing or magnifying inequality. On the other hand, religion is well-placed to contribute towards addressing inequality. The book *The Wealth of Religions: The Political Economy of Believing and Belonging* (McCleary and Barrow 2018) highlights the interface between religion and economics, drawing attention to the importance of religion in creating community. These ideas are important for appreciating religion and inequality in Africa. The urgency of debating these issues from an African perspective is critical in a world where NASA can seek to concretize plans to send a toilet worth $23 million into space (Burton 2020). This is at a time when millions of children in Africa die of hunger and malnutrition!

We are cognizant of the emancipatory power of religion. We agree that Judaism and Christianity were originally constituted as emancipatory movements aiming at the liberation of the dominated from their state of servitude. In these religions, God presents God's self as the agent of subversion of social hierarchies. As per liberation theology, God is the one who liberated the Hebrews enslaved in Egypt. The Exodus-motif in Judaism and in Christianity symbolizes that emancipatory dimension. In Chapter 10 of this book, the emancipatory views on gender and disability in African Traditional Religion among the Ndebele and the emancipatory views on gender and disability in Christian Religion are additionally made explicit. Thus, the focus on religion and inequality in this volume in no way suggests negating the emancipatory role of religion in Africa (and elsewhere). Neither should it be taken as refuting religion's significant contribution to development. Our motivation, however, is to highlight the need to understand the interface between religion and inequality in order to enable different actors to implement progressive policies (where religion promotes inequality) and to deepen current practices (where religion challenges inequality).

Religion and inequality: An overview of the concepts

Scholarship is characterized by perpetual debates over the clarification of key concepts. It will be difficult to achieve consensus on the meaning of words or concepts that are used frequently, such as religion and inequality. This is due to the fact that although the concepts are utilized in everyday communication, any effort to define them with precision generates further controversy. For the purposes of this introduction and volume, we have chosen to operate with open definitions of both religion and inequality. Unlike substantive definitions that have an aura of finality, open definitions tend to be more exploratory, tentative and ambiguous (Comstock 1984; Smith 1987). We understand our operational definitions of religion and inequality as temporary and as only facilitating our entry into the relevant discourses. Other scholars might later nuance, amplify and perfect our definitions of these two concepts.

We approach religion as a system of beliefs and practices where individuals and communities interact among themselves and with unseen beings. Our understanding of religion is that it is a highly complex system, with different dimensions (Smart 1996). Crucially for this volume, we recognize that although religion makes reference to the Sacred or the transcendent, it is lived out or experienced in space and time, in the here and now. Thus, religion has definite consequences for the ordering of society or relationships within society (Bourdillon 1990). We contend that religion is a social fact, sometimes with life and death implications for those who participate in it or others who share the same space with actors motivated by religion. We are aware that most religionist scholars of religion in Africa and many theologians are quite uncomfortable with exploring the link between religion and inequality in Africa. Many of them are products of mission schools, are actively involved in leadership of churches (or are active Muslims and traditionalists) and tend to be ultra-defensive when it comes to critical approaches towards religion.

The religionist identity of most African scholars of religion (Cox 1994) implies that they have a very positive rating of religion. They are keen to present religion as a positive social force. In most of the publications on religion and development in Africa, the focus has been on how religion plays a positive role in improving the well-being of individuals and communities. We do sympathize with the positive approach adopted by religionist scholars in Africa. Faced with criticisms of both their field and its subject matter, they have deemed it necessary to concentrate on the progressive dimensions of religion. However, in this volume, we seek to (re)open the debate between religion and inequality in Africa.

Although the definition of religion remains open to debate, what remains clear in sub-Saharan Africa (the focus of this volume) is that religion is central to the lives of most citizens. Thus, in one study, around nine in ten individuals in the region indicated that religion was very important in their lives (Pew 2010: 3). Further, while we are using the singular, religion in Africa is experienced as a widely variegated and proliferated phenomenon. We find African Traditional Religions, the Baha'i Faith, Buddhism, Christianity, Islam, Judaism, Rastafari and numerous other religious movements participating on the African religious market. Each one of these religions seeks to attract or retain a share of the African religious market (see, for example, Stark, Iannaccone and Fink 1996; Jelen 2002 for idea of the market). Although historical factors mean that Christianity tends to receive greater attention (particularly due to its dominance in the formal Western education sector in Africa), it is important to always acknowledge that the African religious scene is characterized by radical pluralism. Tomalin's edited volume *The Routledge Handbook of Religion and Development* (Tomalin 2015) adopts an expanded definition of religion and is quite helpful in the quest to appreciate the role of religion and development in different parts of the world.

Like religion, inequality is a concept that is widely used but is difficult to define. For the most part, most scholars approach inequality in terms of income. This is consistent with the trend of using figures to measure poverty, income, inequality and other variables. Our review of the literature on inequality globally shows that this is the dominant paradigm. United Nations agencies, development practitioners and other researchers favour this approach due to its scientific and appealing outlook. It confirms the emerging tyranny of numbers, as expressed in the dictum, 'if you cannot measure it, it does not exist'. For example, one study made the following submission:

> Our main finding is that Africa stands out as an extreme income inequality region by international standards: with a top 10% national income share of 54% and a bottom 50% share below 10%, Africa has the highest gap between average incomes of the top 10% and incomes of the bottom 50%.
>
> (Chancel et al. 2019: 1)

As can be deduced from the foregoing citation, Africa experiences serious income inequality. Wealth is concentrated in the hands of the minority, while the majority are struggling for survival. While we appreciate the value of putting figures to human experiences, in this volume we also contend that numbers do not tell the complete story. Qualitative approaches are critical when one is studying inequality because behind numbers are flesh and blood human beings who are living (or trying to live out) the realities that are masked by the figures (see, for example, Messer 2010).

We are also convinced that restricting the focus to income inequality does an injustice to the complexity of inequality as a concept. Although income inequality is a significant dimension of inequality, it is not the totality of it. There are other critical dimensions of inequality that need to be examined. In particular, due to our commitment to social justice, we are equally interested in other forms of inequality in Africa. Politically, we are aware of Africa's exclusion from global processes. We are conscious of the myriad of ways in which Africa is systematically silenced, erased and diminished on the world stage. This is due to historical, political, ideological, economic and other factors (see, for example, Part VII, 'Africa in Global Politics,' Oloruntoba and Falola 2018). Thus, even as we focus on religion and inequality in Africa in this volume, we are painfully cognizant of the inequality that the continent itself experiences. Religion is also implicated in this, although a longer narrative is required for us to explore this. However, for the purposes of defining inequality, we find the following submission helpful in part:

> There are inequalities based on demographic characteristics, such as gender, race, ethnicity, religion, and age. A second type of inequality is regarding assets and income. A third type of inequality is regarding public decision making (political power) and access to public resources, such as publicly financed health, education, housing, financing, and other services. Needless to say, these different types of inequalities are interrelated.
>
> (Islam and Winkel 2017: 2)

Our main contention with the foregoing citation is that it fails to recognize that religion affects the other characteristics in very profound ways. Thus, although at one level it is possible to categorize religion as part of the 'demographic characteristics', at another level it is strategic to explore how religion intersects with the same (as we do in this volume). That the different types of inequalities are interrelated is a very helpful observation. As Tsikata (2015) observes, income inequalities, social inequalities, political inequalities and gender inequalities tend to interface in highly dynamic ways in Africa. Sometimes these forms of inequalities are so intertwined that it is actually not possible to disentangle them, or to identify which one is having an impact on the other. When the theme of ethnic diversity is thrown into the mix, given its historical significance in Africa, the discourse on inequality in Africa becomes even more complex (Alcorta et al. 2018; Ajide et al. 2019).

Contributors to this volume focus on existential inequality. This is inequality that accompanies individuals and social groups on the basis of their identity. Globally, there are categories of human beings that are excluded on grounds of who they are, and religion has played a major role in shaping/justifying their exclusion. For example, historically, Black people and ethnic minorities have been excluded by white people, as well as people of other races (Darity and Nembhard 2000). Women experience inequality in a world that is built on masculine assumptions, with religion providing the ideological support (Klingorová and Havlíček 2015). People with disability face inequality in a world that subscribes to the tenets of ableism and relegating many people with disability into poverty (Pinilla-Roncancio 2015). Thus, according to Therborn in an interview,

> there are three basic kinds of inequality which interact; they are interdependent, but they don't always go together. Vital inequality refers to inequality of life and

death. It can be measured through infant mortality, or life expectancy, or health expectancy, the number of years you can expect to live without serious health problems. And there is existential inequality, which refers to issues of dignity, humiliation, recognition, respect or ignorance, and marginalization. Important manifestations of existential inequality are racism, sexism, patriarchy. And certainly there is inequality of the sources, income and wealth, of course the most important ones, but we also talk of inequalities of power, or social contacts.

(Álvarez 2016: 118)

These observations by Therbon in an interview in the foregoing citation lead us to comment briefly on the close relationship that obtains between inequality and poverty, although the two concepts are different. In many ways, inequality results in poverty, and poverty is often the result of inequality (Peterson 2017; Soudien et al. 2019). It is, therefore, critical to invest in addressing poverty and inequality in order to be on the trajectory for development (Mukharjee et al. 2017). Having provided our operational understanding of religion and inequality, we can now briefly reflect on some of the major concerns/interests that have emerged concerning the interface between religion and inequality.

Scholarship on religion and inequality: A summary

As we noted above, although the output on religion and inequality has not been as consistent as it could be, given the importance of the theme, there is a growing interest. We would like to underscore the point that this is not meant to be a detailed or exhaustive literature review, but that the section seeks to illustrate some of the trends in the field (for a helpful review in the United States, see, for example, Smith and Faris 2005). To highlight the growing interest in the theme, two journals have devoted special issues to reflections on religion and inequality. Although, typically, Africa does not feature in these reflections, we still appreciate the focus on the theme. The journal *Social Inclusion* had a special issue entitled 'Complex Religion: Intersections of Religion and Inequality' (Volume 6, No. 2, 2018). Further, the journal *Religions* had a special issue focusing on 'Growing Apart: Religious Reflection on the rise of Economic Inequality' (Volume 8, No. 4, 2018). It was later published as an edited book (Ward and Himes 2019).

Prior to the special issues referenced above, there had been publications that also sought to explore the interface between religion and development. The book *Religion and Inequality in America* (Keister and Sherkat 2014) provides valuable information on the interplay between religion and inequality in the

United States. On their part, Wilde, Tevington and Shen (2018) highlight that Jews and Mainline Protestants remain on top of the socioeconomic ladder in the United States, with Evangelicals, both Black and white, at the bottom. Focusing mainly on religion and inequality in Europe, *Religion, Equalities, and Inequalities* (Llewellyn and Sharma 2016) also facilitates an appreciation of the extent to which religion is implicated in various forms of inequality. On the other hand, Jordan (2016) advances the intriguing proposition that societies that are more religious are characterized by greater inequalities than those that are not. He argues that powerful religious institutions oppose the state's efforts to address inequalities. Staying in Europe, the volume *Religions, Class Coalitions, and Welfare States* (van Kersbergen and Manow 2009) explores the impact of religion on the development of the welfare state.

How the different religions of the world approach poverty and the poor is an important theme to consider when studying religion and inequality. The book *Poverty and the Poor in the World's Religious Traditions* (Brackney and Das 2019) engages with how the various religions interpret poverty and the poor. How world religions can contribute to human liberation (Cohn-Sherbok 1992) represents a quest for an interfaith liberation theology that addresses inequality in a radical way. This is the same concern expressed in the hope of liberation in world religions (De La Torre 2008). Jaco Beyers (2014) wrestles with the issue of religion and poverty, proposing that religion can, among other things, bring in the ethical dimension in addressing poverty. Further, religion can also promote generosity. Judith Soares (2008) focuses on religion and poverty in the Caribbean, while Stephen Offutt et al. (2016), as well as Emma Tomalin (2018) reflect on how religions seek to promote development. Kim, Yu and Hassan (2020) have highlighted the impact of religion on financial inclusion.

From the foregoing, one would be forgiven for imagining that religion is only found in Europe and the United States. Most of the discourses on religion have been driven by scholars within these spaces and they have generally set the agenda for the religious studies discipline. To be fair, scholars in Europe and North America are not to be expected to champion research into religion and inequality in Africa, since African scholars will typically cry foul (as we should!). It is the responsibility of African scholars of religion (and African scholars in related fields) to lead in reflections on religion and inequality in Africa. To this end, there have been some publications by Africanists and African scholars.

The volume edited by the African-American scholar, Peter J. Paris (2009), entitled *Religion and Poverty: Pan-African Perspectives* provides valuable historical and theological interpretations of the phenomenon of poverty among black communities on the continent and in the Diaspora. For us, it remains one of the most informative and ideologically persuasive publications on the theme of religion and poverty in Africa. Its effort to mobilize Black communities to struggle against poverty is as passionate as it is stimulating. Agbiji and Swart (2015) have reflected on the possible role of religion in social transformation in Africa, while Wood (2019) explores the impact of patriarchal practices in the church. June Dickie (2018) analyses how the deployment of the category of lament, which is steeped in the Bible, can bring healing to youth in South Africa. Öhlmann, Gräb and Frost (2020) have edited the highly informative *African Initiated Christianity and the Decolonisation of Development: Sustainable Development in Pentecostal and Independent Churches.*

As we observed earlier, the Circle of Concerned African Women Theologians has been consistent and highly productive in highlighting the role of religio-cultural patriarchal ideologies in the inequalities experienced by women in contemporary Africa (Chitando 2009). These inequalities, often justified and buttressed by religion, have prevented many women from achieving leadership in business and institutions. However, women have deployed the same sacred text that has been used to exclude them to work for their liberation. Here, the ambivalence of religion in relation to inequality features prominently.

The volume *Religion and Social Marginalisation in Zimbabwe* (Togarasei, Bishau and Chitando 2020) represents a more decisive shift towards a critical appreciation of the extent to which religion is implicated in inequality. Although it is limited in terms of being confined to analysing the Zimbabwean context, the volume breaks new ground by engaging with concepts such as religion and mental illness, disability, children's rights and others. A more sustained focus on disability is found in the book *Disability in Africa: Resource Book for Theology and Religious Studies* (Kabue, Amanze and Landman 2016). The volume highlights the extent to which African Traditional Religions and Christianity have influenced negative attitudes towards people with disability in parts of Africa. On their part, contributors to the volume on Pentecostalism and women's entrepreneurship in Harare, Zimbabwe (Mapuranga 2018) have highlighted how Pentecostalism both promotes and compromises women's active involvement in business.

Overall, therefore, there is a general acknowledgement that religion in its various forms is implicated in discourses on inequality. What has been generally lacking is a volume that retains focus on this interface between religion and inequality in Africa. As the different chapters in this volume will seek to make clear, religion is often a pronounced and significant factor for understanding inequality in different parts of the continent. Religion features as the cause of, interpretation or justification of, and is a resource for resisting different forms of inequality in Africa. Below we reflect on the major conclusions that can be drawn from reflections on religion and inequality in Africa.

Religion and inequality in Africa: Some reflections

Does religion cause inequality in Africa? There can be no simple answer(s) to this question. Insights from the study of religion and violence are helpful in responding to this question (Tarusarira and Chitando 2020). First, there is no disembodied religion. That is, religion is always embedded within the social fabric. It both influences and is influenced by other social factors. Second, and intricately related to the foregoing, religion is always acting within other variables, as well as having other variables acting on it. Consequently, there are many instances where it will always be difficult to pinpoint the dominant factor behind inequality. Thus, for example, a young woman from a geographical region that is far away from the capital city, and a member of a religious and minority ethnic group, might be excluded from an employment opportunity in the capital city of a particular country. Apart from the challenges associated with corruption, we would struggle to isolate the main reason why she experiences inequality. Is it on the basis of her religious affiliation? Ethnic identity? Place of origin? Gender? Age? All, one, or some of these variables? Thus, we will need further creativity to isolate and interpret forms of inequality and how the different types of religion intersect with them.

Third, insights from intersectionality are quite helpful in interpreting religion and inequality in Africa. As we have noted, although religion is a very important factor, it is not the only factor relevant to understanding inequality in Africa (and/or anywhere else for that matter). Feminists have highlighted how the marginalization of women, for example, must be interpreted within different other fault-lines such as ethnicity, class, race, sexual orientation and age.

Fourth, religion intersects with other factors to interact with inequality in very dynamic and complex ways. We might refer to ambiguity and ambivalence as helpful concepts in efforts to understand the relationship between religion and inequality. In one context, for example, women in African Instituted Churches (AICs), religion might be a major factor in causing inequality. However, some urban poor people might use the same AICs to struggle against inequality and assert their right to be heard! In a Diasporan setting, many Africans might be oppressed and excluded on the basis of not belonging to the mainstream religion (for example, membership to the Church of England in the UK). However, they might use their own religion (for example, African Pentecostalism) to struggle against inequality. Historical factors, such as the investment by Christian missionaries in education in specific areas in Africa (see, for example, Alesina 2021), are important as they gave Christians in some areas a head start ahead of fellow Christians and followers of other religions in other contexts.

Fifth, and proceeding from the foregoing, the very same religion that might be providing ideological support for inequality often possesses redemptive windows/raw materials for helping in the struggle against inequality. For example, the same Christianity that uses the Bible to support gender inequality and the marginalization of people with disability can use the same Bible to promote gender justice and the rights of people with disability. Religions are not monolithic; they are diverse and open to different interpretations and applications. According to Schweiger (2019),

> religions can relieve and burden, they can stand against poverty and legitimise resistance, but they can also justify inequalities, poverty and exploitation. It is the case that religious belief systems can frequently be understood in different ways and that they can produce texts, discourses and practices that can be interpreted multifariously.

Therefore, it is not possible to derive one absolute and binding statement on the relationship between religion and inequality in Africa (or anywhere else). However, from the case studies presented in this volume, it is fair to say that the dominant paradigm is that of religion as feeding and lubricating inequality. This does not mean that religion is intrinsically oppressive or that it prevents full human liberation. Far from it, intersectionality cautions us from limiting our perspective to only one variable. Different forms of oppression overlap and immobilize individuals and groups.

Sixth, there is need to invest in analysing the impact of religion and the marginalization of lesbians, gays, bisexual, transgender and intersex (LGBTI) in the different African (and other) contexts. While some work has been undertaken in terms of examining the interface between, for example, Christianity and homosexuality in Africa (Chitando and Van Klinken 2016), there is need for more detailed analyses in relation to the impact on livelihoods. Researchers need to undertake more focused studies on the various ways in which religiously inspired/justified homophobia is impacting on the day-to-day opportunities of LGBTI people in Africa.

Seventh, scholarship on religion and inequality in Africa needs to address the theme of children (see, for example, Togarasei and Kügler 2014). The impact of religious ideologies on children's health and well-being requires more critical analysis. This is particularly urgent, given the fact that adolescents and youth constitute the majority of citizens of the continent of Africa. Therefore, there is need to examine how the various religions of Africa either facilitate or frustrate the flourishing of children.

Eighth, the wanton exploitation of the environment can be attributed to the inequality that it endures in relation to humans in some religious traditions. When the environment is regarded as belonging to a lower rung of creation due to religious interpretations, the tendency to adopt instrumentalist approaches towards it is high. In this regard, religions might be regarded as justifying the exploitation of the environment. However, some religions in Africa, such as Rastafari (Sibanda 2017) and African Indigenous Religions (Tarusarira 2017), have shown appreciable levels of commitment towards conserving the environment and responding to climate change.

Finally, the inequality experienced by followers of African Traditional/ Indigenous Religions in Africa needs to be addressed in a clear and effective way. Although many struggles for independence in Africa utilized African Traditional/Indigenous Religions to counter oppressive religious ideologies and practices, these religions and their followers have found themselves marginalized in the postcolonial period. In particular, elites from Christianity and Islam have taken over the state and only give token recognition to Indigenous Religions and their followers. Thus, a separate volume is required to reflect on the status of African Traditional/Indigenous Religions and their followers in Africa.

Chapters in this volume

The chapters in this volume focus on the interface between religion and inequality in diverse African settings. The contributors approach the theme from various angles, have different thematic concerns and focus on variegated geographical spaces in Africa. We readily concede that there are overlaps in our categorization of the various forms of inequality that we have employed to organize the chapters. Thus, if we use the frame of intersectionality (discussed in an earlier section), we will recognize that the different forms of inequality are often intertwined. In this chapter, the editors introduce the volume.

In Chapter 1, Sokfa John analyses the interplay between religion and inequality in Nigeria. Nigeria, one of the most strategic countries in Africa, has high levels of inequality. Religion is deeply implicated in this inequality. John probes the historical, political, ethnic and other factors that have led to the current challenges. In Chapter 2, Julio Machele and Mário Jorge Carlos review religion and inequality in Mozambique. They draw attention to the impact of the Catholic Church and Protestant churches in reducing inequality and seeking to give many people the chance to achieve upward social mobility. Machele and Carlos discuss the changing roles of African Traditional Religions, Christianity and Islam in addressing inequality in Mozambique. Shifting the debate from within the specific African context, in Chapter 3, Nomatter Sande focuses on religion and inequality in the African Diaspora. Since the African Union has defined the Africans in the Diaspora as the sixth region of Africa, it is strategic to review the interface between religion and inequality in the African Diaspora as it offers insights into religion and inequality in Africa, and in general. Sande contends that religion in its various forms has an ambivalent role in relation to inequality. On the one hand, Diasporan African communities use religion to negotiate the dynamics of migration processes, settlement in host nations, family reunions and the transnational ideologies. On the other hand, religion also contributes to the marginalization of Africans in the Diaspora.

The next set of chapters use the lens of gender to interpret religion and inequality in Africa. In Chapter 4, entitled 'The One Man Jihad: Sarki Sanusi Lamido Sanusi (SLS) and Hausa Muslim Women's Status in Northern Nigeria', Rahina Muazu probes the ambivalence of religion in relation to women's rights. While numerous forces seek to constrain women in Northern Nigeria's access to their rights, there are also some progressive religious leaders who appeal to religion in order to advance the same rights. Loreen Maseno, in Chapter 5, utilizes the case study of Bishop Margaret Wanjiru of the Jesus is Alive Ministries (JIAM) of Kenya to highlight how she deploys charisma and social capital to negotiate the marginalization of women in leadership. Maseno's chapter highlights the resources and strategies that Wanjiru employs in order to overcome the oppressive gender ideology that dominates in her area of operation, namely, the religious sector. In Chapter 6, Alexander Makulilo focuses on sensitivities around religion, as well as religion's role in gender socialization in Tanzania, and how this in turn has influenced the marginalization of women. Utilizing the responses of students registered for the course 'Gender and Politics in Africa' at one university in Tanzania, Makulilo reflects on the significant silence that accompanies the particular section 'Women and Religions'. He argues that if there is to be success in the struggle against inequality in Tanzania, it will be vital to mobilize the religious sector. Sonene Nyawo picks up the same theme in relation to women's political marginalization in the Kingdom of Eswatini (formerly Swaziland) in Chapter 7. Nyawo demonstrates how religio-cultural ideologies have led to women playing a secondary role in the Kingdom's politics. She argues that religio-cultural beliefs have differential effects on the endorsement of traditional gender roles for women and men, which then translate into different orientations towards politics. In Chapter 8, Nicholas Nyachega and Kudzai Biri reflect on how women in Spirit-type Apostolic churches negotiate HIV/AIDS in Eastern Zimbabwe. They show how the African Apostolic Church of Johane Marange (AACJM) contributes to women's inequality and increased vulnerability to HIV/AIDS through beliefs and practices that entrench the low position of women. The theme of religion, gender identity and marginalization is explored further by Jones Hamburu Mawerenga in Chapter 9. Using the prism of homosexuality in Malawi, Mawerenga probes how religious homophobia in Malawi is largely responsible for the lack of well-being for most lesbian, gay, bisexual, transgender and intersex (LGBTI) people. He describes the concrete manifestations of this religious homophobia in Malawi, after which he explores the impact of homophobia on the health and rights of LGBTI people.

The set of chapters on religion, gender and inequality is followed by that on religion, disability, age and inequality. In Chapter 10, Sinenhlanhla S. Chisale and Kesiwe Phuthi examine the impact of religion on Ndebele women with disabilities in Zimbabwe. Adopting an African women and disability approach, they highlight the ambivalent role of religion in relation to women with disability. Chisale and Phuthi propose a more liberating stance, with emphasis on achieving equality, justice and human flourishing for everyone, irrespective of their different bodies. The narrative then shifts to South Africa, arguably one of the world's and the continent's most unequal countries. In Chapter 11, Nadine Bowers Du Toit, Dione Forster, Shantelle Weber and Elisabet Le Roux examine the feelings and stances of religious young people in Stellenbosch, South Africa, in the face of high levels of inequality. They discuss how the reality of inequality causes young Christians (eighteen to thirty-five years old) to struggle with the concept of reconciliation. Their chapter draws attention to how factors such as history, race and age are key to understanding inequality in South Africa. In Chapter 12, Tshenolo J. Madigele and Ronald Tshelametse examine the religion, age and inequality interface through the opposite dimension of old age. They focus on how the Church in Botswana is implicated in the struggles of retirees. However, they also highlight how the Church can be a positive change agent by embracing a positive pastoral contextual theology and practising advocacy.

The chapters in the last set approach religion and inequality from the perspective of Pentecostalism and indigenous knowledge systems/liberation theology. The role of Pentecostalism in Africa's development has generated considerable debate. In Chapter 13, Mookgo Solomon Kgatle analyses how some New Prophetic Churches (NPC) in South Africa have sustained inequality. He argues that the same churches have the potential to address poverty and unemployment. Simbarashe Gukurume retains the focus on Pentecostalism and inequality in Chapter 14. Gukurume examines Pentecostal Charismatic Churches (PCCs) and inequality in Harare, Zimbabwe. Positively, he describes how practices such as entrepreneurship and financial literacy, as well as philanthropy and charity activities, all helped to address inequalities. On the negative side, he identified how practices and rituals such as seeding and partnering often exacerbated socioeconomic inequality. In the concluding chapter, Chapter 15, Mukerrem Miftah reflects on the 'Let Our Voice Be Heard'(LOVB) Movement among Ethiopian Muslims. He highlights the inequality that emerges when the state identifies a particular form of religion as the rallying point and expression of national identity, while suspecting another religion of terrorism. This chapter confirms the truth that a religion can dominate in one place, such as Islam in some West African countries, but can experience marginalization and inequality in other places (such as Islam in Ethiopia).

Conclusion

The world is characterized by very high and unacceptable levels of inequality. Africa is experiencing high levels of inequality, with religion featuring prominently. This volume discusses the ambivalence of religion in interfacing with inequality in Africa. It is clear that religion is deeply implicated in inequality in Africa (as it is in other parts of the world). Religion has nurtured and nourished problematic approaches to gender. In many instances, the exclusion of women and girls from leadership positions is often given religious justification. Religion is also a factor when considering the challenges faced by people with disability, young people, elderly people, LGBTI people and others. At the same time, religion possesses immense capacity to mobilize individuals and communities to address inequality. Africa must, therefore, invest in continuing to reflect on religion and inequality in order to make concrete steps towards the achievement of the SDGs and the continent's own development agenda, as articulated in the African Union's Agenda 2063.

Part One

Religion and inequality in Africa: Exploring the conundrum

1

Sleeping with the enemy

The entanglement of religions with inequalities in Nigeria

Sokfa John

Introduction

Inequalities are pervasive and high in Nigeria. They are multidimensional and interact in complex ways with religion, through which they sometimes manifest (Kuznar 2019). The relationship between Christians and Muslims in Nigeria has been largely defined by competition, conflicts and struggles against perceived inequalities. Members of both religions have accused each other and the government of marginalization. Grievances related to economic inequalities are a major factor in the emergence and mobilization of insurgencies in both northern Nigeria and the oil-rich Niger Delta. Recent agitation for the secession of Biafra (southeast Nigeria), as well as the several conflicts that have been witnessed in the middle belt and the north, can be linked to claims of economic, cultural, political and religious marginalization, contentions around access to the state and resources, and citizenship/indigenship to which such access, opportunities and privileges are tied. While inequalities are manifested in many spheres of individual and social life of Nigerians, ethnicity is often a central factor in assessing them. The strong connection of ethnicity to religion and location adds several more layers of complexity to the question of inequality in Nigeria.

This chapter examines the ways in which religion is entangled with Nigeria's inequalities. I survey economic, ethno-regional and religious inequalities in the country and demonstrate how these are intertwined and reinforce each other. I then explore how the place of religion in the (re)production and sustenance of inequalities may be understood in the Nigerian context. I argue that Islam and Christianity, which shape the core values, lifestyle and choices of millions of Nigerians, partly created structural and systemic inequalities, as the foundations and structures that produced and continue to shape Nigeria emerged out of Christian and Muslim, as well as colonial religious and state-making processes. Due to the ways they have evolved in the Nigerian state, these religions have contributed to the entrenchment of inequalities. At the same time, they offer the spectacles through which inequalities are interpreted, experienced and contested.

Religion in social stratification

That religion is deeply interconnected with inequality is well established among social theorists. This has been partly influenced by Marx's critique of capitalism which depicts religion as reinforcing and promoting socioeconomic inequality by populating the minds of materially poor adherents with beliefs that make them docile and dissolves any motivation to seek change (Pals 2006). Weber's (2002) assigning of religious ideas a key place in the evolution of capitalism, while criticized, also remains a widely consulted resource for engaging the religion-inequality relationship.

The explanation offered by these early scholars is insightful but fails to adequately explain contemporary religion-inequality patterns, especially in non-Western experiences. The contemporary scholarship that exists on the matter mostly provides further evidence of the reality (Keister and Eagle 2014). Such studies also often highlight the strong correlation between religion and inequality that is observable in the fact that societies, such as many African countries, which have the most inequalities, tend to be the most religious (Jordan 2016). Furthermore, these are among the societies with high levels of insecurity, which is viewed as produced by high inequality, and from which poor people seek solace in religion (Jordan 2016).

In such places as the United States, the conversation commonly seeks to examine questions of race, class and ethnicity. One approach insists on *complex religion* as a more nuanced approach to the relationship between religion and these inequalities (Wilde and Glassman 2016). It draws on theories that view social stratification as having multiple dimensions and, consequently, different inequalities as producing different outcomes (Wilde and Tevington 2015). Thus, variables such as religious membership or affiliation become an important social structure for analysing inequality, emphasizing the complex and diverse nature of religion (Wilde and Tevington 2015).

Membership dynamics may prove insightful in some analyses of religion and inequality in Africa, but, perhaps, more useful is the idea, well-known in the study of religion, that religion is an extremely complex fact. Part of this complexity stems from the ability to observe that which is distinctly religious while also being acutely aware of the near impossibility of neatly separating religion from ethnicity, culture, politics, and several other sites of personal and social experience. At the same time, this is a fluid situation where the degrees of connection could be determined by time and space. This assumption can provide a useful orientation and openness with which to approach the ways religion is entangled with inequalities in Nigeria.

Sociodemographic and historical contexts of inequalities in Nigeria

The federal system of Nigeria is three-tiered. The federal government (FG) is the highest level of administration, followed by thirty-six states and the federal capital territory (FCT), Abuja. Each state is further decentralized; thus, there are a total of 774 local government areas (LGAs) in the country which constitute the smallest unit of administration and service delivery (Archibong 2018). The states are organized into six geopolitical zones: north-east, north-west, north-central, south-east, south-west and south-south. This zoning formula maintains the regional structure of colonialism and the three autonomous regional administrative structures (north, east, west) that emerged in the 1950s. Regionalism has also remained a very active and functional system in the psyche of Nigerians despite its dissolution in 1967 (Lergo 2011). The middle belt is a strong and salient political region on the lower axis of the north, although it was not granted the independent regional status that its people have pursued since the 1950s. At the heart of the politics of the middle belt is the struggle of its over 200 largely Christian ethnicities to assert a separate and independent identity from the Hausa-Fulani, the northern region, and, to an extent, Islam. It is also the location of most of the ethno-religious conflicts in northern Nigeria.

More interesting is that the Nigerian federal structure is rooted in and determined by ethnic groupings, which for many Nigerians would be flip sides of regional and religious identities – thus placing ethnicities, religion and region at the heart of every major historical, social and political challenge of the country, including vertical and horizontal inequalities. Ukiwo (2005) observes that ethnicity is vilified as the scapegoat in most assessments of the Nigerian political economy. While it is true that the way ethnicity functions in Nigeria makes it an easy target that is often taken for granted, it is difficult to assess horizontal inequalities without considerable attention to ethnicity. Nonetheless, Nigerian ethnicities cannot be examined in isolation because of their close connection to other modes of being and experiencing life in the country.

With a population of over 200 million, Nigeria's hundreds of ethnic groups are broadly categorized into ethnic 'majorities' and 'minorities'. Like ethnicity itself, these terms are laden with problematic histories and politics. Moreover, this distinction emerged out of power configurations of colonialism and regionalism (Osaghae and Suberu 2005). The 'majorities' are hegemonic ethnicities, each corresponding to one of the three traditional regions of Nigeria (Mustapha 2006). These are the Yoruba in the west, the Igbo in the east and the Hausa-Fulani[1] in the north. These three ethnicities constituted approximately 60 per cent of the Nigerian population in the 1963 census. Subsequent censuses did not include religion and ethnicity as variables. All the other ethnic groups are minorities to different degrees depending on their location and numbers.

Such categorization of people according to numbers and dominance is a manifestation of inequalities. The judicial and constitutional demarcation of Hausa, Yoruba and Igbo as major languages and hundreds of others as minorities directly translates into political and socioeconomic power distribution and status (Garuba 2001). Each of the three major ethnic groups is a pole in the competition for political and economic resources and consistently seeks to maintain dominance and avoid marginalization by the other two (Mustapha 2007). The so-called minorities are 'culturally, linguistically, territorially, and historically distinct groups, which because of their diffusion, numerical inferiority and historical evolution within the modern Nigerian state, have been subjected to subordinate political, social and economic positions in the federation and its constituent units' (Osaghae 1998: 4). Thus, minorities have historically had to accommodate themselves and align with their respective regional majorities to access the state (Lergo 2011).

Strategies such as state creation and the federal character principle have achieved some level of participation and integration of previously marginalized minorities in the Nigerian federation. However, they have also created new layers of minority groupings and problems, and further entrenched inequalities. The federal character principle which aims to prevent the dominance of one state or group over others and to address horizontal inequalities is widely criticized for serving only elite and ruling class interests, promoting mediocrity in public service and advancing ethnic consciousness rather than reducing inequality (Umukoro 2014). The cleavages that have emerged out of colonial and postcolonial state-making processes along ethnic, religious and regional lines are associated with, and coincide with, observable patterns of horizontal inequalities (Mustapha 2006; 2007).

Since ethnicities are closely bound to religion in Nigeria, it is commonly understood that among the dominant groups, the Hausa-Fulani and thus the north are predominantly Muslim, the Igbo (east) is predominantly Christian and the Yoruba (west) is split almost equally between Christians and Muslims, while the minorities of the south-south and those of the middle belt are mostly Christian (Mustapha 2006). This understanding runs the risk of being overly simplistic as it often overlooks members of these ethnic groups who are religious minorities among their own people, for example, Igbo Muslims in the east, Hausa and Fulani Christians in the north, and Ham or Mwaghavul Muslims in the middle belt.

Prominent dimensions of inequality in Nigeria

Relevant work on inequalities focuses more on economic inequalities in terms of wealth and income gaps, and the extensive work on ethnicity and religion is often analysis of social conflicts in Nigeria. Yet, horizontal interactions in terms of religion, region and ethnicity are core to how Nigerians experience other forms of inequalities and conflicts, and are topical in popular and public discourses among Nigerians. In the discussion below, I aim to demonstrate this and to show that inequality in one realm produces inequalities in others. As a result, I also aim to show that while it is not practical to examine the entangled networks of inequalities all at once in order to understand religion's role in them, taking an overly narrow approach that does not take the web of connections seriously will hardly produce a comprehensive analysis. Finding the right balance is a tricky but worthwhile venture, even if it ostensibly raises more questions than answers.

Economic inequality

The vertical and horizontal distribution of assets (wealth) and income in Nigeria is disheartening. The Oxfam Foundation provides one of the most provocative representations of the economic situation in Nigeria. With a reputation of being Africa's largest economy and a 19 per cent wealth rise in the decade between 2007 and 2017, more than half of Nigeria's population live below the poverty line of $1.90 a day (Hallum and Obeng 2019). The Foundation reports that it would cost about $24bn a year to end this extreme poverty in Nigeria, while the combined wealth of Nigeria's five richest men is $29.9bn, and more than the entire budget of the country in 2017. Even if the richest man in the country spends $1m a day, it will take him forty-six years to spend his wealth, and the net worth of the rich in Nigeria is projected to rise at a rate of 16.3 per cent annually until 2023 (Hallum and Obeng 2019).

This sharp contrast between the rich and the poor, in addition to the abundance of wealth-generating natural and human resources, is an indication that economic inequality in Nigeria is due to neither lack of wealth nor absence of economic growth. The fact that extreme poverty exists alongside an expanding economy and accumulation of extreme amounts of wealth by a few attests to the failure of the state to equitably distribute its wealth and resources among its population. Moreover, because income inequality also produces or aggravates other inequalities and tensions, more than half of Nigeria's population does not have access to good sanitation, live in extreme poverty and over a quarter of the population does not have access to safe water and other basic services (Hallum and Obeng 2019; Mayah et al. 2017). It has also increased inequalities in areas such as education, healthcare, between urban and rural areas, as well as gender inequalities. Women are more likely to be uneducated, poor, landless and excluded from the political, social and economic life of Nigeria (Mayah et al. 2017).

Intertwining ethnic-regional and religious inequalities

While wealth is concentrated among a few individuals from different states, regions and ethnicities, several indicators show income inequality and poverty to be highest in northern Nigeria, especially in the north-east (Akpoilih and Farayibi 2012; Ngbea and Achunike 2014). Thus, although the Hausa-Fulani Muslim population has maintained the political dominance of Nigeria, where lawmakers are among the highest paid globally, and have produced several wealthy individuals including Africa's richest man, they are the poorest population in the country (Kuznar 2019). Such high rates of poverty as well as unemployment, low levels of modern education, and other factors have been linked to growing feelings of alienation, violent conflicts and susceptibility to religious extremism in the north (Adenrele 2012; Aghedo and James Eke 2013; Cook 2018).

Another key factor in regional inequality is formal 'Western' education. Geopolitical zones in the north have extremely lower levels of formal education and literacy than their southern counterparts. The Nigeria Demographic and Health Survey of 2013 shows that the net attendance ratio for school age children was lowest in the north-east at 44 per cent for primary and 29 per cent for secondary school levels compared to 81 per cent and 70 per cent respectively in the south-east (National Population Commission 2014). The survey also shows that the proportion of men with no education in the north-west was up to 56 per cent, compared to those in the south-south which was 1 per cent or lower. This is similar or worse for women. Additionally, the figures demonstrated a significant link between wealth inequality and education, generally showing that school attendance was higher among wealthy households. For example, 81 per cent of females and 71 per cent of males in the poorest households had no education nationally compared with 8 per cent of females and 5 per cent of males in the wealthiest households (National Population Commission 2014). The causal link also goes the other way around, whereby having education can be linked to access to opportunities and wealth. Moreover, the Nigeria Demographic and Health Survey 2013 further reported that the level of education was one of the most important characteristics of Nigerian households because this is linked to many factors that significantly influence health and reproductive behaviour and choices (National Population Commission 2014).

The regional disparity in educational attendance and attainment can be explained in several ways, including the often-cited historical preferences for religious (Qur'anic) education over 'Western' education among many Hausa and Fulani Muslim parents in northern Nigeria (Hoechner 2014; Usman 2008). However, the most telling source of regional inequality in education is the decision of the British indirect rule of the colonial northern region. The British, having conquered the Sokoto Caliphate – the Islamic state in the region that became northern Nigeria – adopted policies which made them ban Christian missionary activities, including Western education in the region. It claimed this to be in the interest of preserving Islam and Hausa-Fulani cultures, as part of its indirect rule policy and with the Caliphate to not interfere with Islam (Lugard 2013; Taiye 2013). However, the northern colonial government was also preventing any form of education that could threaten its rule (Mustapha 2006). The east and west which were ruled under a different colonial policy and had had earlier contacts with Europeans, missionaries and consequently Western education continued to build more schools and to educate more people. Although decades later, missionary education and schools began to penetrate the northern region, mostly among the 'pagan' groups of the middle belt, northern Nigeria has never been able to catch up with the other regions educationally.

While this generally indicates that the Hausa-Fulani Muslim (rural) poor are most disadvantaged educationally and in terms of opportunities that result from formal education, Hausa-Fulani Muslim elites have been the target of emancipatory politics among minorities in northern Nigeria (Lergo 2011; Ochonu 2014; Emmanuel and Tari 2015). Being a regional majority and constituting the Caliphate and its emirates, the Hausa-Fulani ethnic group have had a complex relationship with northern minorities, many of whom would consider their interaction to be extremely unequal. For example, due to their close proximity to Zazzau (Zaria), one of the major emirates of Nigeria, so-called pagan groups (currently Southern Kaduna) who had resisted Islam during the jihad of the 1880s, became targets for the fulfilment of the slave needs of the Sokoto Caliphate in pre-colonial times. This relationship was further complicated by what Ochonu (2014) termed colonialism by proxy or sub-colonization. This is the process whereby under the guise of indirect rule British colonizers outsourced the colonization business to Hausa-Fulani Muslim elites, annexing previously independent non-Muslim groups to the Caliphate. While the British considered Islam inferior to Christianity, they saw it as the highest form of spirituality that Black people in the region could attain, and the Caliphate as an indication of civilization. They also saw the Caliphate and its emirates 'both in theory and practice, as the most ingenious, intelligent, cultured and politically sophisticated' (Kazah-Toure 1999: 115). Thus, Hausa-Fulani agents were deployed as Native Authorities to rule and civilize the so-called pagan groups represented by the British as primitive, uncivilized, savages and 'raw pagans' of inferior stock (Kazah-Toure 1999: 116). With the support of the British, these agents ruled with iron fists and brutally suppressed resistance. This way, lasting inequalities and in an already tense context became entrenched in the relationship between the Hausa-Fulani and other ethnicities in northern Nigeria. Additionally, the Hausa-Fulani Muslim emerged to be the face of oppression for members of these minorities (John 2018). When these minority groups had access to Christianity, they converted massively because it appeared to be in opposition to Islam and offered them tools to resist dominance and fight for social equality (Vaughan 2016; John 2018). Since Nigeria failed to dismantle this colonial structure after independence in 1960, relationships between groups such as those in Southern Kaduna and the Hausa-Fulani remained very tense and were marked by struggles for autonomous chiefdoms, independent of emirates until the 2000s when some of these requests were granted.

State creation and affirmative action assisted in the reduction of the hegemony of majority ethnic groups in different regions. However, it has only done so to a limited degree in the north. In states such as Kaduna with a large number of Hausa-Fulani Muslims with whom political and economic power still primarily resides, Christian ethnic minorities continue to agitate for equality in power, access to resources, job opportunities, infrastructure and increased religious freedom. As I have shown elsewhere, recent violent incidences have made some members of these groups to protest that they are being targeted for impending genocide (John 2018). The failure of the federal and state governments to address these fears and grievances has contributed in shaping how Nigerians understand, relate and compete with each other (Kukah and McGarvey 2013).

On a broader scale, partly because of the political dominance of Hausa-Fulani Muslims, Nigerian Christians have expressed concerns that they are treated as 'second class' citizens. The often-cited historical indications of this inequality include government funding of Islamic pilgrimage (*Hajj*),[2] building of mosques and support for Qur'anic schools; placement of Muslim religious leaders on government payroll; Nigeria's membership of the Organization of Islamic Conference (OIC) in 1986; the implementation of Shari'a criminal law by several northern states, and the efforts to achieve this at the federal level – an issue that has caused heated debates since the 1970s (Onapajo 2012; Ebhomienlen and Ukpebor 2013; Kukah and McGarvey 2013). These issues are usually formally contested through the Christian Association of Nigeria (CAN) and the Catholic Church.

Two media reports represent expressions of feelings of inequality among Nigerian Christians. In two interviews in 2013, the then CAN President, Pastor Ayo Oristejafor, reiterated the view that Christians were treated as second-class citizens. He cited the handling of the Boko Haram insurgency; the spending of public funds on the building of 'Almajiri' schools (madrassas) in northern Nigeria when previous governments had seized Christian and missionary schools and converted them to public schools; the appointment of only Muslims to key federal positions; the establishment of Islamic banking by the Central Bank of Nigeria; the ban on the teaching of Christian Religious Knowledge in some northern states and the ban on Christian preaching on their state-owned television, amongst other things (Binniyat and Eyoboka 2013). In 2016 Femi Fani-Kayode, a lawyer who had held several high-level positions in the federal government, reiterated some of these, accusing the government of marginalizing Christians and failing to treat Christians with respect and dignity. He also said that there was ongoing assault by security forces on Christian leaders; suppression of minorities in northern Nigeria and the middle belt whom he said were facing genocide, intimidation, cultural imperialism and slavery; and cited the killings of mostly Christian rural communities by Fulani herders (Fani-Kayode 2016).

These grievances reflect the fears and feelings that several Nigerian Christians have expressed publicly and against which they have mobilized. They are also often coupled with and framed within longstanding narratives about a hidden agenda to Islamize Nigeria. The extent to which some of these claims are true is a subject of debate. However, some of them have been variously addressed (Ibrahim 1989; Kukah 1993; Akinade 2002; Dudley 2013; Malachy 2013).

Muslim groups have also expressed fears and concerns about inequality in government or disrespectful treatment by Christians. For example, in 2005, an open letter titled 'Progressive marginalization of Muslims in Nigeria' written by the Conference of Nigerian Muslim Organizations (2005), signed and distributed through the Global Network for Islamic Justice, was addressed to the then Christian president of Nigeria. The letter drew on several sources to reiterate the claim that Muslims constituted the majority of the Nigerian population but were underrepresented in the cabinet and other government appointments. It also requested that the government reversed the 'irrational' decision to exclude religion as a variable in the national population census, among other things.

Moreover, the popularity of the implementation of Shari'a in northern states in 1999/2000 and the emergence of several reformist and extremist groups, including Boko Haram, can be linked to feelings of alienation from the Nigerian nation-state system, economy, experience of poverty, perceptions of moral degradation, suffering of the poor and pervasive corruption (Ajayi 1990; Adenrele 2012; Cook 2018). Some of these problems are also blamed on Western education and influences. Thus, Shari'a proponents and reformist groups and politics have thrived and are targeted for exploitation because they advanced an agenda to recover the old Islamic State or bring back some Islamic authority in public affairs, thereby producing a more egalitarian, moral, corruption- and poverty-free society (Kane 2003; Miles 2003; Weimann 2010; Loimeier 2011).

Overall, feelings and claims of inequality are mutual and a subject of contestation between Christians and Muslims in Nigeria. African Indigenous Religions are often taken for granted and by-passed in the religious priorities and public discourse of Nigeria, although they are recognized as the third major group of religions in Nigeria. Several other religions and new religious movements also quietly exist in Nigeria and lack significant political voice. Thus, they are hardly heard and almost completely excluded from several key conversations.

Religion in Nigeria's inequalities

So far, I have hopefully demonstrated that religion is deeply entangled in questions of inequality in Nigeria. But how precisely should we understand the role of religion in this entanglement? While different levels and models of causality can be identified, especially in specific situations, it is difficult to speak of a blanket causal relationship between religion and inequality in this context. Religion contributes to the [re]production and sustenance of inequality in several ways, and more specific analysis of cases of religions, religious teachings and practices, specific issues and context would be further enlightening. A considerable body of work exists with regard to gender inequality in Africa. Here, I suggest that (a) religion's role and agency in the inequalities discussed above is better understood in relation to the embeddedness of Christianity and Islam in the structures of Nigerian society; (b) religion through these traditions has come to be a key language and site through which citizenship, access and consequently, inequalities, are experienced, framed and analysed; and (3) like democracy, religion has further emerged in the public sphere to be a system or an asset that offers advantages for competition and a means for channelling grievances and fears of the other.

Olufemi Vaughan, in his historical work, *Religion and the Making of Nigeria* (2016), most convincingly advanced the argument that Christian and Muslim doctrines have consistently been embedded in and shaped the foundations, structures and power configuration of the Nigerian state and society. According to Vaughan, beginning with the reform jihad of Uthman dan Fodio which led to the establishment of the Caliphate in the vast region that became northern Nigeria, and the activities of English evangelical missionaries among the Yoruba in the west through the Church Missionary Society (CMS) in the nineteenth century, religious structures became the foundation on which the colonial Nigerian state was created. As I have also highlighted earlier in this chapter, Vaughan argues that besides transforming and unifying the independent Hausa city-states into a Caliphate, the Jihad of the 1800s immensely shaped the geopolitics and identities of the hundreds of communities in the modern middle belt and the Yoruba in the south-west. Further, Christianity and Islam were also uniquely shaped by the cultural, political and social structures of traditional Nigerian communities in the process (Vaughan 2016).

British rule mostly intensified these structures and their imbalances, especially in northern Nigeria. Postcolonial Nigeria has primarily done the same. It has maintained and built on major colonial structures and logics while at the same time dealing with persistent efforts to reclaim or achieve some version of the precolonial Islamic state in north. The competition, alliances, tensions, structures and consciousness that emerge out of these processes have produced a situation whereby ethnicity, religion and location have become the key tools for navigating life, relevance, politics and power. The salience of these categories is visible beyond the fact that they themselves are layers of inequality. Thus, even other spheres of inequality and contestation such as citizenship (indigene versus settler/migrant tensions) are based on region and ethnicity as well as the expression of affirmative action in practices that exclude settlers, migrants and non-indigenes from access and rights to the local resources and services of a state and or government area (Osaghae and Suberu 2005).

In his influential book on religion, politics and power in northern Nigeria, Kukah (1993) observes that the 'average' Nigerian navigates multiple belongings and through them shapes identity-based relations. According to him the life of the 'average' Nigerian therefore revolves around at least ten institutions to which they belong, and which compete for their attention. These are based on clan, village, income, religion, gender, age and more, and increased by migration to city where such associations can facilitate upward mobility. Several of these are based on the overlapping dimensions of ethnicity, religion and region/location. Additionally, Kukah notes that each of the multiple belonging has its own dynamics. For example, in order to access certain religious spaces candidates must possess certain economic, political or class status, or other symbols of success. In addition to these, Nigerians trade religious and other types of belonging in the process of seeking patronage and in mediating, competing and negotiating power within formal structures such as region, state, local government and bureaucracy (Kukah 1993).

Such embeddedness and functional entanglement of religion in the structures of Nigeria and in the ways many Nigerians do and experience life make Christianity and Islam complicit in many forms of inequalities in the country. I do not intend to undermine the role that these religions as well as faith-based organizations and networks play in struggles for justice, equality and the improvement of lives in Nigeria. I also acknowledge that examples can be found of positive opportunities and outcomes that are not necessarily driven by such identity-based competition and politics. However, the broader context in which these alternatives are experienced appears to be predominantly that of ethnic, religious and regional competition, as well as suspicion and a widely politicized and contested idea of unity and the need to keep Nigeria one.

It follows then that religion becomes a key language and site for the experience, assessment and interpretation of inequalities in Nigeria. Similar arguments have been made in some literature to show that the popular view that the politicization of religions explains their salience in social tensions is not complete. Kukah (1993) argues that religion is a platform on which political and other interests are pursued. Bienen (1986) also pointed out that religions in Nigeria offer groups a set of values, institutions and language for contending within and between communities. This is an obvious conclusion given the way Christianity and Islam have developed and established their salience in the Nigerian political economy. Mustapha (2014) notes that religion is an idiom through which warring groups mobilize and a lens through which broader political and social processes that may not relate to divinity are played out. Additionally, just like democracy, religion has emerged in the Nigerian space to be an asset or system that offers competitive advantage, access and power, and a means for channelling grievances and fears.

This means that inequalities are both encountered and contested through, and on, religion as a site. Yet, religions evolve with other institutions in society and in the context of social change, just as the nature and manifestations of inequalities may change over time. This is an important context for further understanding the role of religion both as an integral aspect of inequalities in Nigeria and as a site for their manifestation and contestation. The logic and structure of the nation-state is mutually demanding for Nigeria and its religions, and no religion has the perfect solution for how exactly to relate to it or what the nation should look like (Clarke 1988). According to Mustapha (2014), Muslims in Nigeria are constantly confronted with questions about what it means to be a good Muslim in the context of social change, which splits them into sectarian groups based on differences in the interpretation of scriptural texts and ritual practices.

Conclusion

One of the powers of religions is their ability to shape the ways that adherents experience the world and how they interpret and relate to their experiences. I have argued that Christianity and Islam are complicit in the structuring and entrenchment of inequalities in Nigeria, while they shape the ways that such inequalities are experienced and contested by Nigerians. This means that in order to overturn the pervasive inequalities in Nigeria, religious actors must critically rethink the ways they position their communities to experience and relate to the world and to each other. This requires thinking and operating outside of the competitiveness and suspicion that frames current interreligious interaction. This is a difficult task, considering that Christian and Muslim groups appear to have different visions of how to best achieve equality, and certain stakeholders in each religion assume that the other necessarily has negative intentions towards them.

An example is the assumption by some Christians that the default objective of Muslims in Nigeria is to Islamize and politically dominate the country or to eliminate non-Muslims. Such intentions may have been expressed by extremist groups or suggested by certain forms of violence or the politics of a few Muslim elites. But believing that to be the aim of Muslims as a whole becomes problematic and stifles potential opportunities for more fruitful interreligious relations and for mutual collaboration to end inequalities. Thus, rather than taking a warring stance, Christians and Muslims could take a more self-critical stance that enables them to re-assess their complicity in inequalities and their failure to produce better realities for their followers and nudge the Nigerian government in the same direction. They could deploy their ability to shape the lifeworld of their communities to create more positive, liberating and egalitarian realities, where adherents are exposed to narratives that promote self-concepts and action that are not based or feed on opposing and negating ideas about the other.

Acknowledgement

The author acknowledges South Africa's National Research Foundation which, through the Research Chair in Sustainable Local (Rural) Livelihoods at the University of KwaZulu Natal, funded the research and time spent writing this chapter.

Religion and inequalities in Mozambique

Júlio Machele and Mário Jorge Carlos

Introduction

Religion, or the interpretation of the environment of individuals based on religion, has always characterized the history of humankind. In the history of Mozambique, although its (re)construction has privileged the political-economic aspect, religion was, and is, omnipresent. Religion has served and continues to serve a large part of Mozambicans to, giving meaning to their lives. However, its fortunes have changed in line with the ideological positions adopted by those with political power. In this chapter, we seek to interrogate the connection between religion and inequalities in Mozambique. Although the insurgency (starting in 2017) by militants who profess allegiance to Islam in Northern Mozambique is important, it requires a separate narrative to do justice to its dynamics. Consequently, it is not covered in this chapter.

An attempt was made during the colonial period to put an end to 'barbarism' and 'primitivism' by 'civilizing' Africans through religion and education, while at the same time sharpening inequalities. In the period after independence in 1975, it was from a Marxist-Leninist interpretation that the project of building the 'new human' was born in Mozambique. It was envisaged that this would be a more humanized person free of inequalities, in which there should be no exploitation of one human being by another. The development policies and strategies adopted by the FRELIMO government were initially aimed at creating equality in Mozambican society and regarded religion as an intrinsically oppressive ideology that would create and intensify inequality.

This ambitious project, which initially mobilized many Mozambicans, came with its own shortcomings. Instead of an egalitarian society, there was the reproduction of the colonial social pyramid (Adam 2006: 380–3).

The privatizations adopted in accordance with the recommendations of the International Monetary Fund (IMF) and the World Bank (WB) increased the disparities from 1987 onwards. Even with the democratization that began in 1990, in an environment where voices about human rights, equality, fraternity, etc. resonated, inequalities increased even more in Mozambique.

Considering that in religion it is common to assume that 'we should delight one another, make each other's conditions our own, rejoice together, lament together, work and suffer together, always having our community before us as members of their bodies' (Myers 2007: 326), this chapter seeks to highlight the relationship between religion and inequality in colonial and independent Mozambique. The objective is to contribute to an understanding of this relationship by focusing the analysis on education and health.

This approach is justified by the fact that the study of inequalities in Mozambique is a field dominated by feminists whose model of explanations focus on the unequal gender relations (Casimiro and Andrade 2009), by economists whose reference is income, wealth and education (Maia 2012; Gardín 2019), and by demographers who consider the relationship between migration and poverty/development (Vletter 2007; Raimundo 2009).

Scholars who have taken religion and analysed it in the context of inequalities have mostly assumed that religions have become a refuge from the growing inequalities faced by a considerable segment of the population (Pfeiffer 2002). They argue that in settings where inequalities prevail, Christian churches, for example, help to improve health, protect and promote well-being (Bonate 2005: 44; Victor and Lambranca 2009). Others who have studied inequalities within various religious groups have postulated that members of mainstream religions have greater opportunities in terms of access to health and education because of the connections of their members with these sectors (Cau, Sevoyan and Agadjan 2013).

In analysing the role of the Christian religion in the face of the inequalities, we maintain that the Roman Catholic Church has made a significant contribution. To maintain this position is to counter some scholars who condemn the Catholic Church. It sought to promote access to modern health and education, thus reducing inequalities in part, but within a context of restrictions, first because of the colonial and racial context in which it operated and second for the postcolonial period because of its 'collaboration' with colonialism until this critique was revised in the late 1980s.

As far as the Protestant churches are concerned, we make the same point, but they did not experience many limitations after independence, since FRELIMO's leadership identified itself with these churches. Concerning education, we concentrate more on *dominical* education (Sunday education) given in the vernacular language. Here the most visible exception is the Jehovah's Witnesses who were treated as an 'abnormal' group and unequal because of their religious convictions.

With regard to Islam, we maintain that its role in combating inequalities was restricted in the colonial and postcolonial periods with the closure of mosques and madrasahs and the persecution of its leaders. Despite the restrictions, some were able to access Islamic education and knowledge, mastery of the Arabic language and great participation in trade, but within Islam itself there are inequalities related to the Islamic diversity in the country.

As for the African Traditional Religions, we contend that they helped to combat inequalities in access to other forms of health (traditional medicine), but within an equally tight climate. Their role in education in a country that has come to privilege Western-style formal education is, it can be assumed, null and void.

This chapter has been made possible by the reading and critical analysis of documentation relating to religion and inequality. These are primary and secondary sources of various formats – published and unpublished. Personal observations were also mobilized. This is an eminently qualitative study that privileges historical analysis.

Religion and inequality in colonial Mozambique

During the precolonial period religion was, par excellence, the monopoly of the kings and emperors who had it as an ally. In fact, 'magical-religious beliefs ... played, in these societies, a very important role, constituting a fundamental weapon of power' (Serra 2000: 19). Although it also served as a fundamental weapon of social cohesion and of apparent immobility, the fact is that only the kings claimed to have exceptional access to the supernatural entities that were thought to populate nature and the world in general, hence the interdiction of the exercise of magical-religious activities without the express authorization of the king (Serra 2000: 42–3). It is to be believed that in the empire of Gaza, the monarchs, in order to better keep their subjects under subjection, also arrogated to themselves – like the Zulu kings – a legitimate monopoly of necromantic powers (Rita-Ferreira 1974: 224). Mediums were strictly associated with political power and were especially relevant during succession processes (Serra 2000: 45).

With the establishment of the colonial administration decades after the Berlin Conference and the alliance of the Portuguese State with the Vatican, sealed with the Concordat of 1940 and the Missionary Agreement of 1941, the Roman Catholic Church came to have health and education as its special qualities. From here on, evangelization became more systematic and rapid; missions and schools, health centres and laboratories that were deemed critical to the task were also created (Vatican News 2019).

Most Africans in Mozambique who have attended rudimentary, elementary and secondary education have a background in the Roman Catholic Church. The assimilated, a complex category of Africans 'admitted' as Portuguese, are the most obvious proof that the Roman Catholic Church has fought, in part, inequality in access to education but within a colonial racist climate.

Some Africans benefitted from this openness and have been able to access modern education. In 1955, out of an estimated total population of 5,650,000, there were 4,555 assimilated (Hedges et al. 1993: 183). Although it can be said that this is a derisory percentage (about 0.08 per cent) of the total population, the fact is that it was this population that served as the starting point for an attempt to level out inequalities in relation to the privileged white population. However, this process simultaneously increased inequalities among Africans.

We can provide one example of such. Thus, Gabriel Chiphiri, interviewed by André Mindoso, was able to affirm, like so many other Mozambicans scattered throughout the country, that 'my father already knew how to read and write properly back in 1930, he studied at the priests' school. He was a carpenter. So he had a civilization far ahead of the people he lived with. He lived in Marara, and that was one of the places where the priests gave a lot of training' (Mindoso 2017: 134).

In fact, one can safely say that the existence of Roman Catholic schools with a leading role in training was common practice in several parts of the colony. The reflection, 'Education in Mozambique: Policies of Assimilation and the Privileging of Portuguese in Teaching', by Sheila Perina de Souza (2019) confirms that the Roman Catholic Church has contributed to reducing the gap between those who could read and write and the 'illiterate'. The group of assimilated people, as well as others like Gabriel Chiphiri's father (cited above) who knew how to read and write, were able to compete for the advantages of an increasingly global world.

Paradoxically, by reducing the inequalities in relation to the colonial population who could read and write, the Roman Catholic Church also widened the gap among the Africans themselves. Because of issues inherent in colonial politics, the few Africans who had access to education 'emancipated' became an elite and thus differentiated themselves from the majority of the population. This became more visible in the access to various privileges (Souza 2019).

Alongside contributing to education, colonization diversified the ways of dealing with diseases and cures by introducing biomedicine into an environment dominated by traditional medicine. The figure of the physician who penetrated the hinterland and lived with the communities was instrumental in this approach to biomedicine in Africa. Accosted by new diseases linked to European expansion, such as venereal diseases and smallpox (Junod 1996), tuberculosis (CEA 1998), flu, like the Spanish flu, Enzootics (Shapiro 1983), the Roman Catholic Church provided access to healing, control and mitigation of diseases in various parts of the colony.

The Protestant churches played a similar role, but on a smaller scale because education and health had become, in part, a kind of monopoly of the Roman Catholic Church. Indeed,

> in some areas, such as the Limpopo Valley, where the Catholic Church took care of long-established state schools, Protestant families were increasingly forced to enroll their children in rudimentary Catholic schools. In the 2nd grade, that is, the "common elementary teaching," the educational system was the responsibility of the Catholic missions, with only one Protestant school [in 1944] in the mission of Messumba in Niassa.
>
> (Hedges et al. 1993: 122)

The role of the Christian religion in increasing the number of those who could read and write continued. The Christian religion continued to be instrumental in reducing this inequality.

From early on, there were examples of Africans who achieved educational success due to the impact of the missionaries. Thus, despite operating under enormous hardship, Aron S. Mukhombo and Elias Mucambe, who were pastors and teachers of the United Methodist Mission, are some examples of the involvement of the Protestant missions in the modern education of Africans. Another example is Gabriel Macavi, a teacher, pastor and poet who attended the Rikatla Teacher Training School linked to the Swiss mission. It was an education more accessible to the Africans and that gave primacy to the use of vernacular languages. As a result, the Protestants contributed towards the vitality of indigenous African languages in contexts where colonialism sought to make them inferior.

Many indigenous people in the rural areas affiliated to the Protestant missions became able to read and write thanks to the work of the missions. Protestant missions have been crucial in reducing inequalities in reading and writing between Blacks and whites, particularly among those who were assimilated. The possession of writing and reading skills has allowed many assimilated people access to public administration positions, as well as other liberal professions. However, like the Roman Catholic Church, the Protestants were also responsible for creating an elite that later enjoyed enormous privileges over the majority of the African population.

The appearance of the Islamic religion in Mozambique dates back to at least the tenth century. As in other parts of the continent, Muslim traders and travellers played a major role in the spread of Islam (Von Sicard 2008). Islam penetrated the hinterland from the coast and in some parts was Africanized, mainly in the matrilineal societies of northern Mozambique. It was a religion closely linked to trade. Access to Arabic, the language of the Quran, opened up enormous possibilities. The madrasas and mosques, the places of learning, were spreading from the coastal zone to the interior. Through the Arabic language many Africans were able to penetrate the webs of commerce and become famous, while others became Sheikhs, Mwalimus, etc., a kind of elite that in turn represented a differentiated segment of the rest of the Islamized population. It was part of this elite that knew how to use the Arabic alphabet that produced the Ajami writing. This refers to African languages written in Arabic script.

The prominence of powerful female figures, such as Queen Achivanjila (Zimba 2005), in the matrilineal societies of northern Mozambique can, in part, be understood as Islam's contribution to the promotion of women.[1] Bonate (2019) has also documented the contribution of Muslim female leaders in precolonial northern Mozambique. Moreover, there is no lack of examples in Muslim society: "during the early days of Islam, women played a distinct and full role in society. In fact, their position was prominent" ' … "In Muslim history, the privilege of being the first Muslim goes to Khadijah, the Prophet's wife"; Fatimah Jinnah, who led the movement in Pakistan and became the symbol of opposition to the military dictatorship (1940s)' was a woman, as was Benazir Bhutto who challenged another military leader in Pakistan and was the first female Muslim prime minister (Ahmed 2003: 115–16).

With the threat of nationalism, some Muslims were co-opted to collaborate with colonialism, while others suspected of involvement with the liberation movement were persecuted and imprisoned. Some mosques and madrasas were closed. The policies of the Portuguese colonial state reduced, in part, the impetus of Arabic and Islamic teaching, which would later have an impact on power relations within Mozambican Islamic society.

Traditional African religions, anchored within society and with explanatory models linking the living with the dead, were guarantors of order, cohesion, prosperity since humans came into existence in the territory that became modern Mozambique. For example, the 1770s and 1780s are full of examples of the roles played by the *Mhondoro* spirits as arbitrators in issues of war and peace, trade disputes and political disagreements between Europeans and Africans as well as among Africans (Mudenge 1976: 35). However, the colonial authorities in alliance with the missionaries responsible for proselytism defended the need for the eradication of African Traditional Religions in favour of a Christianity that identified with European values in general and the Portuguese in particular.

João dos Santos, the Dominican missionary and many others who followed him, gave full support to the 'civilizing mission' under the banner of proselytism. Despite the attitude of Friar João dos Santos and several other missionaries, evidence shows that many Europeans adopted traditional African practices in matters related to health and disease (Mudenge 1976).

As far as health is concerned, one can postulate that African Traditional Religions have been instrumental in promoting access to healthcare through traditional medicine. The pursuit of health, understood here as 'a state of complete physical, mental and social well-being and not just the absence of disease or infirmity' (WHO), was achieved by most Africans who did not have access to biomedicine through African Traditional Religions. For their part, Europeans who faced problems of lack of medical personnel in the early centuries made use of these specialists to bridge the gap, not only with those who remained in the metropolis, but also with those who settled in some urban parts of the colony. In the Limpopo River Valley, for example, there are records of Portuguese white 'specialists' in traditional medicine. In the villages of Guijá and Sagres there are testimonies on the use of various local medicinal plants, divination and witchcraft by Europeans.

Because the administration hardly reached the various rural areas where the majority of the African population lived, it was traditional medicine that ensured health in a context where biomedicine concentrated on urban areas and was unable to cover the entire population. However, in urban environments where repression was most active, African Traditional Religions, including the Ethiopian separatist churches, made a minimal contribution to promoting access to health. For example, in 1941, '[protestant missions] headquarters and branches were ordered to be closed down because of being illegals' (Hedges et al. 1993: 183), but this repression was not effective the rural areas in particular.

Religion and inequalities in independent Mozambique

It was from independence that the new leadership of the People's Republic of Mozambique engaged in the construction of the new Mozambique, a Mozambique guided by 'Marxism-Leninism' and whose approach to this ideology dates back to the period of the national liberation struggle.

It was through this influence that the leadership of FRELIMO sought to create the 'new person', without the exploitation of one human by another, where equality should be promoted, but with a reduced role of religion because it was considered an obscurantist manifestation that served to deceive, cheat and the divide people. Thus, even before independence, during the transition period, FRELIMO prohibited the teaching of religious beliefs in all government schools (Cabrita 2000: 97). In August 1975, a communiqué from the Dinamizadores Groups (1975) revealed that religion was not welcome to be part of the construction of the new Mozambican society.

Although the constitution (RPM 1975) did not deny affiliation or non-affiliation to a certain religion by Mozambicans and did not condemn its practice, the fact is that the secular state that emerged after independence reduced the role of religion in societal spheres such as education and health. By doing so, the State removed the role of religion in reducing inequalities based on health and education.

Since the new leadership wanted to monitor and control the whole process of creating the 'new man/person', previously important actors were no longer relevant, one of them being religion, in this instance understood as an institution that promotes inequalities. In fact, FRELIMO's leadership began to assume that the practice of medicine and private education was a means of exploitation that used illness and ignorance as a means of enrichment (besides the fact that access to medical care was reserved for the elite) (Rita-Ferreira nd: 132), which could go against the project of an egalitarian society.

The discourses linking the Christian churches with imperialism became more frequent. In fact, several religious groups were labelled as 'agents of imperialism' (Guebuza 1975) and they tried to present believers as serving the interests of the exploiters (Dynamizing Groups 1975).

Most of the Roman Catholic Church's possessions, especially health centres and schools, were confiscated through the nationalization process by the State. There was greater control over the publication, importation and distribution of religious material. Religious organizations were prohibited from 'duplicating' the work of State-sponsored mass organizations. The

FRELIMO government also arrested missionaries, sometimes without formal charges (Cabrita 2000: 122).

The Roman Catholic Church has seen its agency diminished in sectors such as education and health. Failures and mistakes in strategies and policies had already created an exodus of health and education specialists and technicians to other regions of the world. The promotion of preventive medicine, which was even praised by the World Health Organization (WHO) in 1977 at the expense of curative medicine, limited the country's capacity to deal with various diseases.

With the deterioration of curative care, only the political elite and other better off individuals could travel to neighbouring countries in search of a cure. The bulk of the population that once used health centres belonging to churches began to face enormous difficulties in accessing curative care, thus increasing inequality in access to healthcare.

As the civil war that began in 1976 increased, the national health system collapsed. Churches scattered in various areas with or without conflict, with an incapacitated government, were unable to provide adequate medical aid as a result, for the most part, of decisions taken after independence. Similarly, the national education system had almost collapsed.

Of the Protestant churches, the members of Jehovah's Witnesses were systematically impoverished after independence. They came to be understood as an anomalous group, different from the others and deserving to be sent to the re-education camps in the most remote areas of the country.

They became part of the bulk of the so-called 'unproductive' and 'enemies of the revolution' because they were accused of denying the achievements of the revolution, of refusing to pay taxes, of not saluting the national flag and of not recognizing the symbols and leaders of the Mozambican homeland. In the re-education camps, poverty raged and accusations of sorcery became common practice. In these remote regions, due to the constant policing, members had many difficulties and promoted well-being among themselves. They did not participate in the struggle against inequalities in health and education.

Protestant churches played a greater role than the Roman Catholic Church because part of the leadership of FRELIMO identified with them. They did not suffer the same confiscations and in some situations they were left to work. Doctors linked to the Swiss mission, such as René Gagneaux, remained very active. René Gagneaux continues to be remembered in southern Mozambique for his courage, determination and altruism during the difficult period of the war. He, like others, managed to bring healthcare to those in need in various parts of the country at a very troubled time (Thoele 2005).

The Islamic religion also found itself in a challenging situation after independence. It became increasingly difficult to teach the Arabic language, the vehicle of the Islamic religion, and to profess one's own religion with the closing of mosques and madrasas (Morier-Genoud 2002; Bonate 2013: 245). In an area where the Islamic religion dominates, in the coastal districts of Inhambane province, on the north coast and the respective hinterland, the dominance of Arabic, important in religious practice and other forms of knowledge, was losing ground to an education that, in part, 'de-Islamicized' those who professed this type of religion.

Thus, these measures gradually broke the line of knowledge transmission. The ability to admit new 'Mwalimu', Imams, etc. into Muslim society became more and more difficult with the restrictions of the post-independence era because a homogeneous education was intended to be monitored and controlled by the FRELIMO government.

Many Muslims who had been forbidden to go to Mecca on pilgrimage no longer felt themselves to be 'complete' Muslims, as they were denied one of the pillars of Islam. The homogenization of society through the prohibition of dress codes almost made Muslims in Mozambique different from other Muslims in the rest of the world.

Traditional African religions, although persecuted during colonialism, resisted and showed great vitality. With independence, when many thought African traditions would be however, 'Marxism-Leninism' and its supposed scientific view of reality dashed such hopes.

Prosecutions continued. Some practitioners were uprooted from their homes or when they went to do their healing and spirit appeasement work from the re-education camps. The official ban on so-called 'magic-religious practices' in some parts of the country left many Mozambicans out of care in the face of the threat of diseases caused by angry spirits. It also left them equally unprotected against witchcraft and against many other diseases whose etiology and healing were in the domain of traditional medicine.

The inequality between those who had access to psychological care and those who did not grew significantly, since a considerable part of the population had to negotiate mental illnesses. This was because the traumatic experiences during the war were closely linked to the spirits and required those who had such knowledge to administer healing.

Isabel Parada Marques, a psychiatrist in Mozambique, went so far as to state that, with regard to issues relating to depression and trauma, traditional medicine is much more capable of interpreting symptoms, of interpreting the patient's speech, of understanding their social environment, of having contact with their family structure, and of systemically finding a way of establish a dynamic that is conducive to the behaviour of the patient. These are things that Western medicine is not able to do (Kotany 2003).

It was these traditional 'psychiatrists' and 'psychologists' who were forbidden from making their interventions and some were expelled to the so-called re-education camps in the remote areas of the country who could have offered the much needed help and care for many victims. The acceptance of traditional doctors as necessary from an official point of view came with the officialization of the Association of Traditional Healers (AMETRAMO), created in 1991. This has gone some way in addressing the inequalities associated with the rating of medical systems emerging from specific religions.

Conclusion

This chapter sought to relate religion and inequality in Mozambique, with a focus on education and health in the colonial and postcolonial periods. The analysis was restricted to the Roman Catholic Church, Protestant churches, Islam and African Traditional Religions. The findings indicate that religions in Mozambique fought inequality in the area of access to health and education in both periods under consideration, but within their own internal logic. The Catholics as well as the Protestant churches have enabled a small part of the population to read and write, thus levelling it with the white population, but at the same time they also increased inequalities among the Black indigenous populations. Both the Catholics and the Protestant sought to promote health, but the Catholics were more effective during the colonial period – a situation that would be reversed with the coming of independence.

The Islamic religion in turn promoted access to the Arabic language and thus to the Quran and related knowledge through the madrasas and mosques that were spread throughout the country. But persecution, the closure of mosques and other limitations reduced Islam's role in levelling out those who did not have the command of Arabic, the Quran and other knowledge connected with those who did not. Traditional African Religion was very instrumental in creating access to traditional medicine for a considerable part of the population that did not have access to biomedicine, but faced many limitations imposed during the colonial and postcolonial periods. Overall, this chapter has confirmed the close interplay between religion and inequalities in Mozambique by showing the role of the State in promoting or restricting certain religions during different historical periods. Additional reflections on the extent to which religion/Islam and inequality have influenced the insurgency in Cabo Delgado (see, for example, Heyen-Dubé and Rands 2021) will assist in clarifying the nexus.

Diaspora African communities, religion and inequality

Nomatter Sande

Introduction

Inequality is a topical issue affecting global development, as well as emerging as a developmental challenge in Africa. Currently, inequality is on the increase across the world (World Inequality Report 2018). The 2030 Agenda for Sustainable Development is using the motto 'leave no one behind' to show the urgency of this matter. Thus, inequality is a phenomenon that is continuing to affect humanity, with negative outcomes. According to the World Inequality Report (2018) there is exponential growth in economic inequality across the globe. Besides economic inequalities, other factors linked to inequality are social, gender, environment and political (Eagle 2014; United Nations 2019).

Apart from these factors, this chapter argues that religion is a critical factor when dealing with the interface between diaspora African communities and inequality. Correspondingly, religion is a critical tool used by diaspora African communities. In particular, diaspora African communities use religion to negotiate the dynamics of migration processes, settlement in host nations, family reunions and the transnational ideologies. There is an increased attention by scholars 'to the resources religion provides in driving and sustaining the migration process' (Burgess 2009: 225). It follows, therefore, that since religion is central to the migration processes, inevitably it has a role in dealing with matters of inequalities experienced by diaspora African communities. Migration processes are heterogeneous phenomena; hence, diaspora African communities experience diverse forms of inequalities across the sectors and parts of the globe. To understand diaspora African communities in the context of religion and inequality, it is important to accept that 'diaspora' experiences are sandwiched between dispersion and religion. According to the biblical definition of the term, it comes from the dispersal of the Jewish community into the new environment. Consequently, with this definition in mind, diaspora African communities strive to settle within a new environment.

To date, there has not been a lot of literature that reflects the relationship between religion and inequality in the context of diaspora African communities. While there is considerable literature on religion and diaspora African communities (see, for example, Ter Haar 1998; Adogame 2013; Pasura 2014; Pasura and Erdal 2016), there is limited attention on the theme of inequality. This chapter fills that gap by exploring how the major religious traditions in Africa impact on inequality in the context of migration. A critical question this chapter is asking relates to how religion is implicated in either perpetuating or reducing inequality in the context of diaspora African communities.

Thus, this chapter acknowledges that the religious traditions in Africa are heterogeneous and their effects differ in diverse African countries and contexts. Therefore, taking a global view about the plight of diaspora African communities, this chapter acknowledges that Africans from different parts of Africa are received differently by their host nations. For example, sometimes Africans from nations that were formerly colonized by a particular host country are appreciated because of their skills and language. In other instances, a shared religious identity facilitates the acceptance of diaspora African communities. Accordingly, the overarching aim of this chapter is to explore the effects of African Traditional Religion, African Independent churches tradition, and Protestantism, including Pentecostal traditions, on inequality in the context of diaspora African communities. The chapter acknowledges the role of Islam in the African diaspora (Curtis 2014), but does not cover this particular dimension.

The context: Diaspora African communities

This chapter uses the diaspora African communities as a case study to understand the relation between religion and inequality. Admittedly, the word 'Africans' is too broad and needs delimitation. So, 'Africans' in this study refers to all African descendants, but does not include those associated with transatlantic slavery who reside in Europe and the Americas. The African Union Commission defines the Africa Diaspora as 'peoples of African origin living outside the continent, irrespective of their citizenship and nationality and who are willing to contribute to the development of the continent and the building of the African Union'. It is clear from this definition that Africans in the diaspora are expected to help to develop Africa. Inevitably, accepting this position promotes inequality. For instance, from an economic perspective, this suggests that those Africans living in diaspora are not equal to Africans living in Africa. This creates economic pressure for Africans in the diaspora to sacrifice for Africans on the continent. Below, the chapter expands on the understanding of 'diaspora' that informs its approach.

The term 'diaspora' is increasingly getting attention in scholarship. 'Diaspora-ness' is a state of being, worth national and continental recognition. Diaspora-ness is a state of being, which should be understood within the specific socioeconomic, political and cultural milieu. Statistics show that Africans in different parts of the world can be estimated as: North America 39.16 million; Latin America 112.65 million; Caribbean 13.56 million and Europe 3.51 million (World Bank 2012). Significantly, the African diaspora consists of approximately 170 million people out of the 1.2 billion people. To understand inequality in the context of diaspora African communities, it is important to reflect on the relationship between African and her diaspora. Diaspora African communities are likely to be affected by the impact of religion and political issues on the continent or country of origin. There is diffusion of material, intellectual and spiritual resources between Africans living in diaspora and Africans living in Africa. In this regard, diaspora African communities are strategically positioned to redefine and reshape Africa. However, they need to negotiate the problematic and reality of nationalism.

Nationalism as a driver of inequality

Nationalism is an ideology that is gaining momentum in the contemporary period. Nationalism is a driver for inequality and is sustained by religion. As mentioned above, religion is at the centre of migration processes. Diaspora African communities are often regarded as 'foreigners' within host nations. The term 'foreigners' has a negative connotation, suggesting a sense of not being welcome. Such social construction and naming propel inequality. Regardless of the contributions of the immigrant to host nations, immigrants are mostly regarded as 'foreigners'. This finding, while preliminary, suggests that immigrants are not equal to people in the host nations.

On the other hand, some people in the sending nations feel diaspora African communities are 'traitors' or 'runaways' who either failed to stand with their countries or want the best of both worlds. Sande (forthcoming) argued that when Zimbabweans speak about people who went into diaspora, they seem to be angry for being left in crises and having bad experiences in Zimbabwe. Diaspora African communities are accused of wanting to remember their roots when all is convenient and exotic, but who are quick to pack and leave when the going gets tough. Be that as it may, people in sending nations expect continuous transactions and relations with the diaspora African communities. One of the resources that diaspora African communities carry with them is their African traditional religious spirituality. Central to this spirituality is the idea of communalism.

However, religious practices which promote communalism can be a source of inequality, if not approached with a sense of balance. For instance, the African Traditional Religions focus on a traditional concept of family. A family unit is not only the immediate family, but the extended family too. Such a practice often makes running a family expensive, relatively making the people poor. Traditionally, African families and extended families are big because they used to cater for labour. The family with the highest number of children was likely to become economically empowered. So, this high fertility facilitated the accumulation of wealth. This is opposed to the Jewish family which owns huge financial status for their families (Brenner and Kiefer 1981). It can thus be suggested that religion aids in producing both social and economic inequalities and these harm diaspora African communities.

Although diaspora African communities use religion to settle in host nations, this is not always easy. Some immigrants maintain their religions from Africa. According to Tettey (2007) there is a continuous engagement between members of African Independent Churches with the socioeconomic and political concerns in Africa. When members of African Independent Churches migrate, they carry their religious identities with them. In most cases, diaspora African communities have failed to assimilate to host nation's homogeneous church traditions, such as the mainline churches. This finding has important implications for sustaining the notion that diaspora African communities are biased towards loving their homeland and religion. However, this phenomenon is popular with first-generation immigrants. In this case, religious affinity promotes inequality. Unlike the concept of 'diaspora' which occupies physical space, religion occupies social and spiritual space. 'Religion and places are mutually influential' (Knott 2010: 476).

The first-generation immigrants struggle with the issue of transnationalism. The concept of transnationalism focuses on the exchanges, connections and practices across borders. This chapter argues that religion acts as an agent as well as a subject of transnationalism. It allows immigrants to engage in transnational activities and practices to either a greater or lesser degree. Such a role of religion makes it a vehicle to promote inequality because diaspora African communities want to maintain closer religious links to their sending nations. African immigrant churches are seen as serving ethnic people in diaspora. In general, therefore, it seems that religion has the potential to hold connected communities through the joining of one diasporic or transnational community or the other. In this case, religions authenticate the racial challenges that exist within communities. However, religion has to use connected communities to challenge inequality within diaspora African communities.

Poverty and economic contributions cause inequality

Poverty is continuously impacting Africans and is a push factor for the migration of many Africans in search of greener pastures. However, faith and religious practices are key elements that give meaning to how diaspora African communities can deal with poverty. Thus, diaspora African communities can be called transnational communities alleviating the effects of poverty. The sending nations through their families will be expecting their contributions. Both the African Traditional Religion and Christianity teach honouring parents and supporting siblings. The teaching of respecting parents is the source of communalism. It may be the case, therefore, that the concept of communalism has the potential to reduce inequality as people can share their resources. However, some diaspora African communities struggle to make ends meet. According to Burgess (2008: 49), in the British context, there is more of an emphasis on hard work and the employment of alternative strategies for acquiring material prosperity, apart from faith and prayer.

Besides, the host nations and the sending nations alike treat diaspora African communities as 'economic resources' that can be tapped, but not embraced. Some African countries do not want to disclose the diaspora's economic contributions to their nations. One of the reasons is that, the leaders do not want to admit that they are financially dependent on the diaspora. A total of 46 billion US dollars were sent to sub-Saharan Africa in 2018. The role of religion in encouraging these transactions cannot be denied. These results suggest that the remittances help to reduce the severity and suffering people in the countries of origin and this helps to reduce inequality amongst countries and individuals. Bettendorf and Dijkgraaf (2010) argued that in high-income countries religiosity reduces income inequality.

Most Africans believe that education is a powerful resource to end poverty. So, education, professionalism and experiences of diaspora African communities are resources for economic empowerment. Therefore, the African diaspora communities indirectly build sending nations' infrastructure and betterment of the homelands. Most immigrants are motivated to work for their families and live happy lives. The question is, what role does religion play to end poverty? In sub-Saharan Africa, Pentecostal prosperity theology has some potential impact on addressing inequality. Burgess (2009) argued that 'Pentecostal prosperity theology' has some positive contribution towards immigrants' civic engagement. In Europe, particularly Britain, African Pentecostal theology presents strategies to reduce economic inequalities for diaspora African communities. Thus, religions that promote the social and economic gospel have the potential to shape ideologies of equality within the society and underdeveloped nations and communities.

African Pentecostals, African religions and African Indigenous churches use rituals like prophecy, healings, miracles, dreams and visions to help the believers to be positive and strive to improve their economic status. Many Christians, especially from the Pentecostal traditions, always use Christianity to legitimize their success and businesses. It is possible to hypothesize that these sermons and testimonies provide coping strategies for the dispossessed diaspora African communities. So, on the positive side, religion offers structural support that benefit diaspora African communities to navigate their daily lives.

However, diaspora African communities cannot function as 'magic bullets' to provide solutions to complex development issues in altering the fragmenting social system in Africa. Religion at times contributes to making the people poor. Distribution of wealth is dependent on some religious beliefs and this affects the earning of religious groups (Picketty 2014). Some religions do not empower their members to pursue higher secular education, which ultimately affects income inequality. For instance, African Traditional Religions use other forms of education which are different from conventional Western education. Consequently, graduates of such education systems endure inequality when their qualifications are not recognized by the hegemonic Western education. The colonial education system, including missionary education, focused on promoting inequality and supporting imperialism. This resonates with findings by Keister and Eagle (2014) who argued that religion creates and maintains social and economic inequality.

Identity and culture enhance inequality

Class, culture and identity emerged as key aspects which drive inequality within diaspora African communities. Identity as a factor affects inequality because it has an impact on how diaspora African communities perceive themselves. Particularly, growing knowledge about migration shows that diaspora African communities fail to quickly adapt and integrate themselves within the host nations. A study on Zimbabwean churches in Britain (Sande and Samushonga 2020: 27) argued that 'it is however uncommon for African diaspora Pentecostal churches to emerge and continue to exist along ethnic lines and not integrate with other cultures'. The Black Majority churches feel comfortable to fellowship on their own, as opposed to fellowshipping with white mainline churches. According to Appiah (2015) African migrant churches in Britain make networks for social, business and other reasons which may have nothing to do with religious thrust. These findings suggest that when this happens, unequal religious relations are enhanced, making religion a means of coping with oppression and legitimizing structural inequality. Consequently, some houses of worship have been marked as 'social ghettos' (Adedibu 2013: 418).

On the more positive side, the second-generation immigrants are likely to adapt to the host nation's culture but, suffer identity crises along the way. According to Sande and Manyanga (2020) the migration process makes the youth vulnerable to an identity crisis. However, the impact of migration processes causes the youth (second generation) to have hybrid identities, while parents (first generation) have dual identities. It is possible to hypothesize that religion has the potential to assist in creating youth identities for the children within diaspora African communities. The fact that religion offers understanding of one's identity gives it opportunities to challenge inequality for diaspora African communities. Most religious traditions teach about a spiritual identity, for example, the Christians believe that their identity will be like Jesus Christ (1 John 3:2–3). According to this text, it can be inferred that the Christian ideology focuses on spiritual identity and gives a sense of equality. It makes believers not to think about national identity but to concentrate on attaining a new spiritual identity. Accordingly, this creates the impression that identity should not be defined by ethnicity, place of origin or cultural background.

Further, identity is interpreted within the notion of language and culture. This is the case, at least in part because diaspora African communities continuously negotiate aspects of culture and language within their host nations, perhaps to both integrate and settle within host nations. As put by Olupona and Gemignani (2007), Ghanaians in Canada use immigrant churches to act as conduits for the construction of dynamic and fluid transnational identities. To put it differently, this observation may support the hypothesis that the ability of religion to embody language and culture helps in reducing inequality. Accordingly, proper use of religious language can be a strategy to reduce inequality. For instance, the notion of 'heavenly citizenry' can balance the conflicting ideologies culture and language for diaspora African communities. Thus, language is central to the social construction of identity. Religious language and faith make believers to abide by specific rules, and these rules of language shape how we understand the world. As a result, religious language is not neutral; it emphasizes certain things while ignoring others, such as issues of equality. Thus, religious language constrains what we can express as well as our perceptions of what we experience and what we know as inequality.

Migration processes for diaspora African communities inevitably cause new nationalities and hybridized identities. In the globalized world, religion aids in promoting equality as the notions of boundaries are slowly fading away. Thus, while African Traditional Religions emphasize the places of birth as sacred and responsible for giving people their identity, Christian traditions employ the birthplace as a neutral place, while waiting for transition to 'heaven'. Hence, it could conceivably be hypothesized that these findings suggest that some elements of Christian teachings like heaven, within limits, are useful to help diaspora African communities to reduce homeland loyalties and promote integration. The settling of diaspora African communities within host nations, in the long run, is likely to give rise to equality. Migration processes indeed move people away from their homes and this can be considered in some way as promoting inequality. Religion and other social ideologies help to construct the idea of 'home' as a place where one spent a considerable time, even working and socializing, and a place where one feels relieved. This chapter suggests that the value of 'home' provides a weak link that may exist between diaspora African communities and inequality. The fact that religion, then, functions to establish the meaning of home to diaspora African communities acts to reinforce inequality. It can create the feeling of alienation among diasporan Africans in their new setting and prevent them from settling down and competing against those who have a more settled notion of 'home'.

The nexus of culture and identity is important for this chapter. African Traditional Religions uphold that culture and personal identities tie individuals to their countries of origin. For instance, in Zimbabwe *midzimu* (ancestors) are regarded as guardians of traditional morality. According to Machoko (2013) Zimbabweans in Canada use rituals, sacrifices, prayers and fetishes from ATR and AIC so that they remain with a sense of identity, security and protection. In this process, religion gives a false consciousness that promotes identity by encouraging cultural values and beliefs. The result, then, is that religion supports and validates structured inequality embedded within host nations' societies.

Racism sustains inequality

Racism emerged as a driver of inequality within diaspora African communities. Racism is prevalent in the context of economic empowerment. In this way, racism creates inequality by categorizing people as 'white' and non-white. One may think that racism is a thing of the past, but racism is embodied within structures. Diaspora African communities experience institutionalized racism especially in the areas of employment and other economic empowerment programmes. According to Small (2018) race-thinking is a multi-faceted phenomenon responding to contemporary conditions. It can, therefore, be noted that there is a correlation between religion and racial biases.

To have a better picture of the experience of diaspora African communities about racism, it is important to accept that religion played a significant role in colonization of Africa. Diaspora African communities merge racism, colonization and religion. According to Small (2018: 1183), 'the UK had an extensive, deeply exploitative and long-standing colonial and imperial intrusion, lasting hundreds of years, in Africa and the Americas; and currently has a relatively large black population (in comparison with other nations in Europe)'. One implication of this is the possibility that there is no hope for religion being part of the solution to promote equality and inclusion of diaspora African communities. However, Christian traditions have an opportunity of revisiting the memory lane, and correct and acknowledge where Christian traditions erred and encouraged colonization. African Independent Churches were at the centre of speaking against colonization. Essentially, as Engelke (2007) argued, African Independent Churches were formed to challenge racism. However, in diaspora settings, African Independent Churches face stigma and discrimination, leading to inequality.

Achieving equality is a daunting task for diaspora African communities involving an inquiry into complex racial relations between the sending and host nations. At the same time, it is important to note that despite the chapter's focus on diaspora African communities, religion and inequality, the chapter recognizes that the hangover of racism impacts other social inequalities such as gender, income and leadership. In a commentary by Braunstein (2017) religious ideologies and ritualized religious practices such as ecumenical prayer help to build effective movements across class, racial and cultural lines. What could be interesting as well following Braunstein's argument is the fact that diaspora African communities tend to be marginalized and affected by global politics, institutionalized racism and postcolonial issues. By way of filling this gap, this chapter goes a step further by arguing that the task of challenging of postcolonialism and racism should not be left to religion alone. The challenges faced by diaspora African communities call for understanding the nature of support that diaspora African communities require from Africa to deal with the challenges and predicament of colonial and postcolonial issues. Or put in other words, are there ways diaspora African communities can assist Africa in negotiating the challenges of postcolonialism or vice versa?

It can thus be argued that religion can create inequality through promoting religious ethnocentrism. It is possible, therefore, that there is infiltration of traditional values and social conformity based on racial boundaries. According to Machoko (2013: 476), Zimbabweans arriving in Canada face '… racial discrimination, high unemployment, and an inability to obtain permanent residency and citizenship … all of which lead them to maintain their adherence to African Indigenous Religion and African Independent Churches act as vehicles of attachment with Zimbabwe'. This present study raises the possibility that the continued existence of racial biases and rhetoric amongst the churches shows that Christianity often sustains racist attitudes.

The fact that diaspora African communities are coming to new territories, from Africa whose economic systems are often deemed as inferior to those of the host nations, leaves them disadvantaged in the context of economic empowerment. This agrees with Marxist theorization about the relationship between religion and class. Karl Marx argued that, religion within capitalist societies legitimizes the status quo, making sure that the working class will not recognize the roots of their alienation. The diction 'religion is the opium of the people' (Marx 1978: 54) is a reality to diaspora African communities. Diaspora African communities turn to religion to meet their means of survival, potentially forcing the idea of using religion to promote equality to the periphery. For example, as in the case in Ghanaians in Canada, Zimbabweans also had 'Visa pastors' (Tettey 2007: 235). As defined by Machoko (2013: 487), 'Visa pastors' were 'special' pastors of AICs who were believed to be anointed by God to pray for Zimbabweans so that they could easily get visas to go to

Europe, North America, Australia and New Zealand. Thus, one of the issues that emerges from these findings is the fact that religion can deepen inequality by generating unrealistic hopes and aspirations. However, on the positive side, one finding by Adogame (2013: 101–9) studying African Nigerians in Britain demonstrated that African Pentecostal churches in the diaspora are critical wellsprings of social, cultural and spiritual capital.

The role of sacred texts in deepening inequality is yet another dimension critical to this study. For instance, the Bible is somewhat at the centre of the discourse about inequality. The starting point in the context of diaspora African communities is to accept that many of the facts about inequality can be traced to the emergence of Christianity in Africa. Christianity promoted inequality in Africa through the distinct dichotomy between whites and Blacks, and this was exacerbated by colonization. According to Hondius (2014), Africans were considered as heathen, inferior and subordinate. These findings help us to understand that religion can create or sustain and promote class divisions and inequalities that are in line with values and beliefs. In the same vein, biased interpretation is used to justify inequality as something divine. Mostly, the story of Noah is used, saying that Noah cursed Canaan, who was a descendant of Ham. This is regarded as African(s) who were cursed and are supposed to serve their (white) brothers. Such stories show that Christianity can be used to justify racism in the diaspora, thereby deepening inequality on the part of Africans who have migrated in search of greener pastures.

Conclusion

The present chapter was designed to determine the relationship between religion, inequality and diaspora African communities. In the context of migration and transnationalism, the diaspora African communities are increasing across the globe. As such, the African Union has defined the Africans in the diaspora as the sixth region of Africa. Therefore, this population implies that it has the potential to bring other dynamics to understanding the nexus between religion, inequality and diaspora African communities. This chapter has identified that diaspora African communities experience diverse inequalities across the globe and sectors, and that religion plays a critical and strategic role in issues of inequality. In particular, religion has an ambivalent role in inequality in the context of the diaspora African communities. So, the effects of different religious traditions on inequality are mixed; they can either be negative or positive.

The other perspective, which is the second major finding of this study, showed that nationalism, culture and identity, and racism, are factors interfacing with religion and inequality in diaspora African communities. For instance, this study showed that African Traditional Religion, Protestants, including Pentecostal traditions and the African Independent Churches, play a role in trying to mitigate inequalities for diaspora African communities. Overall, this study strengthens the idea that religion permeates the dynamics of migration processes, settlement in host nations, family reunions and the transnational ideologies. It is imperative to accept that although there are some negative elements about the impact of religion on inequality, many religions and versions of Christian traditions are positive in their claims to equality in the public domain and make a broader contribution to the nexus among religion, inequality and diaspora African communities. For future research, there is a need to focus on understanding some of the challenges to the development of a strong Africa-diaspora nexus, with religion as a mobilizing force. Such studies can establish how Africa can continue to help advance diaspora causes and vice versa, utilizing the social capital that religion avails.

Part Two

Negotiating religion, gender and inequality in Africa

The one-man Jihad

Sarki Sanusi Lamido Sanusi (SLS) and Hausa Muslim women's status in Northern Nigeria

Rahina Muazu

Introduction

This chapter analyses gender and Muslim Hausa[1] women.[2] It focuses on Sarki Sanusi Lamido Sanusi (SLS), the fourteenth Emir of Kano Emirate's efforts to use Islamic legal tradition to achieve equality for women. Sarki Sanusi Lamido Sanusi has spoken publicly about the situation of women and advocated for the passage of a Bill to protect the latter from various forms of gender-based abuse. The goal of the Bill is to cover what he sees as the biggest gap in Islamic jurisprudence in Nigeria, that is, the lack of understanding of the fundamentals of Islamic law and the inability to use it to bring the Muslim community into the twenty-first century. Through the objectives of the Islamic law (*maqasid al-Shari'a*), public interest (*masalih al-amma*) and restriction of what is permissible (*taqyid al-mubah*), the Bill aims to regulate, amongst other things, the age of marriage, divorce, reproduction, child custody and fight for equal treatment for Muslim women. This chapter draws on interviews, audio-visual material and an analysis of the Kano State Muslim Code of Personal Status. Its central goal is to analyse religion and inequality with particular reference to the status of women in Islam in a northern Nigerian context.

Gender in Muslim majority contexts has attracted a lot of academic attention (Marnissi 1985; 1993; Ahmed 1992; Wadud 1999; Barlas 2002). In trying to explain the persistence of high levels of gender inequality in Muslim majority countries as they rank low on gender equality indexes,[3] many factors have been explored. These include family/kinship structure (Spierings 2014), 'Islamic culture', Islamism, the impact of oil, the patriarchal state (Kandiyoti 1991; Charrad 2009; Ross 2012), economic factors (Moghadem 2005), government policies (Spierings, Smits and Mieke 2009) and the impact of colonialism (Muazu 2019).

In northern Nigeria, the poor condition of Muslim women is evident through a low level of female education, low female labour participation, poverty, diseases, easy access to polygamous marriages, a high number of divorces, among others. In many cases, female divorcees, who are mostly financially ill-equipped, are suddenly left to fend not only for themselves but for their abandoned children. There is also no state law forcing the fathers of their children to provide financial support, nor is there any organized welfare assistance. This rampant divorce and lack of maintenance have resulted in many young, divorced women living in difficult situations and millions of out-of-school children begging on the streets. All these problems have been connected to the kind of gender regime present in the Hausa Muslim society.

In this chapter, I take gender in Hausa society as a social construct derived from certain notions of femininity and masculinity that both the culture and religion have shaped. As defined by Connell (2002: 10), it is also a 'structure of social relations that centers on the reproductive arena, and the set of practices that bring reproductive distinctions between bodies into social processes'. In the Hausa society and others, gender relation is not a coincidence but a structural relationship. The gender orders or regimes form a pattern of structural inequality, shaped by many factors that include the perception of women, economic factors and specific interpretations of Islam.

Scholarly works in the field recognized as Islamic feminism have focused on gender relations and the struggle for full equality between women and men. These studies, which are based on the discourse of Islam, especially its sacred text, the Qur'an, have investigated the historical roots of women's oppression (Ahmed 1992), endeavoured to reinterpret the Qur'an from a woman's perspective (Wadud 1999; Barlas 2002), disputed ethnocentric presentations of Muslim women and mounted a detailed critique of patriarchy (Ahmed 1992; Barlas 2002; Badran 2008). The knowledge approach it brings uses the concept of gender to understand how Muslim communities view biological differences between men and women and how perceptions of women's roles influence male-dominated religious interpretations (Muazu 2019). However, the above studies concentrate mainly on Arab Muslim women, and the Black African Muslim women of West Africa, despite their large population size, have been chiefly excluded (Edwin 2016). This is also consistent with the general trend of overlooking female Muslim scholars in Africa (Frede 2020).

These works by Muslim feminists are essential because they have recognized that to have a meaningful change in the Muslim majority context, Islam should be part of the solution. As the society is Muslim and the women whom they fight for take their religion seriously, therefore, the Qur'an, with its egalitarian values, should be used to argue for full equality for women. They also maintain that scholars and activists could work together to bring fresh perspectives on Islamic teachings (Wadud 1999). The advocacy of SLS could be placed under this category, as he argues that Islamic legal tradition must be used to bring about gender reform in the Hausa Muslim society. Although he differs from scholars such as Wadud and Hosseini, who concentrate on the egalitarian aspects of the Qur'an, SLS argues that it is *fiqh* we need and a 'jurisprudence intelligence' that needs to bring the Hausa society along with gender equality into the twenty-first century.

Sanusi Lamido Sanusi (SLS)

In July 1961, Muhammed Sanusi Lamido Sanusi was born in Kano to the Kano royal emirate family. He grew up in the royal court and received both Islamic and secular education. He has degrees in Economics and Islamic studies and worked as an academic and later as a banker. He gradually climbed to the rank of the Governor of the Central Bank of Nigeria (CBN). In 2014, he was suspended from CBN by the then Nigerian President Goodluck Jonathan after exposing a 20-billion-dollar oil fraud in the Nigerian National Petroleum Corporation (NNPC). Afterward, SLS was crowned as the 40th Emir of Kano in 2014. The Kano ancient city-state has been in existence for more than 2,000 years, and SLS's dynasty, the Dabo dynasty, has been ruling Kano for over 200 years. In postcolonial Nigeria, the emirate continues its religious and traditional role, advising political authorities and collaborating to deliver public services. On his accession as the new Sarki, SLS became one of the most influential Muslims in Nigeria. However, on 9 March 2020, he was dethroned after a conflict with the Kano State Governor Abdullahi Ganduje, who accused SLS of being a 'celebrated social critic that has not understood the responsibilities of a traditional ruler and could not control his tongue'. On 10 May 2020, he was appointed as the leader of the Tijjaniyya Sufi order in Nigeria. At the time of the data collection for this chapter, SLS had four wives and fourteen children.

SLS spent most of his reign (8 June 2014–9 March 2020) calling for cultural, social and religious reforms, particularly gender reforms for women. In his public talks and writings,[4] he criticized various forms of gender inequality and abuses against women, such as 'forced marriage, careless polygamy and reckless children reproduction'. All these, he says, result in a 'high number of divorced women, irresponsible men and neglected children that end up on the streets, into drugs, political thuggery, and violent extremism'. SLS has also critiqued the re-implementation of Shari'a by the twelve northern states, starting in 1999. He argues that in all those twelve states, apart from the Muslim criminal law, no other law has been codified:

> It is almost as if, if you are not a thief; if you don't commit assault, if you are not a criminal, then the Shari'a does not apply to you. You will not go to any of those states and find a law written that talks about consent in marriage, the rights of wives and husbands. What does Islam say about domestic violence if you beat your wife? What is the right of a wife when she is divorced? What are the responsibilities of the husbands if a child is found on the street? Is the father responsible, and can the state hold him accountable? These are all Shari'a, and they are far more important than just talking about cutting off the hand of a thief.

Although SLS criticized the Shari'a re-implementation (which he feared might be a political project) for its lack of codification of a law that regulates the lives of Muslims, particularly the institution of marriage, the only solution to women abuse, according to him, will be a return to the Shari'a. During his reign, he set up a committee that looked at the Islamic legal tradition, putting together scholars from various fields and non-governmental organizations (NGOs) to come up with a bill to be passed by the Kano state house of assembly. The bill they produced covers the personal status of Muslims, including marriage, divorce, child custody, inheritance, will and testimony. SLS wants marriage, polygamy and divorce to be regulated. He believes that the inability to do that in the past became the root cause of women's abuse in the Hausa society. Men allowed to practise polygamy must also take responsibility and face the consequences in case divorce occurred, he stated.

The failure of the society which led to these forms of abuses is because 'men have enjoyed privileges of having many wives and refused to take responsibility'. Quoting from Ibn Taymiyya's (*al-siyasa al-shar'iyya*), he states that the Qur'anic verse 57:25 must be followed:

> Certainly, We have sent our apostles with clear arguments, and sent down with them the Book and the balance that men may conduct themselves with equity; and We have made the iron, wherein is great violence and advantages to men, and that Allah may know who helps Him and His apostles in secret; surely Allah is Strong, Mighty.

He explains that the messengers and scriptures are sent by Allah to create balance and maintain justice in this world, justice in our relationship with our Maker and justice in our relationship with fellow human beings. 'Justice in a marriage means that if a man takes the privilege of being the head of the family, he takes the responsibility of being the maintainer and provider of the family' (Qur'an 4:34). He states that one cannot take the privilege and abandon the responsibility. If he does, then the reference to iron in Qur'an 57:25 is a reference to state power, which must ensure that the rules are followed, and wrongdoers are punished.

SLS recognizes the intersectional[5] nature of women's oppression. In his lecture, 'how to stop manufacturing poverty on an industrial scale', he maintains that particular religious interpretation and culture are not the only causes of women's abuse. He expanded his argument beyond the religious paradigm. It was the mainline of thinking until the late 1970s, which gives religion a privileged explanatory power and subsumed people only under religious categories of thought. The complexity of their lives is reduced to one or two symbols deemed representative of their culture, for example, veil or polygamy. Within this context, it is difficult to appreciate and identify how religion, politics, economics and gender interact under specific historical conditions (see Marnia 1990). In the context of the Hausa Muslim society, SLS states that poverty, illiteracy, child mortality, population growth, out-of-school children, low women labour participation, malnutrition, maternal mortality all come together to produce the kind of gender inequality that is being witnessed. The worst of it, however, is low girls' education:

> I believe that the single silver bullet that will solve 70% of our problems in Africa will be the education of the girl child and an opportunity for women to earn a living. Because that deals with malnutrition, infant mortality, maternal mortality … child spacing … extreme poverty. All the human development indexes that today are embarrassing us will basically begin to disappear once we keep girls in school longer, improve the quality of education, and then allow them to earn something. So ensuring inclusive and quality education, especially for girls, and promoting sustained inclusive and sustainable economic growth, full employment, and work for all, especially for women.

To place his statement above in a larger picture, SLS started by looking at how enormous improvement in the living standard of people globally has been achieved, and hunger, poverty, illiteracy and child mortality have all been reduced by 40–50%. 'In every region of the world, based on the Goal Keepers and Bill Gates reports, poverty has decreased except in sub-Saharan Africa, and according to the Gates Foundation, by 2050, 85% of extreme poverty in the world will be on the African continent, and half of those will be in Nigeria and DRC.' One of the significant drivers of poverty, he continues, is population growth. As projections show that by 2100, Africa will cross the 2 billion mark if it continues on its current highest fertility rate. Nigeria leads the regional variations, with much higher fertility rates in the north. This is also where there is the highest level of poverty. Within the north, the northwest has the lowest level of girl child education, the highest number of out-of-school children, and the highest fertility rate.

What is alarming to SLS is that even though the Nigerian population has been growing at the rate of about 3.4 per cent annually, doubling every twenty years, he states that the people in northern Nigeria, which is overwhelmingly Muslim, have since the Nigerian independence in 1960 grown eight times, while still competing and conflicting on the same resources (such as herders and farmers conflicts). In Kano state alone, he states that there are 3 million children out of school, which the system cannot cope with. In addition, '58% of all under-five children suffer from malnutrition, 48% of all women of reproductive age are anemic due to iron deficiency, we have one of the highest infant mortality and maternal mortality rates in the world'. What is important to note here is that SLS has tied all these problems to the root cause of women's gender-based abuse. He argues in many of his public talks that the inability of society to respect girls and women, educate them and accord them the rights and opportunities they deserve is what leads to all the problems. An effective solution, he says, lies not only in building more hospitals and schools but in codifying a Muslim family law.

The Kano State Muslim Family Bill

The Kano State Muslim Family and related matters Bill (1440 A.H. 2019) is a 137-page document that aims to provide a law for the regulation of marriage and related matters. The purpose of the Bill is to address the myriad of problems affecting the marital institution in society, to regulate it, improve it, and protect the rights of spouses within a subsisting marriage and after divorce. When passed into law, it will apply to any marriage contracted under Islamic Law within or outside Kano, provided the spouses are living within the state. It also applies to any union between Muslim spouses or between a Muslim man and a woman from the People of the Book (*ahl al-Kitab*, in this case, usually referring to the

Christians, but also Jews). Non-Muslim spouses may consent to the application of the law. In the course of application of the provisions of the law, a judge may refer to the rules of Islamic Law as expounded by Maliki jurists and contained in the corpus of Islamic Jurisprudence. The Bill also covers polygamy, rights of children and orphans, maintenance (*nafaqa*), lineage, deceit in marriage, absence of a partner (*ghaybah*), the waiting period after divorce (*idda*), custody of children (*hadana*), legal capacity (*ahliyya*), guardianship (*wilaya*), bequest (*wasiyya*), endowment (*waqf*) and inheritance (*mirath*).

One dimension that is vital to SLS, which is also very controversial, is the question of regulating the age of marriage for girls. Many people have criticized SLS for publicly pursuing that. Part of their argument is that there is no Islamic ruling which prevents parents or guardians from marrying off their daughters, even at the age of three. SLS argues that under Islamic jurisprudence, there is

> *taqyid al-mubah*, regulating that which is lawful. I will give an example that we can all understand. We all have freedom of movement; you have the freedom to drive your vehicle, you have complete freedom. It is permissible, [but] someone says to you, if you see a red light, you must stop. He has not stopped you from driving, but he has regulated driving because if you keep going through those red lights, you can kill someone, you can cause accidents, you can damage society. That is the principle of *taqyid al-mubah*. If you say wait until a girl has reached a particular stage before you marry her, you have not stopped the marriage; you have not stopped the sunna, you have simply regulated a certain element of it that has been shown to cause harm to society at this point. We have seen all the harm associated with all these, but having that conversation is very difficult … Shari'a intelligence is the most crucial intellectual component that we lack as an Umma.

Another controversial issue is lowering reproduction. SLS thinks incentives, just like in Egypt, could be used to keep the number of children low, 'they don't have a one-child policy, but if you have only one child, the state will pay for the child's education up to university level. If you are a welfare recipient, you cannot have more than two children.' SLS argues that it makes sense to implement a similar thing in Nigeria. 'If you know you cannot feed one [child], … why go and have more … those who cannot maintain one wife in northern Nigeria will go and marry three wives and have ten children … the poorer you get, the more wives you marry.' He has publicly stated that although men have the right to marry four wives, they do not have the right to starve the wives, and the whole institution has to be regulated.

Concluding remarks

This chapter has analysed some Hausa Muslim women's gender concerns in northern Nigeria by focusing on the advocacy of SLS. As the fourteenth Emir of the Kano Emirate, SLS has used most of his reign to advocate for social change concentrating on gender equality for women. As northern Nigeria is marred by poverty, insecurity and corruption, SLS has always tied all those problems back to the problems faced by women. In his attempt to bring about social change, he initiated and supervised the writing of a Bill (the Kano State Muslim Code of Personal Status) under Islamic law that covers marriage, divorce and child maintenance, amongst many others.

SLS is a social thinker and arguably the most outspoken elite on Muslim women's rights in northern Nigeria. His views have, however, been controversial. The reason lies not only in his scholarly positions but in his non-conservative approach. While he advocated for the use of Shari'a and Islamic jurisprudence to 'emancipate' women, in most of his public talks and writings, he discusses the various 'traditional' positions taken by scholars and then subjects them to critique. SLS states that 'an argument's popularity among the faithful is not necessarily based at all times on superior validity of its truth-claims'. With this viewpoint, he has publicly critiqued popular practices such as polygamy, reproduction and divorce and has received his fair share of criticisms.

He has maintained that the bulk of the problems associated with public intellectual discourse on Islam and gender reforms in Nigeria have their roots in the failure of the academic faculties of Islamic studies in the universities that trained the participants, especially in Nigeria and Saudi Arabia. This is because modern research in Islamic studies has transcended the purely religious, and in most universities, Muslim societies are studied from perspectives in social sciences-anthropology, sociology, political economy and international relations.

SLS is right in his attempt to get women's rights obtained through the Shari'a because no meaningful change could be achieved for women without engaging the Islamic legal tradition. The population is Muslim, and it takes its religion very seriously. Therefore, it would only be wise to utilize the Islamic concept of justice to achieve equality for women. However, as SLS was dethroned, and the Kano State Muslim Code of Personal Status Bill is yet to be passed into law. On women's rights, any close observer knows that there is a very long way to go. The reason is simple. Those with authority are not yet ready to engage themselves with the right question. Any advocate of women's rights or gender equality could be easily painted as pursuing a 'Jewish or a western propaganda' (Hausa: *yahudanci*). They are often accused of attacking Islam of depriving women of their rights. On the contrary, many Muslim feminists and pro-women's rights working on ground are certain that Islam has accorded women their full rights, but the question is, have Muslim men, the society or women (as one of the main reproducers of patriarchy themselves) accorded women those rights? Until this question is sincerely asked, no meaningful change or even a sincere conversation can begin.

Negotiating gender inequality in religious fields

Bishop Margaret Wanjiru's use of charisma and social capital in Kenya

Loreen Maseno

Introduction

Gender inequality in the Kenyan religious arena has been attributed to various factors. A number of these inequalities stem from cultural references and (mis) interpretations of religious canons. Three gender models are introduced to highlight the diversity within gender in Christianity. This chapter explores how Bishop Margaret Wanjiru of the Jesus is Alive Ministries (JIAM) in the face of gender inequality in the Christian religious arena negotiates her standing by use of charisma and social capital. It focuses on the overflows between charisma and capital and the way Bishop Margaret Wanjiru mediates both to negotiating gender inequality. The charisma Wanjiru displays works to her advantage to minimize explicit gender inequality and to accord her additional symbolic capital which she further reinvests for even more social prestige and honour. The central argument in this chapter is that charisma as exemplified by Wanjiru when routinized serves the end of negotiating gender inequality and legitimizing her in the religious field.

Setting the scene

The religious field is but one variant of social fields (Bourdieu 1991: 2). The Kenyan Christian religious field serves as the context for our investigation. Within this field, 'social forces and social struggles based on the relations of exchange between religious actors and the laity, and on the competition amongst the (religious) specialists' (Bourdieu 1991: 17) come to play. Therefore, religious actors try to outsmart each in order to claim superiority over the rest.

Religious specialists in Kenya comprise both men and women. A number of women have observed and experienced myriad challenges when operating in this religious field. A prominent experience is that of gender inequality which advantages males over females when handling matters pertaining to the divine. This is due to the presuppositions which draw from the cultural context and the use of (mis)interpreted canonical teachings.

Gender inequality can be seen in various cultures in Kenya. This inequality is also noted as overflowing for Wanjiru in religious circles. According to John Migwi (2016) in his study, 'The Place of Women in African Pentecostal Churches in Limuru, Kenya', there remains a tacit influence of traditional culture on the leadership potential of many women in churches, even when unspoken, as many are conditioned by their culture which upholds traditional positions for women. Citing from Gikuyu culture extensively, Migwi notes that roles were demarcated in Gikuyu society, with women cooking, washing and nurturing children and the girl child taught to respect and obey men, regarded as breadwinners, even as men led in all social political activities, including leading prayers. Religious ceremonies were commonly led by 'fathers' (Migwi 2016: 94–5). Clearly, granted this background, leadership for women remains negotiated grounds.

Gender inequality in Christianity

Gender inequality has some historical basis in Christian history which understood the male as the norm. For the purpose of this section, a rendering by Salomonsen (2003) is explored to highlight the situation in Christian thought where she adopts Ruether's three gender models in Christian history at length. First, she describes the Gnostic model. In this model, the soul is considered unsexed whilst the body is sexed. Herein, the soul is considered of eternal value which does not come to end. The soul as unsexed follows through the worldview given that in the end, there shall be no marriages in heaven. Gender differences here are said to be limited to the physical body which is temporal and soon fading away. Within this constellation are overflowing implications and restrictions on sexed bodies and their worth.

The Romantic model has it that both the body and the soul are sexed. Here, both women and men are sexed throughout, both body and soul. Herein in terms of religion derives the logic of inequality, where it therefore follows that there is a more noble gender. According to the African theologian Mercy Oduyoye, souls as sexed,

> Women are persons-in-communion, not persons who 'complete' the other. There are female souls and there are male souls. We may need to reorient our thinking so that we see communion as a relationship devoid of hierarchical relations and power seeking.

(Oduyoye 1992: 23)

In the Liberal model, the whole idea of sexed beings is denied. Being sexed therefore remains irrelevant owing to the belief that all humans are created in the image of God (see Salomonsen 2003: 107–09). These three different models in part capture the ways in which gender in religion has been explored. Depending on which model is taken up, it has implications for gender inequality in the religious arena.

Jesus Is Alive Ministries (JIAM)

Pentecostal Christianity in Kenya traces its roots from the East Africa revival with the Balokole movement that spread from Rwanda into western parts of Kenya (Maseno 2015). There is a general consensus that there are three broad categories of Pentecostal and Charismatic Christianity in Kenya, namely: classical, independent and the Charismatic/Neo-Pentecostal church (NPC) types. Independent Pentecostal churches as those founded by Africans themselves are self-funding, self-propagating, self-supporting and have limited or no links with Western founded churches. Classical Pentecostals uphold their links to early American and European Pentecostal churches, and stress faith healing, exorcism, speaking in tongues, spontaneous prayer, prophecy, as well as laying an emphasis on visions and dreams (Parsitau 2014). Common to these churches is that they all respond to existential needs according to an African worldview, offering a personal encounter with God through the power of the Spirit, healing from sickness and deliverance from evil in all its manifestations (Anderson 2002).

According to Mwaura, citing examples such as Gaudencia Aoko, co-founder of Legio Maria Church, Reverend Teresia Wanjiru of Faith Evangelistic Ministries, Mary Senaida Dorcas Akatsa of Jerusalem Church of Christ, Bishop Margaret Wanjiru of Jesus Is Alive Ministry, Elizabeth Wahome of Single Ladies International Ministries, Bishop Margaret Wangare of Church of the Lord among others, there are several female religious leaders, particularly in the Neo-Pentecostal churches subsequent to the establishment of Christianity (Mwaura 2002).

JIAM is a ministry started by Bishop Wanjiru. Margaret Wanjiru was born in 1961 into a polygamous family in Kahuguini, Kiambu Kenya. Wanjiru herself repeats often in her church services that as a youth she was a member of the Anglican Church of Kenya. She also explains in her messages, drawing support from her experiences that she always had to fend for herself and her two children. Since her father was an alcoholic, her mother had to fend for the family. They found themselves impoverished and having to live within Nairobi's Kangemi slums where she grew up in poverty, even as her mother made and sold illicit brews to educate and feed the children. Kangemi is located in a small valley on the outskirts of Nairobi city, on the road connecting Nairobi and Naivasha. It has a population of over 150,000 people and its southern border connects with another large slum known as Kawangware.

By the age of sixteen, Wanjiru was pregnant. Before she knew what was happening she conceived the second time, despite the many warnings she had received from her mother (Kalu 2008: 150). Indeed, studies indicate that living in extreme environments like slums impacts sexual and reproductive health. This is essentially so since slum communities are often characterized by a lack of basic infrastructure, high risk of sexual and gender-based violence, high levels of substance abuse, poor livelihood opportunities and poor schooling facilities, all of which negatively impact young women aged between fifteen and twenty-two years (Beguy et al. 2014). In Kenya, it has been indicated that over 13,000 girls drop out of school annually, due to early pregnancy.

However, this account provided by Wanjiru has been contested to date. There seems to be inaccuracies and imprecisions in some of the information Wanjiru has over the years supplied to interviewers and researchers. Some researchers use the age seventeen (Parsitau 2011: 134) as the age at which she became pregnant. However, a certain James Kamangu came to the media light and insisted that he actually formally married Wanjiru according to Kikuyu traditions. His much broadcast account brings her age to about nineteen or twenty. These discrepancies came to light from media revelations following her debut on to the political arena in 2007. Consequently, the age at which she became pregnant differs and remains contested (Maseno 2017). In general, though this chapter considers the JIAM founder, it is not from a position of exceptionalism and perfection. Rather, the aforementioned denotes that a closer look into the personal lives of popular and charismatic leaders who negotiate their standing by use of charisma and social capital could possibly open up aspects of inconsistencies and cover up.

Following through Wanjiru's life course, she has worked in several places, first as a house help in Nairobi, in order to feed her children (Mwaura 2002: 202). While working as a helper, she returned to school and completed her elementary education. She later tried professional cleaning companies as her second job opportunity. Here the wages were regularized and her work station now in the commercial buildings. While doing professional cleaning jobs, she indicates that she enrolled for a marketing diploma course. She later got a job, which she did so so well, as a marketer that she moved up the ranks (Kalu 2008: 150–1).

During the marketing course, Wanjiru learnt the process and technique of promoting, advertising, selling and distributing a variety of products or services. These skills have been well utilized in her ministries through publicity, adverts, video sales, TV and radio broadcasts so that her brand name was built across Kenya and beyond. JIAM is on social media and Ustream. The JIAM website states that her discipline and determination to succeed resulted in rapid promotions and various accomplishments until she became a sales and marketing executive for a multinational firm in Nairobi. She later went on to form her own business in the city, excelling as an entrepreneur.

Wanjiru's conversion has been vividly captured. In March 1991, Wanjiru attended a crusade by the Nigerian preacher, Emmanuel Eni, where she converted to Christianity and turned away from the path she had earlier walked (Kalu 2008: 151). Eni is a Nigerian evangelist renowned for his book (Eni 1987), *Delivered from the Powers of Darkness* (Ellis and Ter Haar 1998; Corten and Marshall-Fratani 2001).

Charisma and symbolic capital

The concept of charisma emerged from Max Weber's discussion of religion (Riesebrodt 1999). Max Weber's theory of charisma describes charisma as a type of authority not based on inherited, rational or traditional power but on a supernatural gifting of power and the perception of such gifting among those who follow the leader (Fabian 1971). Thus, Wanjiru's charisma stands out as one type of legitimate authority even as her individual personality has a quality considered extraordinary and is treated as one endowed with supernatural or superhuman powers (Jentges 2014: 5).

Weber accentuated the opposition that is encountered between those with the spontaneous character of charisma and the institutionalized forms of authority.

This links closely to Bourdieu's views on the prophet as an independent who exercises authority outside of any institution, one who invests and enjoys capital by primarily depending on the value of their discourse to mobilize a religious following (Bourdieu 1991: 24). Since capital is a factor that can be invested and enjoyed to mobilize, this chapter considers these scenarios within the framework of JIAM for further discussion towards the end of Wanjiru negotiating gender inequality in religious arenas.

Capital, in its various forms, may be deemed both as something to be exploited towards religious legitimation (a means to an end) and as the product of religious legitimation, in that, capital becomes something to be enjoyed by the religious player(s) who has risen to a considerable level of religious legitimation. In this case, capital becomes the privileges that come with legitimation, the very dividends that legitimation pays to the player(s). Bourdieu differentiated various forms of capitals to include cultural capital (knowledge, educational and skills), economic capital (money and property), symbolic capital (socially recognized legitimation) and social capital (those networks of influence and support base) (Bourdieu 1991). It also follows that these forms of capital, including social, cultural and symbolic capital, do convert back into economic capital, and therefore enable one to enjoy, invest and maintain followers.

To exemplify Wanjiru's symbolic capital, it is obvious that she and other JIAM female ministers in her congregation have risen to and enjoy a significant level of acceptance, especially in the context of JIAM. The masses of the faithful who flock their services every Sunday and sit under their teaching (male ministers also speak in a significant share of Sunday services every month) are evidence of this accrued legitimacy. Many of these congregants look up to, especially, Wanjiru as a (spiritual) mother and mentor, and as a one with a word for their issues, whether socioeconomic, spiritual, personal, etc. It is this kind of overwhelming, and at times seemingly fanatical, loyalty that charismatic ministers get, that feeds from their legitimation for their enjoyment, or even exploitation towards sustained negotiation of gender inequality and the acquisition of even more symbolic capital.

Wanjiru's symbolic capital when reinvested continues to give her access to the high and mighty in the land, such as politicians and senior civil servants. These connections she strategically exploits, and enjoys, for the growth of her ministry and the much needed infrastructure and image.

Clearly, while mobilizing a following, Wanjiru invests and enjoys symbolic capital in myriad ways. In one performance, with her carefully selected words, she puts on display or, in other words, makes a careful performance in which she achieves several things. The first is to indicate that Honorable Members of Parliament have decided to worship at her church as members. This speaks to status, that of those honourable members and her own status to be able to have them in her church. As a charismatized person, Wanjiru is placed in opposition to other Pentecostal outfits ranked lower. This display works to reinforce and assert her claims of status.

Her oratory performance achieves another goal. As a charismatic figure, Wanjiru sustains and establishes clear authority structures between herself as leader and her followers, displaying a clear hierarchy with the audience. Indeed, by placing a demand and sending the honourable member, she is letting the audience know that she is the one with authority to send this honourable member with the message that they should fund a section of her construction ambitions (Jentges 2014: 7).

Such speech acts in general have a far-reaching impact. The words declared are not just put out there but perpetuate her performance. Clearly, with regard to Weber the concept charisma is heavily dependent on the performance of the leader. Wanjiru as a leader has to keep her followers anticipating for more, be it in construction and other projects, Church ministry and the like. All of which have a bearing on her symbolic capital accumulation and reinvestment.

Wanjiru and charisma

Charisma as one type of legitimate authority is linked to Bourdieu's symbolic capital (i.e. the attaining of high status, accumulating social prestige and honour). It takes a group to ascribe charisma to a person whom they treat with acceptance and one befitting as their symbolic representative. JIAM and its followers, partners and friends deem Wanjiru as one whom they regard as a leader, a mentor and a pace setter. As a leader, she is regarded as one with influence and a certain degree of popularity.

Indeed, Wanjiru can speak for long hours and keep crowds waiting for more. Her performance is mainly oratory in nature. Trained in marketing, she learnt at an early age to package her items, in this case the message of the gospel, selecting words carefully and using a right tone to communicate her arguments. This oratory performance developed over charisma is based on individual performances (Jentges 2014: 1) which make the person gain acceptance as a symbolic representation for a group of persons.

Charisma can to a certain degree be learnt and improved upon by engaging in certain behavioural routines or skilled plays. Indeed, for the charismatic person a central marker is the important connection between a speaker and audience which depends on aspects of charisma, especially verbal skills, but also voice intonations, hand gestures and emotions (Antonakis et. al. 2012). These are some endowments that Wanjiru's father took note of and pointed out in her earlier days.

Her oratory performances in evangelical crusades, Church services, philanthropic missions and the like are perceived by her followers as supernaturally driven. Whether she be found acting in the capacity of evangelist, pastor or prophet, she finds herself aptly utilizing oratory skills again and again. As one with charisma, she is deemed to have the extraordinary personal quality and ability to create emotional dominance (Collins 2014).

But, Wanjiru's Charisma within JIAM is further routinized so that it acquires a legitimizing effect through the continued processes of creating and reinvesting symbolic capital. It is clear that charisma as one type of legitimate authority as exemplified by Weber may be interfaced with Bourdieu forms of capital. In Bourdieu's rendering, authority is related to symbolic capital. In other words, charisma is neatly linked with what Bourdieu called symbolic capital (i.e. the attaining of high status, accumulating social prestige and honour) (Jentges 2014: 7). The charisma Wanjiru exemplifies works in a way to add to her legitimacy and to accord her additional symbolic capital, which she further reinvests for even more social prestige and honour.

Charisma routinized at JIAM and deployed to overcome gender inequality

Charisma intrinsically serves to add to forms of capital enjoyed at JIAM in diverse ways.

Since authority deriving from charisma is not based on traditional authority such as culturally prescribed gendered power, Wanjiru can negotiate gender inequality within the religious arena. Wanjiru has over the years established herself and her ministry across Kenya and beyond. She is considered as one with specially endowed grace, much like what charisma entails to not only pull a crowd but also maintain it. She happens to now be a household name in Pentecostal charismatic circles in Kenya and beyond. Weber envisioned charisma as spontaneous (Weber 1978) and this is experienced in JIAM often times.

Just like Charismatic Christianity emphasizes the working of the Holy Spirit and giftings (Anderson 2002: 4), so do the charisma claims at JIAM present the framing that Wanjiru has direct, personal access to the spiritual and religious. Gender inequality in religious circles deriving from the claim that souls are sexed and are in hierarchy is undermined at JIAM. In JIAM, Wanjiru and the souls of others are considered of eternal value which do not come to end. As unsexed souls, there is opportunity for access to the spiritual and religious in equal measure. The gnostic model presents this option for JIAM members in their consideration of their leader and founder. This claim by Wanjiru, to spontaneity, sensing what God would want to say, feeling in the spirit and the like is founded on a claim to access supernatural powers and these claims are perceived and validated as such by JIAM followers.

Different typologies have been worked out on charisma, such as the construction and amplification of charisma, extraordinary, routinized and everyday charisma, charismatic giants and aspirants (Schweitzer 1984). Over the years, it is also evident that Wanjiru's charisma has been amplified through her international linkages and active usage of new media.

According to Fabian, charisma may be routinized. In this he implies that charisma takes new forms and formal structures are adopted (Fabian 1971). An interpretation of this concept brings to fore such routinizations and more institutionalized forms of performing her charisma. Her religious practices at JIAM create charisma and arise from charisma. Previously, she only held interdenominational meetings without having her own outfit, but with the formation of a church, her charisma is shifting into more institutionalization. These types of religious experiences attract many in Kenya to these congregations, thus serving to act as catalysts towards her negotiating gender inequality. Indeed, her charismatic outflows inform ways of perceptions to downplay gender inequality from her congregation.

Further, at JIAM, religious events flow after a fixed pattern and sequence, thus becoming formalized. This is noted in all Sunday services, as certain things such as early morning prayers and intercessions are done before the service begins. These fixed patterns of services arrangement are intended to achieve a particular outcome, which is a spiritual experience by the members. This in the charismatic Church circles is referred to having experienced 'the touch of God' or the 'hand of God'. The charismatic leader Wanjiru in mass gatherings is perceived to facilitate communal and spiritual experiences.

Strategies in performing charisma to negotiate gender inequality

Charismatic Churches have been known to constitute highly motivated and mobilizing communities with great participation opportunities. Wanjiru reinvents the category of status and power as one with charisma to affirm her rightful place of spiritual authority and revelation. This strategy silences those critics who would use the gender card against her. This strategy works since her congregation focuses on and emphasizes her charismatic and spiritual authority over and above her gender.

Wanjiru's demonstration of charismatic and spiritual authority in her congregation best fits within the Gnostic model. It is clear that in the physical dimension, Wanjiru is sexed, and that gender difference is limited to the physical body which we see and does not in any way limit her soul in view of eternal dimensions. It will seem best captured in that as a seeker of souls for the kingdom and through her Charismatic evangelistic efforts, she seeks out more souls as a fisher of souls. Within the Gnostic model, Wanjiru's work and efforts are not deterred since souls are not sexed and through this worldview she is on top of things and well able to raise many unsexed souls under her spiritual authority undeterred. The gender card does not, therefore, work against her and her mission.

In general, in the Gnostic model, Wanjiru's soul is considered unsexed whilst the body is sexed. At the same time, it is her soul which is consequently considered of eternal importance over and above the physical which does come to end. The soul as unsexed follows through the worldview given that in the end, any gender differences are but limited to the physical body, the physical arena which is temporal and soon fading away.

Visual representations of Wanjiru on book covers or magazines and posters serve as signifiers of a lifestyle and what Charismatics may call 'blessings'. Her strategy to exploit modern media technologies such as Facebook and Ustream for her charisma display serves to propagate performances which in the end assist in her negotiating gender inequality in the religious arena.

The exercise of charisma is mediated through a series of performances which create an outlook and inform the perception of followers. Her stage performance have great effect and impact on those in the immediate audience have a way of re-enforcing her charisma. Indeed, whether one is using charisma as a means to legitimacy, or is stepping on legitimacy to access, enjoy and exploit symbolic capital, strategy (the meaningful exploitation/use of what is at hand) is most important. Wanjiru as an actor and performer is at risk of losing out on her ends (legitimacy or the fruits of legitimacy) if she be deemed to lack the strategy to manoeuvre her way.

Being strategic in exemplifying charisma and in the exploitation or enjoyment of symbolic capital in the religious field is a self-defeating concept until we allow ourselves to see, and appreciate how it plays out alongside the 'disinterestedness' (as opposed to interestedness) expected of religious actors. In my view, borrowing from Bourdieu's (1998) assertion that the religious field is 'associated with disinterested, selfless actors' (see also Echtler and Ukah, 2016: 4) is that it is actually the acts of selflessness or disinterestedness on the part of the followers, admirers and others that win and deflect gender inequality for female religious actors. Bourdieu (1998) writes:

> Agents that clash over the end under consideration can be possessed by those ends. They may be ready to die for those ends; independently of all considerations of specific, lucrative profits, career profits, or other forms of profit. Their relation to the end involved is not all the conscious calculation of usefulness that utilitarianism lends them, a philosophy that is readily applied to the actions of others. They have a feel for the game; for example, in games where it is necessary to be 'disinterested' in order to succeed, they can undertake, in a spontaneously disinterested manner, actions in accordance with their interests. There are quite paradoxical situations that a philosophy of consciousness precludes us from understanding.
>
> (Bourdieu 1998: 83)

Therefore, Wanjiru as an actor should not pose as consciously working towards or seeking legitimation. Neither is she to pose as though she has succeeded in securing gender equality. She must continue to nurture her followers, who enjoy the fruits of her legitimation, no matter how successful she may become. Strategy demands that her conduct in JIAM and elsewhere, as she journeys towards continued legitimation, and consequently after attaining it, should reflect a selfless commitment to humble service. Anything short of this is considered a pride and egocentricism, and would threaten the very legitimation she has been working towards, or may have actually attained.

Conclusion

Wanjiru in the JIAM context exemplifies charisma to the extent that she can reinvest her gained symbolic capital in other fields besides the religious field. She deployed symbolic capital to negotiate gender inequality within the Pentecostalism and to attract high-profile politicians and the media to her events.

Yet, charismatic authority is generally not an ideal type as it tends to fade over time when one cannot keep up with performances that match the ascribed status. Over time, more formalized and institutionalized forms of leadership set in, which describes the JIAM metamorphosis to the present day and its current state where the charisma that Wanjiru accumulated is now getting more displayed as formalized and institutionalized.

Wanjiru employs strategies towards attaining, accruing and maintaining her place in the Kenyan religious landscape, wherein she negotiates gender inequality. There is no apparent reason to suspect that she is going to lose it any time soon. If anything, she is likely to keep creating, re-investing and reinventing symbolic capital over the years into the future, negotiate inequality and present herself as a legitimate and acceptable woman religious leader in Kenya and beyond.

Interrogating the 'spiritual puzzle of silence' on religion and gender inequality in Tanzania

Alexander Makulilo

Introduction

Religion is a major identity marker in Tanzania. This chapter examines the impact of religion on women's political participation in Tanzania. It highlights how religion has had an indelible impact on gender inequality in the country. This has resulted in the marginalization of women in national politics. For example, women are under-represented in both Parliament and the Executive. The chapter proceeds to deploy a case study of a class of 'PS 342: Gender and Politics in Africa' at one university in Tanzania to reflect on strategic silences on the section on 'Religion and Gender Inequality'. The section focuses on Islam and Christianity and their influence on gender identity in Tanzania. The chapter analyses the hesitation by students registered for the course to actively identify the extent to which religions are implicated in women's marginalization. It concludes by calling for greater investment in interrogating the impact of religion on gender construction in Tanzania. Although Tanzania is one of the few countries in Africa (and the world) that now has a woman president (Samia Suluhu Hassan, who succeeded former president, the late John Magufuli in 2021), the status of women remains low, mostly due to religio-cultural socialization of girls and women.

Women and religion: An overview

Interest in the 'women and religion' theme has evolved across time and space. In the 1960s and 1970s many European and North American women researchers involving mainly the fields of sociology, history of religions and feminist studies began to focus on the analysis of female religious experience, often starting from a feminist point of view internal to the most common religious traditions (Giorgi 2016: 52). The 'women and religion' theme has become increasingly appealing in the European academic world, especially since the second half of the 1990s. This increasing resonance is due to the fact that religion and its role and place in contemporary societies in general are attracting growing interest among non-specialized scholars (Beckford 1996; 2000). Moreover, the experience and the role of women in religion became more relevant, especially when compared with non-Christian religious traditions (Giorgi 2016).

Unlike in Europe and North America, 'women and religion' theme is still gaining momentum. The Circle of Concerned African Women Theologians (the Circle), established in 1989, has been playing a leading role in this regard. The Circle has undertaken valuable work in exposing the ambivalent nature of religion in relation to women's quest for justice and equality. However, most male African scholars of religion have been hesitant to take up the challenge. The lack of interest in the 'women and religion' theme is owing to the fact that Africans are very religious and deeply attached to it. As a result, the treatment of religion as a variable in explaining occurrences or non-occurrences of social phenomena is largely limited to topics like development, peace and conflict. Yet, religion, unlike any other social cleavage, is deeply rooted in peoples' experiences and influences the socioeconomic and political direction of societies (Peach 2006; Stump 2008).

In Tanzania, religion is said to be 'pervasive, useful and seemingly powerful' (Mukandala 2006: 1). Indeed, Tanzania, like many other African societies, is described as a deeply religious society (Chabal 2009; Makulilo 2019; Ukah 2019). It is on this basis that people use their religious identities to advance their spiritual, material and political interests. Religion is one of the most powerful agencies of socialization and varies across time and space. It is fair therefore to argue that the status of women in society is an outcome of the interpretation of religious texts and of the cultural and institutional setup of religious communities (Klingorová and Havlíček 2015). The literature on gender has established correlation between religion and gender (Moghadam 1991; Hopkins 2009; Seguino 2011; Chaudhuri 2013). The first strand finds that religion promotes gender equality while the second one establishes that gender inequality is an outcome of religion (Inglehart and Norris 2003; Klingorová and Havlíček 2015; Page and Yip 2017). Thus, gender roles are primarily constructed through religion, culture, lifestyle and upbringing (King 1995).

This chapter examines the 'spiritual puzzle of silence' in religion and gender inequality theme in Tanzania. Specifically, it interrogates the silence of the academia in studying religion as the most powerful agent of gender socialization in Tanzania. In accomplishing this endeavour, this work is divided into six major parts namely the introduction, situation analysis of gender inequality, methodology, explanations for the spiritual puzzle of silence, deconstructing the puzzle and conclusion.

Gender inequality in Tanzania: An overview

Tanzania is signatory to several international instruments that set standards which bind it legally to observe equity and non-discriminatory policies and practices. As a member of the United Nations, it is bound to adhere to principles of equality as spelt out in the Universal Declaration of Human Rights and the Bill of Rights which ban discrimination based on race, gender and ethnicity. Tanzania is also a signatory to the Convention on the Elimination of All Forms of Discrimination against Women (1979), the African Charter on Human and People's Rights (2001), the New Partnership for African Development (2001), the African Peer Review Mechanism (2003), the Protocol to the African Charter on Human and Peoples' Rights on the rights of women in Africa (2003), the SADC Protocol on Gender and Development (2008), and the Constitutive Act of African Union (2000) to mention just a few.

Yet, the Constitution of the United Republic of Tanzania 1977 claims to provide for full and equal participation of women and men in all aspects of life. Article 9(g) of the Constitution provides that 'the Government and all its agencies accord equal opportunities to all citizens, men and women alike without regard to their colour, tribe, religion, or station in life'. This provision is founded on the fact that the constitution, through Article 12, affirms that 'all human beings are born free and are all equal'. In fact, Article 21 stresses that 'every citizen' of the United Republic of Tanzania has a right to participate in the governance of the country directly or through their elected representatives.

Despite the implementation of these frameworks, there still exists some notable gender inequality in several aspects of life. Between 1990 and 2015 Tanzania's human development index (HDI) value rose from 0.370 to 0.531, an increase of 43.4 per cent (UNDP 2016: 2). However, when discounted for inequality, this falls to 0.396, a loss of 25.4 per cent. Women in Tanzania form a larger share of the working age population, but a smaller share of the economically active population: women account for 52 per cent of the working age population (fifteen years and over), but labour force participation rate is higher among males (89.4 per cent) than among females (84.2 per cent). Women thus constitute a greater proportion of the economically inactive population: of the 13.3 per cent of the population in this category, 8.2 per cent are women and 5.1 per cent men. Yet, agriculture is the largest sector of employment in Tanzania Mainland. Self-employment in agriculture is the most common form of labour deployment among rural populations, in particular rural women. A 2014 study by the Food and Agriculture Organisation highlights significant gender inequalities in rural employment (FAO, 2014). Men form the majority of landholders: in Tanzania Mainland, 73 per cent of landholders are men, whereas only 27 per cent are women. Agriculture accounts for the largest share of employment in Tanzania: a greater proportion of women than men (69.9 per cent vs 64.0 per cent) work in agriculture. Unpaid family helpers constitute 34.5 per cent of those employed in agriculture – there are more than twice as many females as males in this category. There are significant gender gaps in own farming, with far fewer women landholders, having smaller plot sizes, employing fewer people and farming more for subsistence rather than income generation as compared to male landholders. Males are more likely than females to be employed in formal sectors, including government service – implying that women are more likely to be engaged in employment with less income and less security. Women in employment are significantly more vulnerable than males (88.7 per cent vs 78.2 per cent). The share of males in senior and middle management occupations is 82.6 per cent compared to 17.4 per cent for females.

Similarly, in political terms, women are significantly underrepresented in all major decision-making organs. Women are underrepresented in the Parliament when one considers that they are the majority population in the country. Women have very few members of the Parliament. In the 9th Parliament the number of women MPs was 99 (31 per cent) out of 320 MPs. The number and percentage increased in the 10th Parliament but remained steady in the 11th Parliament, thus 130 (37 per cent) and 144 (37 per cent) respectively. The number of women chairpersons of Parliamentary standing committees has been very low. For instance, during the 9th Parliament (2005–10) only three (17 per cent) committees out of eighteen were under women chairpersons. The number of women chairpersons increased to six (33 per cent) out of eighteen committees in the 10th Parliament. Sadly, this number has decreased just to three (17 per cent) out of eighteen committees in the 11th Parliament, promulgated after 2015 general elections. Similarly, the number of women deputy chairpersons of committees has been very low. For example, during the 9th Parliament only five (28 per cent) committees out of eighteen had women deputy chairpersons. As for the 10th Parliament, just two (11 per cent) committees out of eighteen had women deputy chairpersons. The number of women deputy chairpersons of committees has, however, increased in the 11th Parliament where nine (50 per cent) committees have women deputy chairpersons.[1]

The situation is relatively worse in the executive branch of government. This seems to be the most powerful branch constitutionally in terms of policy and decision making. However, it is overwhelmingly headed by men. Since independence in 1961 the country has been headed by male presidents and vice-presidents except after 2015 general elections where the vice-president was a woman. The rise of President Hassan changed this trend, although she is surrounded by men in the executive branch of government. The number of women deputy ministers between 2005 and 2012 decreased to 10 per cent from 33 per cent, though it later increased to 20 per cent up to 2015. This number increased slightly to 24 per cent after the 2015 general elections.[2] The situation is not different in directorates, boards and management positions in selected ministries. For example, between 2009 and 2016 the number of women in the Ministry of Health, Community Development, Gender, Elderly and Children has been constant or declined. In 2009 there were three women and one man as directors while in 2011 the number of men increased to five while that of women remained the same. Disappointingly, the number of women declined to two while that of men remained at five. Since 2016 the number of women has been three while that of men is four. The situation is worse on the position of assistant directors. For example, in 2011 the number of women was six while that of men was nineteen. In 2013 the number of women decreased to four and that of men to sixteen. Since 2016 the number of women is three while that of men is thirteen.[3]

Moreover, the number of women who were appointed as Regional Commissioners in 2011 was six (28.5 per cent) out twenty-one regional commissioners. Their percentage decreased to 23 per cent after the 2015 general elections. Similarly, in 2016 only six women were appointed as Regional Administrative Secretary out of twenty-six Regional Administrative Secretaries. Likewise, the number of women District Commissioners up to 2015 was 47 (35 per cent) out of 133 District Commissioners. Moreover, out of 123 District Administrative Secretaries that were appointed in 2010/15 only seventeen (14 per cent) were women. Similarly, for the 2015/17 out of 131 District Administrative

Secretaries only thirty-one (23.6 per cent) are women.[4] This indicates a slight increase of women in the respective position.

For women to have meaningful participation in decision-making processes, the principles of equality and non-discrimination against discriminatory traditions among other things must be established in the nation's constitution. This is because in countries such as Tanzania, customs, traditions and public attitudes not only determine how many women are considered and nominated for office, but they have a direct and indirect influence on how many female candidates win a general election. During the 2011–14 constitution-making process in Tanzania, women consistently demanded for prohibitions of discriminatory customs and traditions, which, for a long time, have placed them on unequal footing with men, particularly in the decision-making arena.

Equality guarantees are often followed by a non-discrimination provision and contain a list of grounds on which discrimination is prohibited, including gender. The Committee on the Elimination of Discrimination against Women has consistently recommended that state parties incorporate the definition of 'discrimination against women' into their constitutions from Article 1 of CEDAW, which provides the following:

> For the purposes of the present Convention, the term 'discrimination against women' shall mean any distinction, exclusion or restriction made on the basis of sex which has the effect or purpose of impairing or nullifying the recognition, enjoyment or exercise by women, irrespective of their marital status, on a basis of equality of men and women, of human rights and fundamental freedoms in the political, economic, social, cultural, civil or any other field.

The 2014 Proposed Constitution includes critical elements of Article 1 of CEDAW in defining discrimination against women as seen in Article 33 (5) of the 2014 Proposed Constitution. Articles 12 (a) and 33 of the 2014 Proposed Draft Constitution of Tanzania prohibit all forms of discrimination including sex. Also, Articles 8 and 14 (b) of the Proposed Constitution require national authorities to provide equal opportunities to both women and men, without discrimination. Hence, the 2014 Proposed Constitution successfully provides and protects the women's right to political participation, by including non-discrimination provisions that are important to safe-guard women against discriminatory traditions, customs and beliefs that for a long time have kept women away from electoral decision-making spaces.

The women's rights clauses are important tools for advancing gender equality. In equality and non-discrimination guarantees, constitutions should contain provisions dedicated to setting out women's rights only in addition to every right elsewhere in the constitution that also applies to women. Article 54 of the Tanzanian Proposed Constitution guarantees every woman the right to: (i) be respected, valued and their dignity recognized; (ii) protection against discrimination, harassment, abuse, violence, sexual violence and harmful traditional practices; and (iii) participate in elections and all stages of decision making without discrimination. Specific provisions for women's rights provide for active measures to improve the position of women, which is usually lower in the society, to enable them to achieve gender equality through women's social, economic and political empowerment.

Methodology

This is a case study of a class of 'PS 342: Gender and Politics in Africa' at one university in Tanzania. I had been teaching this undergraduate course for about ten years between 2008 and 2019, except two years in 2009 and 2010. The course had a class size of between 100 and 150 students for each academic year. In terms of composition, the class had about 60 per cent male and 40 per cent female students, reflecting the societal gender imbalance. This course provides an overview of some key topics in politics and gender. It examines the way political life and power are shaped and reshaped by gender constructions. In specific terms, it seeks to understand how femininity and masculinity are socially constructed in all domains of society and how they inform people's mind-sets and practices. The course interrogates the historical and current processes of women's subordination and discrimination in contemporary politics in Africa. One of the specific topics covered is 'Discrimination against Women', where one of its subtopics focused on 'Religion and Gender inequality'. Two major readings around this thematic area included 'Fatina Mernissi 1991. *Women and Islam: An Historical and Theological Enquiry*, Blackwell Oxford', as well as 'Letty M. Russell 1985. *Feminist Interpretation of the Bible*, Basil Blackwell'.

Students were assigned to read relevant chapters to prepare for informed discussion during class and seminars. What was found consistent across all the classes and seminars throughout the ten years is that students were uncomfortable to critically engage with this topic. As indicated from the beginning, Tanzanians are deeply religious and religion is historically a sensitive issue. Christians, just like their Muslim counterparts, did not want to share how their religion treats women in principle and practice. Most often they could simply pinpoint those passages from the Bible or Qur'an that presumably seem to be about gender equality, thereby defending their respective faiths. This is what I term as 'spiritual puzzle of silence'. Therefore, the first source of data for this study is drawn from discussions and observations from 'PS 342' classes over a past decade. In addition, this study reviewed relevant documents in relation to the topic, particularly reports, previous studies and laws. Interpretation of data drawn from the two sources was qualitatively done to understand the 'spiritual puzzle of silence' in perpetuating gender inequality.

Explaining the spiritual puzzle of silence

There are a number of dimensions that need to be analysed in trying to understand factors that perpetuate gender inequality. This chapter explores the major ones below.

Religion as a system of Holiness

There is no clear definition of religion. However, common to all definitions there is 'holiness' of the system. As a belief system in and worship of a superhuman controlling power, especially a personal God or gods, religion commands obedience to 'God or gods'. It is therefore a sociocultural system of behaviours, practices and ethics and morals related to supernatural or spiritual elements. There is an assumption that followers of a certain religion are not allowed to question the existence of God or gods and related teachings and practices. These are given by the spiritual elements and hence are not questionable. During the 'PS 342' classes, it was discovered that students from their respective religious affiliation were deeply socialized right from their childhood. Through religious texts, teachings and practices, students seemed to fear their God's authority. There was a feeling that going against God's or gods' teachings is a commitment of sin. However, questioning the teachings was as good as denouncing the existence of God or gods which could attract Godly punishment and deaths.

The embeddedness of patriarchy in religion

All world religions today maintain male social dominance within societal structures (Young 1987). On the other hand, women are more inclined to participate in religious life (Renzetti and Curran 1999). Likewise, religious norms and prejudices may reflect patriarchal values which are characteristic of all societies of the world religions (Seguino 2011). The role of God, or a creator of a religion, is always taken by a male and the woman is primarily valued as a mother. Her place is in the household, less so at religious ceremonies or in public positions (Klingorová and Havlíček 2015). The voice of women is rarely heard, due to the patriarchal dispositions of societies in which these religions emerged. It is against this background that the influence of women on the formation of religious norms and traditions is small, even though in certain doctrines, we can find women who succeeded in having their normative views accepted, or men who advocated equal integration of women into religious ceremonies (Klingorová and Havlíček 2015; Page and Yip 2017).

In a recent study conducted among young adults in the UK from diverse religious backgrounds assessing how religious young adults understood and managed the tensions in popular discourse between gender equality as an enshrined value and aspirational narrative, and religion as purportedly instituting gender inequality it was noted that, despite varied understandings, and the ambivalence and tension in managing ideal and practice, participants of different religious traditions and genders were committed to gender equality. They viewed gender-unequal practices within their religious cultures as an aberration from the essence of religion and they firmly rejected the dominant discourse that religion is inherently antithetical to gender equality (Page and Yip 2017: 249). Tanzania is largely a patriarchal society. This implies that patriarchy is embedded in religion. This mixture is strong in terms of socialization of men and women. Starting from the family to the public domains, the effect of patriarchy-religion is omnipresent. During 'PS 342' classes, students seemed to have normalized the culture whose core is male dominated. Those who attempted to engage in the discussion around this theme simply ended up selecting sections of texts, teachings and practices which seem to favour equality of all the people before God or gods. They strategically avoided a holistic approach of analysing the discourses around the theme despite advancing them relevant literature to spearhead the debates.

Fear of religious violence

Tanzania is a secular state. Article 19 (1) of the Constitution of the United Republic of Tanzania states: 'Every person has the right to the freedom of thought or conscience, belief or faith, and choice in matters of religion, including the freedom to change his religion or faith.' Subsection (2) further states: 'Without prejudice to the relevant laws of the United Republic the profession of religion, worship and propagation of religion shall be free and a private affair of an individual; and the affairs and management of religious bodies shall not be part of the activities of the state authority.' Yet, Section 129 of the Penal Code provides that

> any person who, with the deliberate intention of wounding the religious feelings of any person, utters any word, or makes any sound in the hearing of that person, or makes any gesture in the sight of that person, or places any object in the sight of that person, is guilty of a misdemeanour, and is liable to imprisonment for one year.

It has to be stated that the relations between Christianity and Islam in Tanzania present moments of cordiality and at times tensions (Mesaki 2011; Makulilo 2019). Religious issues are therefore very sensitive issues. The government, for example, has avoided to include a question in its census so much so that one religious group could plan for any action adversarial to the peace and tranquillity of the nation. Being mindful of this, students were cautious to talk of their respective religious texts, teaching and practices or those of the counterpart religions. It was thought that during discussions, one would have uttered statements which the other students would not have been comfortable with. Each religious group would more likely mobilize for support from its followers. Hence, in defence of peace and harmony, most students decided to be silent.

The divide between divine and scientific knowledge

The foundations of scientific and divine knowledge are typically different. The former is premised on empiricism and experimentation. This kind of knowledge is testable and verified empirically. In contrast, divine knowledge is God centred. Most of its assumptions are God given and in most cases it is unquestionable. In the academia, researchers shied away from religion themes since Marxism was the dominant paradigm at the particular institution and other institutions of higher learning from mid-1960s to mid-1980s. However, starting from 2000s, religion as a theme has been included in other topics on development, peace and security. The idea was to use religion to promote development, peace and security. This means that religious institutions were comfortable to be part and parcel of state-building projects. Nonetheless, the theme of religion and gender has not yet been included in the curriculum. Hence, the two arenas have been treated separately. During the 'PS 342' classes, students thought that since religion was being run by religious leaders, it would be prudent to leave such affairs to them and their followers.

Monitoring of religious behaviour at the University

The University where the study took place, unlike any other university in Tanzania, has built a Church and Mosque for students and staff who stay at the main campus. These institutions have their respective leaders, notably priests, pastors and sheiks. Prayers are conducted every day. Moreover, there are students' religious associations headed by selected leaders from among the students. Students' leaders work closely as links between Church and Mosque leaders. These associations have their social media accounts through Facebook, WhatsApp and blogs. This facilitates day-to-day students' life and affairs. As can be seen, apart from having a praying function, the Church, Mosque and students' religious organization monitor behaviours of students and counsel and advise them spiritually. During my class with the students, it was discovered that some students' leaders were in the class and it was difficult for them to engage in the discussion freely. In case a student challenged religious texts, teachings or practices, there was the fear that he or she could be reported for sanctions. Therefore, students felt they had to obey and respect their religions.

The parent effect

The place of parents in religion is central and special. Parents have to be respected and their guidance to children should be respected. In Islam, whether one is a child, teen or adult, he or she should never disrespect his or her parents. Allah says in the Quran, 'Do good to your parents. If any one of them or both of them reach old age, do not say to them *uff* and do not scold them, and address them with respectful words' (Q. 17:23). Similarly, in Christianity it is written: 'Children, obey your parents in everything, for this pleases the Lord' (Colossians 3:20).

From childhood to adulthood, the impact of parents on socializing their children in religion is excessive. While experiencing campus life, they continue to get shaped and reshaped about religious values. In this way, parents continue to act as authority over their children. Children normally listen to their parents more than to other sources of authority. As a result of this they continue to respect religious texts, teachings and practices. During the 'PS 342' classes and seminars, it was evident that some students were open to sharing the advice given by their parents. Parents are always suspicious that university is the level where students enjoy the latitude of independence and through literature, especially from the Western tradition, they be able to challenge religious foundations. Moreover, because the students were still dependent on their parents in their daily life and support to their education, this tended to enhance compliance and obedience to their parents.

Deconstructing the spiritual puzzle of silence

When dealing with women's rights, equality and the deconstruction of gender roles, religion is often perceived as an obstacle. Indeed, many religious agents involved in the public debate take a firm stand against some typically feminist issues and against the concept of gender itself (Giorgi 2016: 52). Yet, religious feminism as a movement emerged in the 1970s to undertake interpretations of religious texts and traditions that support gender equality. However, the acceptance of such interpretations has been hindered by the dominant interpretations of religious teachings and conservative interpretations by a significant number of believers. This is worsened by the lack of women scholars who are trained to undertake this kind of work. Moreover, these scholars may be seen as elite, Western-influenced or educated women, who have little connection with ordinary women.

In Tanzania, the feminist movements in 1980s following the Beijing Conference were much concerned with addressing the gender gaps in socioeconomic and political spheres. However, it has not interrogated agents of socialization, including religion. Nonetheless, the 'Women and Religion' theme is very sensitive to research effectively in Tanzania, although it has been undertaken successfully in other African contexts. It is not surprising therefore that almost all civil societies have never approached the issues surrounding religion and gender. Yet, education is regarded as a tool for emancipation. The 'PS 342' has clearly indicated the difficulty of transforming an aspect of gender inequality. This is so due to the fact that Tanzanians are very religious. This situation is made worse by the dominance of a patriarchal culture. Hence, the discourse of gender inequality in the context of religion is yet to emerge with full force in Tanzania, although the signs of this happening are beginning to appear. The ascendancy of a woman, Samia Suluhu Hassan, as the president of the United Republic of Tanzania, implies that gender has been placed on the agenda.

Conclusion

This chapter set out to examine the 'spiritual puzzle of silence' among students at one university who studied 'PS 342: Gender and Politics in Africa' between 2008 and 2019. The purpose was to find out why were they silent when we discussed 'women and religions' theme. In the literature on gender, it is admitted that the interest in 'Women and Religions' theme is a relatively more recent development, particularly in Europe and North America. Within this development, one of the first works to be published with a specific focus on religion from a gender perspective was the volume on *Religion and Gender* edited by Ursula King (1995). It collects analyses of the experiences of women and men as well as of the construction of the male and female subject in several religious traditions, along with a variety of theoretical considerations and interdisciplinary empirical studies. In her introduction, King stressed the fact that, although in the 1970s and 1980s studies on the female religious experience flourished, in the literature on religion there was yet neither a specific focus on male experience nor a gender perspective (Giorgi 2016: 52). In contrast, in Africa, the 'women and religions' theme is yet to find its grounding beyond Religious Studies. This is owing to several reasons, notably the fact that Africans are very religious and therefore some tend to avoid critical discourse on religion. Furthermore, Tanzania, like many other societies, is a patriarchal in nature. This implies that women continue to suffer from cultural and spiritual values.

There have not been any serious attempts to interrogate the 'spiritual puzzle of silence'. My experience of teaching students a course on "Gender and Politics" and a subtopic specifically on 'Religion and Gender Inequality' shows that many students were not comfortable to discuss religious matters since they considered them private to religious denominations and that they were sensitive. Indeed, they have normalized this system. Moreover, the legacy of Marxism at the university where the study was conducted has overstayed to prevent academic interests to emerge around these topics. As a result, feminist movements in Tanzania have shied away from touching this sensitive matter. As a starting point in revisiting the relationship between religion and gender inequality in Tanzania, it would be valuable in other disciplines to interact with the publications of the Circle. In addition, activists from diverse fields must invest in understanding this dynamic in order to promote gender justice in Tanzania and beyond.

Religio-cultural beliefs and women's political participation

Gender dimensions in post-constitutional elections in Eswatini

Sonene Nyawo

Introduction

Women are potentially a solid voting bloc in Eswatini politics, but their representation in the decision-making arena remains on the margins. Powerful socialization forces connive to influence societal perceptions about a woman's place. This has far-reaching implications for political behaviour. Analysis in this chapter reveals that the Swati religio-cultural orientations favour men and obstruct women's participation in politics. In the post-constitutional elections in Eswatini, women have generally been part-players whilst men have enjoyed dominion. Women's marginalization in such a predominantly Christian setting is systematic and deep-rooted in culture and religion. Thus, even after close to fifty years of independence, women's primary role in the electoral process is still only to offer their vote to men. Surveys conducted in the country on general elections and women's participation in decision-making positions all confirm that women continue to be under-represented in Parliament, the Cabinet, as well as the public and private sectors where their voices and contributions matter the most. The chapter advances that religion, in partnership with culture, represents fundamental identities that shape political behaviour in Eswatini. As such, religio-cultural beliefs have differential effects on the endorsement of traditional gender roles in women and men, which then translate into different orientations towards politics

(Bartkowski and Hempel 2009). Eswatini post-constitutional elections are used as evidence in this chapter to illustrate the intersection between cultural and Christian gender consciousness which promotes a masculine model of politics. The chapter highlights how this leads to women's under-representation in Parliament.

Outlining the context

The United Nations has launched a series of dialogues on how to build a global partnership, as it celebrates its seventy-fifth anniversary in 2020. Subsequent to the launch the UN Resident Coordinator and the Gender Unit in the Deputy Prime Minister's Office in Eswatini held a Women Empowerment Forum aimed at addressing challenges faced by women and girls in the Kingdom of Eswatini, as well as identifying opportunities for empowerment. It came out clearly from the key speakers' submissions at the dialogue that Eswatini has made strides in addressing gender inequalities that exist in various spheres of the socioeconomic life of the people. However, it was also pointed out that the country still lags behind in giving women political power. Several speakers from the floor expressed strong sentiments against the skewed gender consciousness amongst Emaswati in response to these submissions. They made particular reference to the 2018 national elections where of the fifty-nine constituencies, only two women won the race to Parliament. They blamed this scenario on numerous factors, which included women being not supportive of each other, lack of confidence, socialization agencies, cultural norms and religious beliefs. However, divergent sentiments were also shared and echoed. Some speakers justified the status quo, claiming that it is 'divine' and cultural that women should not occupy positions of power. They cited Bible verses that God ordained men to lead in all spheres of life, including politics. It is this debate that intrigued my mind to explore how religion, Christianity, in particular, has partnered with cultural orientations in shaping people's political behaviour in the post-constitutional era in Eswatini and how this leads to the marginalization of women from leadership positions at various levels.

By post-constitutional elections, the chapter refers to the elections of 2008, 2013 and 2018 conducted under Eswatini's new Constitution that was promulgated in 2005. The most recent elections were held in 2018 to form the 11th Parliament. The Constitution of 2005 sets out broad principles concerning the conduct of elections, and it outlines the context within which the general elections take place. Under Section 79, the Constitution states:

> The system of government for Swaziland is a democratic, participatory, *Tinkhundla*-based system that emphasises devolution of state power from central government to the *Tinkhundla* areas and individual merit as a basis for election or appointment to public office.
>
> (Constitution of the Kingdom of Swaziland, Act No.1 of 2005)

Although there is a strong view, especially in the higher echelons of Swati society, that the electoral system is democratic, a number of Election Observer Missions to Eswatini have made a critical assessment of the 2008, 2013 and 2018 Parliamentary elections in their respective reports. In its assessment of political pluralism and inclusiveness, the Commonwealth Observer Mission, in particular, found the electoral process in Eswatini to have glaring democratic deficits. Recognizing that women constitute over 50 per cent of the population in Eswatini, but are still lagging behind men in leadership positions, the Southern African Development Community (SADC) Observer Mission also appealed to the Kingdom of Eswatini to take measures and develop mechanisms to achieve increased representation of women in elective public positions, in accordance with the Constitution of Swaziland and the African Charter on Human and People's Rights on the Rights of Women in Africa, as well as the CEDAW. However, it was noted during the debates at the Women Empowerment Forum that the National Gender Policy, the Constitution and other legislations do provide guidelines for attaining gender equity and reverse gender disparities in the country. It was, however, regretted that in spite of all these efforts women's political participation has not made significant strides, as women are still underrepresented in Parliament. In every election period the Head of State has had to exercise his powers under Section 94 and Section 95 of the Constitution and appoint a number of women to both houses of Parliament in order to increase the proportion of women in the legislature.

Conceptual framework

Our reflections on the sparse representation of women in Swazi politics are premised on the role congruity theory featured within the gender frame theoretical framework. The wider gender frame embraces the experiences of both women and men which are often viewed in binary terms and are communicated through sex role stereotyping (Nyawo and Nsibande 2014). These cultural stereotypes limit gender-appropriate behaviour to a range of rigid roles which are assigned to women and men, and they are deeply ingrained in people's attitudes (Connell 2005). With regard to women leadership, Eagly and Karau (2002) have used the role congruity theory to explain prejudice and discrimination against women in decision-making processes. They describe this theory as having been grounded in the social role theory's treatment of the content of gender roles and their importance in promoting sex differences. However, they claim that role congruity theory reaches beyond social role theory to consider the congruity between gender roles and other roles, especially leadership roles. It further considers factors and processes that influence congruity perceptions and their consequences for prejudice and prejudicial behaviours (Eagly et al. 2000).

In the area of national government, representative democracy takes the form of elections to congresses, parliaments or similar national bodies. Traditionally, the concept of political representation was not considered to have a gender dimension. But today there is a strong argument in democracies that Parliament must not just be the main debating chamber for the nation but must also be the forum where all voices are heard. Fair representation of both men and women is fundamental in a country that is aspiring to uphold democratic principles. The absence of women in Parliament undermines democracy, legitimacy and public confidence in Parliament since women are an important and big constituency. Democracy dictates that people of all ages, races, religions, classes and sexes be effectively represented in the public bodies where major decisions are taken. Women should participate fully as citizens and as decision makers within governments to be able to influence policy. The quality of representation suffers when women are excluded from decision making, especially in legislative bodies. Research indicates that men and women hold different views on issues and exhibit different policy preferences for dealing with public problems (Ford 2002). It is, therefore, the gender and representative democracy frameworks that inform the chapter's interpretation of the aspects discussed below on women's political participation and representation in the post-constitutional era in Eswatini.

Our reflections in this chapter are also informed by the theory that religion does influence people's political orientations, at both macro- and micro-levels (Elshtain 1982; Rinehart and Perkins 1989). According to some theorists, religion can be viewed as a structural macro-level socialization process in which organized religion represses women's politicization through its power to enforce women's closely confined status. At micro-level, religion can be characterized as an internal source of attitude constraint and structuring, 'as religious beliefs can be thought of as a cognitive schema of great potential, important in the development of women's political orientations because it harmonises well with other aspects of gender differentiated political socialisation' (Rinehart and Perkins 1989: 35). It is, therefore, within this theoretical framework that the chapter advances the argument that gender frames ingrained in women through cultural socialization which relegate women to the bottom of the hierarchal ladder intersect with religious orientations, and they directly influence women's political behaviour – hence their under-representation in positions of power.

Realities on gender dimensions in post-constitutional elections in Eswatini

Both internal and external observers of the 2008, 2013 and 2018 parliamentary elections raised concern about gender inequalities in political spaces of Eswatini. The elections of 2008, 2013 and 2018 stand out from all previous elections because they were held under Eswatini's new Constitution. Whilst applauding the large number of women participation in the electoral process as staff and voters, observers deprecated the women's invisibility in elected offices. The Commonwealth Election Observer Mission to Eswatini, in its report on the 2013 elections in particular commented on the gender dimension of elections. It acknowledged the provisions of Section 84 and Section 86 of the Constitution which seek to ensure effective participation and fair representation of women in the political process. However, in its assessment of participation and representation, the Commonwealth Observer Mission noted that Eswatini had experienced a decline in women's representation in Parliament during the 2013 elections, compared to the 2008 elections, despite the country's commitment to increase women's representation in the legislative chamber to at least 30 per cent. It was observed that only one woman candidate had won a seat in Parliament at the conclusion of the 2013 general elections, representing a significant drop from the five women who won seats during the 2008 elections. The Head of the Commonwealth Elections Observer Mission noted: 'Isn't it surprising that there is a high turnout of women and only one woman won a seat in the August House?' (*Times of Swaziland*, 23 September 2013).

A similar scenario happened in the 2018 elections; the number of women contesting for parliamentary and local government seats was low, thus negatively impacting on their representation in Parliament. During the primary elections the figures indicated that there were 670 candidates in election standing for both MP and *Indvuna Yenkhundla* (constituency headman) categories. Of this figure, 98 (14 per cent) women contested against their male counterparts. In total, 331 candidates were in the race for being Member of Parliament (MP). The number of women against men stood at a very low 13.2 per cent, while the males were at 87.8 per cent. Winners from the fifty-nine constituency ballots that eventually took seats in 11th Parliament were all males, except for two women.[1] This was a duplication of the very low women representation in earlier national elections, despite all aggressive efforts from the civil society, advocating for gender equality in the highest levels of political decision making. During the 2018 election period, civil society conducted a 'Vote for a Woman' campaign, which had included conducting awareness-raising activities at community level and amongst women's groups, as well as some capacity building of aspiring women candidates prior to voter registration. However, all these empowering strategies did not yield the expected results.

A study on women representation in Eswatini by Nyawo and Mkhonta (2016)[2] confirms this observation, as it revealed that Emaswati women remain largely on the margins of the political process in spite of the Government's declaration to promote equality between men and women in decision-making positions. It was shown in the study that there are formidable obstacles to women's effective participation and equitable representation in government bodies, especially the legislature. The role and place of women in politics, it is argued, have been shaped by powerful socialization forces. Swati culture and traditions impose restrictions on women's participation since the rule and command function is ascribed to men, and women are considered to be subordinate to men. Parliament is viewed as 'a masculine decision making territory' where important decisions concerning the country's governance are made, predominantly by men. The women's tendency to shy away from Parliament is, therefore, consistent with the assumption that decision making in Swati society is a male preserve. Because of the patriarchal nature of Swati society, men are reluctant to allow their wives to venture into politics or to seek public office.

Other studies conducted locally have confirmed Swati cultural traditions which emphasize women's primary roles as mothers and housewives do have an influence on people's perceptions on politics. For instance, Daly (2001) claims that women's gender consciousness is anchored on a strong, patriarchal value system which keeps sexually segregated roles in place. This is otherwise known as the masculine model of politics (White 1997). According to Ntawubona (2013), it is the responsibility of women as mothers and wives, as well as their domestic duties, that complicate women's involvement and participation in politics. But for some scholars, women are rendered helpless given that the political arena is organized according to male norms, values and lifestyles. Most women would then shun politics because of this male-style approach to governance. Also, the inflexible work schedule of masculine politics works against them since it has serious implications for women's multiple duties.

Most women would struggle to combine politics and family responsibilities, and still be productive. Furthermore, with their primary roles as mothers and wives, and their competing domestic and professional tasks, they are left with little time to participate in politics (Nyawo and Mkhonta 2016). It is worth noting that a cultural setting such as the Swati society still dictates that women should be pre-occupied with domestic and family obligations that take up a large portion of their time. They are expected to continue to play the triple role of producers, maintainers and reproducers in their families (Nyawo and Nsibande 2014). To cope with all these responsibilities, women have to operate on an elastic concept of time. Sometimes, this elasticity is not high enough to allow them to participate in public activities.[3] Apart from these cultural impediments, many women's meagre financial resources also inhibit their political participation. They would need money to finance political campaigns in order to compete with their male counterparts. Nonetheless, men would always win the election race because they have more avenues to raise finance and are able to outspend women competitors (Nyawo and Mkhonta 2016).

Patriarchal assumptions on women's political participation

A high proportion (53 per cent) of Eswatini's population of 1.2 million people is made up of women (Government of Swaziland 2007 Swaziland Population and Housing Census Vol.4 Analytical Report). Reports by the Commonwealth, EU and AU Election Observer Missions and the Elections and Boundaries Commission, have shown that it is mostly women voters that record the highest turnout during national parliamentary elections. The women's receptive response to voting shows that politics is a subject of great importance to them, given the centrality of the state and the overall impact of government action on their lives (Nyawo and Mkhonta 2016). Issues of political participation, as observed by Senath (2013: 26), generate great interest amongst women because they are well acquainted with the needs and aspirations of their communities and are also the major users of the public goods and services provided by the state. However, the few women who break the norm and compete for Parliamentary seats fail to make it through the race, as the foregoing has shown.

Patriarchal systems are ancient in origin and ubiquitous in their reach. They empower men regardless of their individual ability to exercise power wisely, whilst disempowering women irrespective of their innate abilities for leadership and wise exercise of power (Ford 2002: 10). Male-dominated societies, such as the Swazi society, have adopted certain assumptions that govern female-male relationships, which, when summarized, are as follows: women and men have fundamentally different psychological and sexual natures; men are inherently the dominant or superior sex; and male-female difference and male dominance are both natural (Bem 1993).These are societies where phrases such as 'man-leader/man manager' seem tautological, whereas 'woman-leader/woman manager' have become so normalized; 'that it goes without saying' whenever they are used. Scholars have rightly identified culture as a significant obstacle to women's political engagement and participation, which has led many women to leave politics or activism.

Women get pressure from social institutions such as the family, school and church to conform to traditional gender roles, pervasive use of negative stereotypes and other patriarchal norms that set boundaries to all genders. Women would therefore shun active participation in politics because they have been socialized to believe that their domain is the home and politics is a male domain. Ntawubona (2013) attributes women's limited occupancy of political positions to the limited nature of participation in political activities. With reference to parliamentary elections, she asserts that by not participating in activities such as campaigning and attending meetings, access to power centres such as Parliament and councils where selection of decision makers and representation is made, women's chances to occupy political seats and decision-making positions become limited (Ntawubona 2013: 45). These boundaries that control the social space of a woman are by and large set by culture.

Swati societal perceptions about a woman's place in politics, as it is the case in most traditional societies, have therefore been shaped, amongst other factors, by sociological and philosophical theories that have continued to shape societies down the generations (Daly 2001). Such theories justify the minority status of women. Aristotle, for instance, writing in the *Politics*, ascribed society's rule and command function to men since, according to him, women are naturally subordinate to men, and the male is naturally fitter to command than the female

(Ford 2002: 8). Thus, Parliament is viewed by a Liswati woman, not as part of their territory, but as a remote masculine institution where important decisions are made. She would rather push men to make decisions for her as if she is incapable of representing herself and the interests of the entire women population.

Religiosity and cultural norms on gender as an intricate web

Generally, males in Swati society are accorded priority over females in the various cultural and religious pursuits. Both religion and culture author systematic norms about the sexual division of labour, and hence about the inappropriateness of women as independent political actors (Elshtain 1982). Religious beliefs have differential effects on the endorsement of traditional gender roles in women and men, which may translate into different orientations towards politics. Elshtain (1982) captures what he says is a popular conception of women, namely, that 'they are beautiful souls, pure, chaste, not quite in or of the world, and thus remote from its tawdry violent and political concerns' (Elshtain 1982: 36). He further argues that social institutions reinforce one another as they promote gender variations. He singles out religion, saying that it acts in concert with other socialization agents which send concomitant and reinforcing cues about femininity that women internalize. Some theorists blame these societal perceptions on what they refer to as biblical literalism, which is the widespread belief that the Bible is the actual word of God, to be taken literally. Drawing on the system justification theory, they argue that biblical literalism is the core interpretative framework through which people understand gender relations, which subsequently determine political behaviour among women.

Christianity, which is the dominant religion in Eswatini, is tinged with cultural elements that are male-centred and patriarchal, such that it is sometimes difficult to draw a line between Swati culture and Christianity. The affinities that Swati culture and the Judeo-Christian traditions are believed to share are chief contributing factors to the knotted relationship between culture and religion, which subjugates women (Nyawo 2014). Both traditions assign unequal status to women and men, thus placing women on the margins of society, whilst men enjoy their 'divine' right of dominion. As rightly observed by Kabeer (1996: 16), inequalities are interlinked through interaction between different traditions or institutions, creating situations which disadvantage individuals and groups in multiple ways. Furthermore, they are internalized and accepted through mainstream values and norms justified by arguments derived from culture and religion. These inequalities can also be subtle and pervasive, to such an extent that legal reforms enacted to redress them tend to have minimal success.

In Eswatini, it is mostly cultural and religious impediments that limit women's participation in politics. Both traditions assign men what Giddens (2005) calls an 'ascribed' status, on the basis of their biological factors. This status has decision making right as part of its package, such that only men, as first-class citizens, can be trusted with parliamentary seats, not second-class citizens. It, therefore, appears abnormal, irreligious and unSwati that men, who exhibit God's image, would compete with women in a parliamentary contest (Clifford 2001; Rakoczy 2004). The church and culture often reinforce each other on issues like political participation, which safeguard decision making for men. The Bible, for instance, emphasizes respect and obedience, but, actually, the popular imagination is women and not men who are expected to be obedient, submissive and subservient. Under these interpretations of the Christian tradition, a woman is not expected to occupy a position of authority, and if one aspires to do that, one is labelled a rebel (Nyawo 2014).

The creation story in the book of Genesis which describes how Adam, the man, was created first to rule over Eve, the woman, who was his partner and subordinate, is often cited to reinforce gender disparities. Other verses include 1 Timothy 2:12 – 'I do not permit a woman to teach or to exercise authority over a man; rather, she is to remain quiet'; Colossians 3:18 – 'Wives, submit to your husbands, as is fitting in the Lord'. This confirms Nyawo's observation that there are those parts in the Bible which are convincingly in harmony with the patriarchal traits in culture, and they are quoted over and over again to be and are instilled in the women's minds (Nyawo 2014). This is to ensure that male dominance and authority is accepted as God-given and, therefore, an unquestionable right. Men become decision makers, and women readily abide by men's decisions. So, according to norms and teachings of culture and religion, which preserve any leadership or decision-making position only for males, Parliament is not a woman's territory; parliamentary seats are only reserved for men as they are divinely ordained leaders to control all social structures. It is in such scenarios where we observed Christianity sanctioning patriarchal values deeply entranced in Swazi culture. Clifford (2001: 29) explains this type of Christianity as a Christian theology, which is

> 'a gender blind' concept because it is faith in God being brought to understanding from the perspective of male experience … this is the type of theology that only

incorporates the lived experiences of relationship to God of Christian men, and women's experiences of God relatedness are excluded.

Matei (2013), Rakoczy (2004) and Clifford (2001) associate the patriarchal Christian theology with the development of the biblical texts and cultural contexts that were under the influence of Greek and Latin classics by early and medieval church fathers. They argue that over the centuries many Christian theologians have treated women not only as 'dissimilar species' but also as a defective one (Clifford 2001: 30). They would make reference to the Old Testament narratives where women were treated as second-class citizens, and were segregated and prejudiced in society. Taking a leaf from Christian traditions that have permeated all facets of life down the generations, and in conjunction with culture, Emaswati perpetuate male dominance in political participation and representation.

In a nutshell, the point that needs to be emphasized in this section is that Swati culture, being patriarchal, resonates with the patriarchal tenets in Christianity, and the two become accomplices in both causing and deepening women's inequality (Nyawo 2014). That is, there are certain sanctions and expectations imposed on women in the name of culture, and Christianity affirms and conforms to them (Asamoah-Gyadu 2007). The duo, therefore, becomes an inseparable pair in defining the status of women as subordinate actors of history, thus shaping the societal perceptions of the political behaviour. Also, it gives men the status of heads of households and decision makers, all of which gives them control over members of that family (WLSA 2001), including women's ability to represent their constituencies in parliament.

Conclusion

It has been several decades since gender entered the development discourse and many African countries have increasingly taken the concept on board in policy and practice (Prah 2013). However, gender inequalities between women and men still persist in political participation, despite constitutional provisions and signed international conventions that promise gender parity. The chapter has attempted to establish that the women's role and place in politics have been shaped by patriarchal assumptions. The rule and command function is ascribed to men since women are adjudged to be subordinate to men. Parliament is viewed as an exclusive domain and a masculine decision-making territory where important decisions concerning the country's governance are made by men. The women's tendency to shy away from Parliament is consistent with the assumption that decision making is exclusively a male preserve. Swati cultural traditions and religious convictions based on a narrow interpretation of Christianity limit woman's political participation.

The church and culture often reinforce each other to safeguard decision making as a male function. Both traditions assign men an ascribed status with decision making as part of a total package in terms of which only men, as first-class citizens, can be entrusted with parliamentary seats. Swati traditions emphasize women's primary roles as mothers and housewives. Women's triple role as producers, maintainers and reproducers reduces their chances of joining politics and serving in elected office. Given their adherence to Swati culture and religious traditions founded upon historical antecedent, some women are reluctant to mix their 'wifely' duties with politics. This works against the reasonable assumption that if women are fairly represented in parliament, they will use the opportunity in government to advance the cause of women and push the women's agenda in addition to other competing dimensions of representation. The active participation of women is also indispensable in a country that is still developing. Without the active participation of women and incorporation of women's representatives at all levels of decision making, the goal of equality and development cannot be achieved. When women are absent from the legislative bodies, their perspective is absent and missed, robbing the country of valuable perspectives that could enrich the politics.

The chapter, therefore, advocates women's empowerment that goes beyond economic projects that would increase market and profitability for their income, and thus alleviate poverty. This is internal development, which would enable Christian women to stand against any intentional or unintentional prejudicial treatment that blocks their way to positions of power in politics. This calls for the church to critically engage with the religious beliefs that, in partnership with the cultural ones, reduce women to only wives and housewives. This would contribute immensely towards overcoming the current inequalities and grant women their full voice in politics.

Policing boundaries of the body? Spirit-type African Apostolic churches, HIV/AIDS and inequality in Eastern Zimbabwe, 1985–2015

Nicholas Nyachega and Kudzai Biri

Introduction

This chapter uses the African Apostolic Church of Johane Marange (AACJM) in Honde Valley, as a site of analysis to explore the responses of spirit-type churches in Zimbabwe to the HIV and AIDS epidemic. In contrast to widely accepted views that Apostolic churches have leniently or passively responded to the epidemic, we argue that spirit-type churches have responded in many ways and employed several instruments in the struggle against HIV and AIDS – key to these instruments is spiritual healing with water. The opening sentence shows the deep-seated belief that was taught by the founder of the church and has survived to date. This belief and claims of healing HIV and AIDS with water are the focal point of our probing of the long-held sociocultural beliefs of the AACJM. In particular, the chapter seeks to underscore the dynamics of inequality within the AACJM. It draws attention to the challenges emerging from the emphasis on faith healing (while some of the male religious leaders clandestinely access the same Western medicine which they condemn in their preaching), as well as the policing of women's bodies in the context of HIV and AIDS. In order to protect the identities of the study participants, the chapter uses pseudonyms.

Besides, we examine 'no-sex before marriage' teachings as instruments to police the boundaries of young girls' and women's bodies. There is strict monitoring of girls to ensure that they do not indulge in sex before marriage, which the study queries because boys do not go through the same monitoring. While the AACJM men can engage in sexual intercourse with various women, it is girls and women who are often at the receiving end of the practices and regimes of policing the body. This is largely because of male-patronizing approaches to religion and vulnerabilities created by unequal socioeconomic and cultural practices. The restricted social autonomy of women and young girls reduces levels of awareness of their rights to resist different forms of exploitation that make them vulnerable to infection. To appreciate these dynamics, it is imperative to provide a brief background of the AAJCM. This enables us to see how related diseases have shaped their attitude towards HIV and AIDS.

A growing body of literature has explored the origins, establishment and expansion of the AACJM (Jules-Rosette 1975; 1979; Murphree 1969; 1971). Chitando (2007) discussed the problem of HIV and AIDS in a broader way that facilitated a better understanding of the spirit-type churches' worldview in Zimbabwe. Daneel (1971) has written on Shona Independent churches, noting that a good many Marange in the then Umtali region were educated in Methodist schools. He also focused on leadership schisms in the church following the death of its founder Muchabaya Momberume (known as John/Johane Marange). Bourdillon (1976) and Hastings (1979) have also explored the origins, establishment and expansion of the AACJM. The converging point of the significance of their works is on how girls and women are powerless in decision making both at home and at church, despite the large numbers that they constitute. However, many scholars have paid much attention to the church's growth across Africa, overlooking the role church practices play in shaping communities' responses to the HIV and AIDS crisis.

However, Jules-Rossette (1979), using a feminist approach, explores how women in the Marange church act as ceremonial leaders, also exercising agency and control of their lives. She argues that indigenous churches in Africa provide an ideal situation for examining the role of women and their status as cult leaders, especially among the AACJM where women constitute the majority of church membership. This numerical strength is significant, as we examine the plight of many women in relation to beliefs and practices that relate to HIV and AIDS. Similarly, Murphree (1971) has also observed that the AACJM, in the Budjga communities of northeastern Zimbabwe, seek to insulate themselves from the communities in which they live, claiming to be the most faithful embodiment of Christ's religion and organization. Musevenzi (2017) examines the AICs more generally, focusing on how they have had to negotiate the agendas of non-governmental organizations (NGOs) and their human rights discourses in the contemporary period.

We provide new insights into these scholarly conversations through emphasizing the AACJM members' responses to HIV and AIDS. We draw inspiration from Chitando, who in *Living in Hope: African Churches and HIV/ AIDS* (2007) broadly examines how African churches have effectively responded to HIV and AIDS. His conceptualization and discussion of spiritual healing in spirit-type churches versus HIV and AIDS are useful to our study of the AACJM. He opined that the era of HIV demands that the contemporary generation takes a critical look at some African cultural beliefs and practices. Utilizing these insights, we argue that the AACJM's claim of healing HIV and AIDS with water needs to be questioned because it falls within the doctrine of the church that was birthed during the colonial era to shun Western medicine as a protesting strategy. This was long before the HIV and AIDS epidemic. Being critical of religio-cultural beliefs is crucial; hence, we probe the use of water in healing HIV and AIDS in order to explore and expose some underlying inequalities that are couched in religious garb.

Researches show that HIV and AIDS occurred earlier in Africa. However, it was not until the 1980s that governments began to acknowledge it (Chitando 2007; Ucheaga and Hartwig 2010). Before the 1980s, many conspiracy theories defended 'African integrity' by arguing that HIV and AIDS were developed by outsiders as part of the broader biological warfare to eliminate blacks (Chitando 2007). Many people thus viewed HIV and AIDS as non-existing, and often very dismissive attitudes became prevalent because of such theories. AIDS was often being interpreted as 'American Idea to Discourage Sex' and HIV appeared remote and far removed from African realities (Chitando 2007). However, many people began to suffer from the epidemic such that by the 1990s, many Africans from all walks of life began to give attention to the HIV and AIDS problem. In this vein, Chitando (2007) noted that, after waging bitter struggles against colonization, HIV and AIDS forced Africans to 'get back to the road again' and embark on another struggle with suffering and death. Churches began to respond differently, but many viewed HIV and AIDS as a form of divine wrath or punishment, and the AACJM embraced the same belief.

Origins of the African Apostolic Church of Johane Marange and the emergence of the doctrine of spiritual healing

The AACJM was founded by Johane Marange in the region of Umtali (now Mutare). It emerged as a holistic healing movement, with its leader declaring, 'If you pray for water and give the sick to drink, they shall be healed of their illness. You shall cure all the diseases with your hand and water' (Marange 1973: 5). Most historians and theologians subscribe to the year 1932 as a year of the AACJM inception. Maxwell (2006) highlighted that the Marange Church first appeared in 1932 under the leadership of Johane Marange. According to the Native Commissioner's report of Umtali of December 1932, 'a peculiar sect calling itself the Church of the Apostles appeared in the Marange Reserve. The members disclaim any connections with the Apostolic Faith Mission' (National Archives of Zimbabwe, Native Commissioner's Report, Umtali District 31 December 1932). From the 1930s, the Johane Marange Church began to sprout across Zimbabwe and other parts of the continent. Hastings suggested that 'African Apostolic Church began its work in Zimbabwe then Transvaal and the Orange Free State but then went north towards Luluaburg in Zaire' (Hastings 1979). The growth fulfilled the founder's vision to convert many people in the country and beyond its borders.

The emergence and development of the AACJM, like many other African independent churches across Africa, should be understood within the context of broader colonial politics of cultural domination and social control in Africa. Further, it must be located in Africans' desire to resist such domination through forming their own churches where they would have autonomy. Yet the colonial officials denied this view, arguing that the AACJM was not an offshoot of the then existing white controlled churches such as the Methodist and Anglican (Native Commissioner's Annual Report, Umtali 1929). In addition, the Native Commissioner of the Umtali region in 1932 suggested that the Johane Marange Church denied any connection with the Apostolic Faith Mission in the region. On the other hand, some scholars see little evidence for the church to disclaim its connection to other churches. For instance, Murphree noted that the founder of the church, Muchabaya Momberume, was a Methodist layman of visionary temperament who took the name Johane when he launched the church (Murphree 1969).

Prior to the formation of the Johane Marange Church in 1932, there had been wars and disasters world over. In 1918, the Spanish influenza had reached Africa and both the 'traditional medicine' and 'Western medicine' failed to find remedy for the problem. The Native Commissioner reports of Wankie, on 22 October 1918, noted that the Spanish influenza appeared and spread rapidly, claiming over 1,700 victims (National Archives of Zimbabwe, Native Commissioner's Report, *Report of Wankie*). Many people were left confused by such societal problems. When the influenza reached the Umtali region, Muchabaya Momberume, who was later christened Johane Marange, the founder of the AACJM, was still young. It was not surprising that such disasters largely influenced his attitude towards epidemics and other societal problems. Thus, from 1932, his church (the AACJM) began to emphasize spiritual, and not medicinal, healing. However, we assert that the doctrine of spiritual healing in the AACJM began in 1930. Muchabaya Momberume claimed that in 1930, at the age of nineteen, while he had completed thousands of prayers in Umtali town, God's messenger said to him:

> God chose you before you were born to perform his work. From now onwards you must not be treated with any kind of medicine or drug when ill. Never you try to. In fact, you shall not be ill after these two years. Now stand up and preach to the people.
>
> (Marange 1973: 17)

We use this narrative a reference point to trace how AACJM members have embodied this incident to be part of their daily 'religious rituals' and approaches to 'discipline the body'. Doing so allows us to historicize the AACMJ's body policing practices, underscoring the doctrine of spiritual healing in the face of HIV and AIDS. Using this as his 'calling event', Johane Marange preached across Eastern Zimbabwe that 'the kingdom of God was at hand and many people repented' (Marange 1973). After working tirelessly in the Marange Communal area, Johane Marange instructed Simon, Cornelius and Arnold to set a leadership that was to administer different parts of the Southern Umtali, and he sent a convoy of preachers to Honde Valley. The Simon Mushati led group of evangelists arrived in the area around 1940, probably coming from Penhalonga (*Interview*, J. Masamvu). The Honde Valley area, then known as Holdenby, became strategic for AACJM evangelists. The area shares borders with Mozambique; thus, it offered the shortest route for the Johane Marange preachers to reach Mozambique. Eventually, the AACJM became a religious group without borders, spreading into Mozambique and other parts of southern Africa.

Colonial displacements were also an important factor to the growth and spread of the AACJM. For instance, Native Commissioner of Umtali indicated a series of displacement-induced migration, noting that a company called Lonrho bought land in the Marange area which belonged to the Zimunya people. An estimated 1,250 residents were evicted from their former lands and became landless (National Archives of Zimbabwe, Native Commissioner's Annual Report, Umtali, 1929). These displaced populations migrated northwards. Beginning in early 1930s, this northwards movement facilitated the spread of the AACJM gospel as the early converts took the gospel into new territories, including the surrounding areas (*Interview*, A. Samaringa 2012).

The doctrine of spiritual healing: A body policing tool?

The Christian church certainly cannot remain silent in the face of HIV and AIDS, and while pastoral and medical care of those infected remain crucial in response to this crisis, we Christians in our deep faith in the incarnation and resurrection, must go further and seek to eradicate this virus totally form the world. We have a very distinctive contribution to make to the whole area of prevention, because of the faith we proclaim.

(Igo 2009: 11)

HIV and AIDS shocked many African communities and many societies remain puzzled and traumatized by the epidemic. While there were different responses across social and political divides, the AACJM has responded differently, explaining the coming epidemic in spiritual terms. They believe that all answers and solutions to diseases are found only from the Holy Spirit (Interview with Dodzo 2012). On this note, one is often confronted with many questions, for instance; is spiritual healing the solution to the HIV and AIDS and is it effective?

As argued previously, the doctrine of spiritual healing in the AACJM is based on the claims made by the church's founder that he encountered God in 1930, who told him never to take any medicine. In addition, in 1931, Johane Marange's friend, Andisew, instigated him to take a supernatural drug or boxing charm (*mangoromera*) which would enable him to win the boxing tournament in Mutare (Marange 1973). *Mangoromera* has different meaning among the Shona, but in most parts of Manicaland, it refers to a boxing medicine or charm for invulnerability. The use of this boxing charm was heavily condemned by the colonial officials who thought that it gave African boxers exaggerated opinions of themselves (National Archives of Zimbabwe, S1542/12). Yet *mangoromera* was so common that Johane Marange, who soon was to be a founder of a church that criticized the use of medicine, could not resist. Marange claimed that his use of fighting medicine led him to break the spiritual laws that God gave him in 1930 and punishment eventually followed. Marange claimed that God came to him and asked, 'What have you done today?', 'I have taken a drug', he replied (Marange 1973). 'What did I tell you in 1930?' (Marange 1973), God is said to have added. Marange went on to narrate his ordeal, saying that after the confrontation, he was burnt so terribly by a tremendous fire and God told him never to use any drug again. Marange claimed that the fire that God showed him was the punishment and end of the sinners.

From today, keep the Sabbath, if you put your hand on the head of a person with demons, they shall come out. If you put your hand on the sick, they shall be healed. If you pray on water and give the sick and drink, they shall be healed of their illness. You shall cure all the diseases with your hand and water.

(Marange 1973: 6–7)

The above vignette reveals the genesis of the doctrine of spiritual healing among the members of the AACJM. This doctrine, apart from Marange's claims, was also influenced by the political contexts of the emergence of the AACJM. The combined protests against colonization and Western medicines and hospitals as effective way to disengage their domination on the continent also shaped the AACJM beliefs and practices. This serves to establish the deficiency of the theology of spiritual healing in relation to HIV and AIDS. Emerging in a context where African Protestant churches criticized Western missionaries' hegemony over Africans who were denied chance to exercise their innovations and creativity, the emphasis on Western medicine was also critiqued by the AACJM. Hence, while Johane claims divine visitation and spiritual healing, colonial contexts of medical history and anti-colonial perceptions seem to have inspired him and the rise of the AACJM. The question remains: Is spiritual healing the only way to defeating HIV and AIDS? To follow and implement spiritual healing, the AACJM set up an administrative system to complement the doctrine of spiritual healing. This saw the emergence of offices and ranks of people who eventually became custodians of spiritual healing. These administrative offices were occupied by both males and females who acted as sacred practitioners mainly as healers, prophets and *hakirosi* (singers).

Ranks and administrative posts in the AACJM

The highest rank is the Priest or *Mutumwa* which means 'the one who is sent' or 'the chosen one'. Because the AACJM members believe that Johane Marange was sent to them, he became the first priest. His successors also assumed the same rank and title (Interview, Masamvu 2012). Marange became the highest authority, the *Mutumwa* from 1932 to 1963. After a long period of power struggle, Abel Momberume (Johane Marange's eldest son) took over and Noah Taguta was the priest at the time of writing. Murphree (1969) asserted that from the inception of the church, Johane rested authority upon four credentials: his revelations, his claim to foretell events, his claim to be able to heal diseases and his charismatic personality. To secure in his authority, Johane collected around him a nucleus of men and women who assisted in evangelism and administration.

Several men and women occupied positions in the administration of the church, and *Paseka* (Passover) was instituted as a unifying factor. These ranged from the office of the evangelist, baptizer, prophet and healer as functionaries in the spiritual court of *Mutumwa* Johane (Interview, Madzitire 2012). The offices have different grades to the top rank. The evangelists have badges on their gowns written AP, APE and APE *Liebauma*. APE stands for Apostle, Preacher and Evangelist. *Liebauma* was a secret word that was revealed to Marange in a dream, which is of Hebrew origins meaning 'top rank' (Barrett 1968). The ranks go up to the office of the baptizer who is identifiable by the Mercedes Benz lookalike marks (junior grade), followed by the six-star mark. The office of the prophet follows, and it is often distinguished in the same criteria. Finally, the office of the Healer or *Murapi* follows abbreviated MR. The highest rank in this office has a P and *Liebauma* extension. These are the four basic offices that occupy and play a central role in AACJM, especially in upholding the doctrine of spiritual healing, and policing Marange member's bodies. The doctrine is preached but *murapi*, prophets and *liebaumas* are responsible for converting the 'word' into practice and they are therefore custodians of spiritual healing.

These custodians play the role of advisors in the *Dare* (a 'court') in which the contentious issues and cases are brought to be judged (*Interview*, Marekwa 2012). The AACJM replicates their hierarchical structure of the political court systems. Cases that are brought to the *dare* include cases to do with failure to abide by the laws governing the doctrine of spiritual healing, especially getting vaccinations. The *New Testament of the Apostles* is thus used as the 'constitutional document' to try and judge whether one could be excommunicated or not. Excommunication is feared so much that the AACJM members 'will continue till death' in order to abide and believe in spiritual healing (Interview, Chimuswe 2012). Getting medication leads to disciplinary hearing where one gets sanctioned on behaviour, and reminded about the divine word that

> if you put your hand on the sick, they shall be healed. If you pray on water and give the sick and drink, they shall be healed of their illness. You shall cure all the diseases with your hand and water.
>
> (Marange 1973: 5)

Protest voices

One ex-Johane Marange Church member cried and said:

> It is painful to see these people condemning hospital services. They tell people that do not go to hospital, but the leaders go during the night. Since 2008 I lost four sons and my wife all because of malaria and diarrhea. My wife died last year

at the point of expulsion from the church because I had told them that Masamvu and Masere had been going to Hauna hospital.

(Interview, Kuchocha 2012)

While all the AACJM members are not allowed to seek medicinal treatment, our findings in 2016 show that the 'big men' in the AACJM have been clandestinely visiting the hospital in Hauna and Zindi clinic for STI injections (Interview, Marira 2016). This scenario exposes the hypocrisy of leaders who do not live up to their claims. Besides, it exposes the deficiency of claims of spiritual healing in AACJM. Some women expressed their defiance as they visit clinics privately for family planning injections and pills. This has been confirmed by other women from the same Church who reside in Harare. These women also pointed out that it is important for them because they avoid pregnancy when they have HIV and AIDS.[1] First, it shows the deficiency of claims of spiritual healing by the leaders. Followers are hesitant to protest openly, therefore, they resort to defence mechanisms that do not place them at loggerheads with leaders. Second, it shows the subservient position of women, who are mostly victims of patriarchal doctrines, and how they are affected more than men because of reproductive health challenges.

Such protests should also be read positively as steps towards combating HIV and AIDS. It exposes the deficiency of teachings towards issues of health and well-being that infringe with the plight of women. However, the vulnerability of girls and women to HIV and AIDS and other sexual and reproductive health issues means that they suffer health issues more than men. Critics expect members to quit the church, especially when members die. However, it is an area outside the purview of our study to establish why members remain in the church despite evidence of the failure of water to heal the sicknesses. What is clear is the resilient belief in the power of the 'holy water', which seems to be more of an imagination than reality. While members claimed that water can heal HIV and AIDS, no one could give an example of those who were healed, which raises suspicion and, at the end, it appears members strive to live faithfully to the confession of the doctrine of holy water even where they could see otherwise.

Living the doctrine: Polygamy, child marriages and sanctions on sex

Apart from the doctrine of spiritual healing, there are many other practices for scrutiny. There is need to analyse religious societies' practices and beliefs because no generalized account will do justice to this since churches and ecumenical institutions do adopt dogmatic positions which hamper the dissemination of information or the acquisition of knowledge (Josephine et.al. 2001). The marriage institution is vital to the ongoing analysis on polygamy, child marriages, and *bondwe* (a traditional custom of giving a son-in-law another wife-of-appreciation). It is also relevant for understanding sanctions on behaviour, specifically the 'no sex before marriage' concept. The paradox of women in AACJM must be explored since the marriage institution is patriarchal and determines the position of women in the face of the HIV and AIDS scourge.

The AACJM Church promotes polygamous marriage. Research has shown that in every twenty families of the AACJM, fifteen are polygamous. The remainder of five families of twenty were newly married families who by the time of Paseka (Passover feast) wished to marry a second wife (Dodzo 2012). The roots of polygamy in the AACJM are debatable but also have their origins in Africans' pre-colonial marriage practices. Members of the AACJM give spiritual and biblical interpretations about polygamy. The accounts of Dodzo and Marekwa confirmed that polygamy is inherited from Johane Marange, who had thirteen wives. Dodzo, who has ten wives, said he wishes to reach thirteen to fulfil God's promise to Abraham to multiply like the sand (Interview, Dodzo 2012). This shows that there are attempts to justify polygamy in the AACJM by appealing to the Old Testament. However, Chitando (2007) argues that many AICs have sought to integrate the Christian teachings with the African cultural realities. Chitando (2007) adds that the marriage institution is important in the fight against the HIV and AIDS epidemic and demands the contemporary generation to take a critical look at African cultural beliefs and practices.

Polygamous marriages run the risk of spreading HIV through sexual networks in which the virus can be rapidly spread and go unnoticed and untreated. In addition, the doctrines and belief systems of extreme Independent African Churches such as the Johane Marange have been perpetuating doctrines that continue allowing the spreading of HIV, increase child mortality rates, deaths related to child births, child marriages and general deaths rates due to the non-seeking of biomedical health system (Musevenzi 2017). However, it can be pointed out that the question surrounding the AACJM's polygamous practices cannot be satisfactorily answered from an outsider's view. The narratives we gathered, however, reveal how the marriage institution is treated by the church members as a fulfilment of the founder's divine mandate. Members claim that their polygamous marriages are ordained by the Holy Spirit and cannot be a problem to their health. They cite examples of leaders such as the founder who had thirteen wives by the time of his death. Dodzo said,

> Mutumwa Marange had so many wives. He had 13. To us and the whole church he is quite an interesting example. He is our role model. The belief that women are carriers of HIV and AIDS is for the heathens. We don't believe in that. No, we don't. Wives are a blessing from God and with all that I do for Him, why would he forsake me and give me an infected wife?

(Interview, Dodzo 2012)

Mrs Dupwa, former head of the HIV and AIDS Department in the Ministry of Health and Child Welfare, also shared the same view:

> I don't think that the Johane Marange marriages are problematic in the context of AIDS as we usually think. They are even safer because the people have come in the open and have open marriages. What do you say about those men and women who are married but they still have small houses, and some are sweet mummies and sweet daddies? I think people must stop stereotyping apostolic churches.

(Interview, Dupwa 2011)

However, the chances of HIV infection are high if the husband has extra marital affairs without protection. This can lead to the spread of the virus to all the other wives. Yet, if there is sexual integrity, the marriage institution is instrumental in the fight against HIV and AIDS. As Chitando (2007) pointed out, HIV competent churches continue to stress the importance of marriage and family life. Stable families and marriages are a strategic resource in response to HIV. As Phiri (2006) contends, the era of HIV and AIDS demands that urgent steps be taken to change the status of married women since they are most endangered people because of the lack of power over their own sexual lives that are controlled by their husbands. This explains why some women visit clinics privately in fear of their husbands and the church doctrine which shows that there are contradictions between the church doctrine and the realities of life. In cases where women do not have the courage to have such protests, they can contract HIV; get impregnated under unhealthy conditions and live with the virus in ignorance.

The AACJM members also deny the preventive measures such as use of condoms. For years, condoms have been viewed as one of the central measures to prevent HIV. These views are not exclusive to the Marange church, as other Christian organizations such as Catholics also talk about the 'evils' of condoms, maintaining, amongst other points, that they offer little protection against the transmission of HIV, because they promote promiscuity and trivialize sex (Flint 2011: 132; Moswane 2013: 8). Hence, many NGOs and HIV and AIDS activists have strongly advocated the use and free distribution of condoms as a more radical way of combating the virus (Igo 2009: 30). Dodzo argued:

> 'We do not use condoms. I and my wives are one in flesh and spirit; condoms are for the "world" and the heathen who are unrighteous. Move around our rubbish pit ... you will never see any condom wrappings or used condoms ... Momberume never used condoms but he survived till old age (Interview Dodzo 2012).
>
> (Interview 2012)

Child marriages also affect young girls in the AACJM. According to Sibanda (2011: 3), 'child marriage, is any marriage carried out below the age of 18 years, before the girl is physically, physiologically and psychologically ready to shoulder the responsibility of marriage and childbearing'. In Zimbabwe, child marriage is illegal, and perpetrators should ideally be charged and jailed. Yet in AACJM, child marriages continue under the guise of customary marriages. Child marriages are prevalent among the AACJM despite the fact that Zimbabwe has laws that govern marriage practices for both girls and boys (Sibanda 2011). Early marriage practices continue mainly in the AACJM where the Holy Spirit is used for indoctrination and intimidation of church members. Besides, the Holy Spirit is used among the AACJM members to validate child marriages because of the belief that men are 'directed' by the Holy Spirit to marry young virgin girls (Sibanda 2011). Through 'prophecies' and dreams, marriages are endorsed and viewed as divinely ordained and the Holy Spirit is used to endorse the marriages of young girls. Hence, a channel in which older men that have been exposed to sexual sprees can infect young girls at the point of marriage. The girls are usually married when they do not even understand marriage and do not have control over their sexuality. The cross-generational nature of marriages is also problematic because young girls cannot demand safe(r) sex or take part in the decisions that affect their health such as child spacing (Sibanda 2011). To add on, Makoni (interview 2012) reiterated:

> Child marriages in the African Apostolic Johane Marange are quite prevalent and disappointing because we do not enroll girls from this religious sect. Many of them end in grade seven and this keeps them marginalized for decades. The old men who marry the young girls do it because they claim the Holy Spirit wants them to do it.

Betty Makoni (2012), the former director of the Girl Child Network International (GCNI), branded the AACJM as a paedophile syndicate because of its members' propensity to marry under-age children. Makoni wrote, 'Johane Marange Apostolic sect sexually enslaves girls, it has ruined the lives of the innocent girls, and I am going to explore what I have found in their bedrooms in my book *Never Again*.' While outsiders such as activists and academics may view child marriages in the AACJM as 'enslavement', some young girls and their mothers or even senior wives do not explain their child marriages within these lenses. Young girls were, however, reluctant to speak about their experiences fearing that their husbands and fathers would punish them if heard. Senior women in Dodzo's family expressed some sense of security and happiness because they had young girls recently married to their husband. For Emilia and Ruth (both Dodzo's senior wives), having young girls married to their husband meant they would be seniors, and this means they would not have to do more work in the fields, home and in bed. Their husband wound spend more time with the young wives to meet their *duty* (a term often used to refer to sexual intercourse) demands.

Apart from all these practices that increase vulnerability in the face of the HIV and AIDS epidemic, the AACJM members emphasize the notion 'no sex before marriage' which is endorsed by the *gedhe romweya* (spiritual screening) and *zemeni* (virginity test). The unmarried girls are seen as 'Virgin Marys', figuratively pointing to virginity, moral uprightness and purity. The notion of 'no sex before marriage' has no roots in the coming of HIV and AIDS. The AACJM members are strict law observers and have laws that guide them and sanction their behaviour as they prepare themselves for '*Jerusarema yaMutumwa*' (the Prophet's Jerusalem) (Interview, Phiri 2011). By and large, the 'no sex before marriage' principle emerged as a tool to sanction the members as they prepare for themselves the way and 'write their passports for eternity' (Dodzo 2012).

To effect the policing of bodily boundaries and desires, members deploy another practice, *gedhe romweya*, whereby prophets, often standing in pairs, make people pass by them. Those who would have sinned, for example, committing adultery, witchcraft and stealing, among other vices, will be caught and will be brought to the *dare* (church court) for interrogation. The *gedhe romweya* is done on Saturday services and *Paseka* (Passover). There are several cases that have been recorded in different sects, for example, Mukubva and Katseye, about adultery. The *munyori* (secretary) of the Mukubva sect disclosed that from June 2010, there were cases of adultery caught by the 'great prophets' of his sect.[2] Thus, *gedhe romweya* becomes one of the most vital body policing tools and to weed out the adulterous members. In a way, it helps in the fight against HIV and AIDS as people are embarrassed to be caught up and denounced in public; sexual networks outside marriages may dwindle. However, the *gedhe romweya* practice does not emerge primarily as a response to HIV and AIDS. Both the *zemeni* (virginity tests) and *gedhe romweya* can be traced as far back as the 1930s. Although these practices do not project a direct response to the epidemic, the practice minimizes the chances of HIV and AIDS infection and spread because of the regulation of sexual behaviours.

Zemeni is a patriarchal practice employed by the church to police girls and women because few, if any men, have been subjected to punishment of witchcraft and adultery. It focuses on young girls only and while girls are protected from sex before marriage they can still be married by young men and old men who have been vulnerable to the virus and disease. *Zemeni* ensures the Marange elders, both males and females, total control, largely over sexuality of the young girls. Chigweshe (Interview 2012) noted that *zemeni* can simply be defined as a virginity test for the Marange women. Chigweshe added that 'girls are taken to the rivers, usually under the escort of old women, and they are tested. After some lengthy cross examinations, they are taken back to the church and the names of those who would have failed will be announced in the public ... they are also given pierced leaves'. The pierced leaves mean that the girls have 'failed' and are now marriageable to anyone, but most preferably old(er) men with white beard. The young boys who could have attained 'marriageability' will not go for the 'failed', but scramble for the virgins. Since this practice forbids girls from having premarital sex, it also exposes the girls who would have failed since they will not have choices of marriages as compared to the virgin. Their status will be reduced and are rejected on the 'marriage market' (Interview, Phiri 2012). However, it has been observed that the *zemeni* practice did not emerge out of the need to curb the spread of the pandemic in the AACJM. Yet, the practice protects girls against the HIV and AIDS epidemic since it requires them to keep and guard jealously their purity and virginity. It minimizes the spread of HIV and AIDS through sexual intercourse by protecting the girls. While *zemeni* has been important in curbing the chances of the rapid spread of HIV and AIDS, there are loopholes. Therefore, the gender politics in the AACJM deserve attention in the quest to address inequality and to promote gender justice.

Gender politics and inequality

The interpretation of the Bible, policing of women's bodies and the under-age marriage of girls (discussed above) is a manifestation of how religion facilitates gender inequality and abuse, alongside closing off avenues of empowerment. Religion enables and explains gender-based and sexual violence and bolsters patriarchy that effectively places women at the bottom of the socioeconomic and political ladder, to their exploitation in every facet of lives. Despite constituting the bulk of the membership, women continue to groan in faith. One would then ask why women continue to flock to such churches. While Mwaura (2008) has explored the struggles of women and their stigmatization in African initiated churches in the face of HIV and AIDS, it is important to see how women are trapped within culture, tradition and teachings that are claimed to be sanctioned by the Holy Spirit. Women and girls in the AACJM often struggle against male domination, and they are usually silenced and exposed to HIV and AIDS under the guise of the Holy Spirit and strong emphasis on spiritual healing

As pointed out by some activists, the issue of HIV and AIDS is accompanied by externally funded and managed projects that aim at disseminating knowledge, change practices, and provide care for HIV positive persons and those vulnerable. This means the extension of ideas of health, sexuality and gender relations through sexual networking. It means most women and girls in AACJM remain devoid knowledge of HIV and AIDS prevention and management. They are not empowered to challenge existing male dominance that put their health and well-being at risk but are socialized and conditioned to be subservient to their oppression and sexual exploitation. Mukonyora (2007) correctly describes their plight – 'wandering in a gendered wilderness' of poverty, sickness and being victims of oppression. The scriptures and the Holy Spirit have been used as a tool to silence women, put men on a pedestal and to practise and promote gender inequalities which negatively affects women and girls in the HIV and AIDS era.

Conclusion

There are two important observations which emerged from the foregoing discussion. First, it is inappropriate to view Apostolic churches as merely passive societies in the face of the HIV and AIDS epidemic. However, their theology on spiritual healing is problematic in the sense of increasing their members' vulnerability to premature deaths in the wake of the availability of antiretroviral therapy, and their practices such as polygamous and child marriages risk them in the face of HIV and AIDS. Prominent figures in the church are aware of this risk and do not stand by what they preach. Ironically, the leaders and others clandestinely visit hospitals when they suffer from diseases such as malaria and even get tested for HIV. Some of the leaders, thus, act hypocritically, misleading and deceiving followers, thereby deepening inequality.

While the AACJM's theology against the use of Western medicine emerged in a colonial contest, to resist domination in mainstream Christian churches such as the Anglican and Methodists, their practices remain very deeply entrenched in the old colonial politics and ways of knowing. Therefore, employing such an approach in the HIV and AIDS era proves dangerous. The doctrine of spiritual healing is important in explaining the responses of the church; however, it is not as effective as some leaders sneak privately to seek medication in modern health centres. The doctrine of spiritual healing does not emerge as response to HIV and AIDS, but it is rather enshrined in the origins of the AACJM. This means that ignoring medicines for those living with HIV because of the founder's teachings at the inception of the movement is both a wrong deployment of teaching and disastrous to the health and well-being of girls and women. Most of the practices and beliefs are stumbling blocks in the fight against the HIV and AIDS epidemic. The effectiveness of spiritual healing against diseases and other epidemics remains questionable. Further, the policing of the bodies of girls and women deepens inequality and entrenches the patriarchal culture of the movement. Clearly, therefore, religion is deeply implicated in women's marginalization and vulnerability within the AACJM, although it also provides some redemptive windows by protecting them from HIV infection through a few beliefs and practices.

Religious homophobia and inequality in Malawi

Jones Hamburu Mawerenga

Introduction

Most discussions on inequality in Africa overlook the impact of sexual orientation and gender identity. Many lesbian, gay, bisexual, transgender and intersex (LGBTI) people experience high levels of inequality. In particular, deeply entrenched religious ideologies contribute to the marginalization of LGBTI people. This chapter examines how religious ideologies exacerbate the inequality experienced by LGBTI people in Malawi. It explores how religion sponsors, justifies and intensifies the inequalities experienced by LGBTI people in Malawi. The chapter describes the different expressions of religious homophobia in Malawi and reflects on how this affects the well-being of LGBTI in relation to health and civil rights. The central idea articulated in this chapter is that religious homophobia leads to negative outcomes for LGBTI people in Malawi.

The chapter explores how religious homophobia leads to socioeconomic and political inequality of LGBTI people in Malawi. Earlier publications on religion and homosexuality in Africa (for example, Chitando and Van Klinken 2016) have highlighted the marginalization of LGBTI people. Although these efforts are commendable, they have not gone far enough in demonstrating how religious homophobia has a direct impact on inequality in relation to LGBTI people.

Inequality in this chapter refers to the unequal treatment given to LGBTI people at work, school and society in general, based on their sexual orientation and gender identity – in other words, a predisposition towards heterosexual people which is biased against LGBTI people. Badgett et al. (2014) explain that religious homophobia has a direct bearing on the discussion of inequality in Africa since the continued marginalization of LGBTI people undermines their contribution to the continent's socioeconomic growth. In the introduction to the volume on churches and homosexuality in Africa, Van Klinken and Chitando (2016) point out the role of both local and international religious actors as both framers and agenda setters of the religio-political homophobia debate. This chapter builds on these insights by showing how different categories of local religious actors have fuelled homophobia in Malawi.

The chapter is divided into two sections in order to demonstrate how religious homophobia leads to socioeconomic and political inequality of LGBTI people in Malawi. The first section presents the manifestations of religious homophobia by the faith community in Malawi. The second section presents a discussion of the impact of religious homophobia on the well-being of the LGBTI community in Malawi.

The manifestations of religious homophobia in Malawi

Adams et al. (2007) argue that homophobia encompasses a range of negative attitudes and feelings towards homosexuality or people who are identified or perceived as being LGBTI. McCormack (2013) contends that homophobia involves contempt, prejudice, aversion, hatred or antipathy towards homosexuality which is based on irrational fear and ignorance and is often related to religious beliefs. Its expression can range from verbal abuse to violent attacks or criminalization.

I have identified at least five ways in which religious homophobia has manifested itself in Malawi. These are: (a) the condemnation of homosexuality by ecclesiastical bodies in Malawi, i.e. the Episcopal Conference of Malawi (ECM), the Malawi Council of Churches (MCC) and the Evangelical Association of Malawi (EAM); (b) the 'Citizen March for Life and Family'; (c) calls for the execution of gays in Malawi; (d) national interdenominational prayers for the rains; and (e) the Public Affairs Committee (PAC) and the Young Pastors Coalition of Malawi (YPCM) fights against the repeal of anti-gay laws in Malawi.

The condemnation of homosexuality by ecclesiastical bodies in Malawi

I hereby present a discussion on the ecclesiastical bodies' engagement with homosexuality because it provides insights into how religious homophobia in Malawi re-enforces socioeconomic and political inequality of LGBTI people in Malawi.

The Episcopal Conference of Malawi (ECM) condemns homosexuality

In January 2015, Archbishop Thomas Luka Msusa, chairperson of the ECM, advised Catholic Members of Parliament to defend the Christian family unit, which he said is composed of a man and a woman, against what he called destructive evil forces promoting homosexuality (Nyasa Times 2015). Alava (2017) argues that the Catholic Church has contributed to the debates on sexuality through a heteronormative and patriarchal family and gender system. In practice, the Church's emphasis on traditional marriage creates a system of violent exclusion that silences the very possibility of any other form of sexuality – particularly, same-sex sexualities. This ideology reinforces a local understanding of homosexuality as a foreign practice that goes against national, ethnic, cultural and religious identities in Africa. Consequently, the adherence to a heterosexual normativity as the only form of sexual orientation and gender identity leads to marriage inequality for LGBTI people.

Gwede (2016a) recounts that Catholic bishops in Malawi met with the former president, Peter Mutharika, at the Kamuzu Palace where they advised him to resist the pressure to legalize homosexuality in the country. They further observed that the controversy and undue pressure on LGBTI rights were alien to most Malawians and were being championed by foreigners. Therefore, they said president should not bow to foreign pressure on LGBTI rights but should follow what the Malawi constitution says. The politicization of the homosexuality discourse in Africa has a common tendency of describing it as a foreign intrusion threatening the stability of African culture. Thus, African politicians and the religious community use bigotry in mobilizing people against what is said to be an affront to African cultural values.

The Malawi Council of Churches (MCC) condemns homosexuality

Mawerenga (2018) intimates that the MCC made a twofold resolution on homosexuality in 2012. First, it argued that homosexuality violates gender complementarity of males and females (Genesis 1:27, 28; 2:18-25). Second, it undertook to uphold the criminalization of homosexuality in Malawi. It identifies gender discomplementarity as the primary reason for what it says is the Bible's rejection of homosexuality. The MCC's first resolution is clearly influenced by the notion of gender discomplementarity, and it contributes to marriage inequality for LGBTI people.

Chirombo (2012) recounts that the MCC made two objections against the government's narrative that the anti-gay laws moratorium would help in reducing the rate of HIV transmission in Malawi. First, contrary to the view that acknowledging homosexuality helps in curbing HIV/AIDS, the Church argued that the promotion of homosexual relationships is in itself the promotion of HIV transmission. Second, there is no law that denies gays the right to medical access and treatment. Therefore, citing lack of access to the healthcare system in Malawi could not be a basis for legalizing homosexuality in the country.

Contrary to the approach of the church in Malawi, Reddy et al. (2015) present a unique effort to examine the knowledge about homosexual transmission of HIV in South Africa. This reverses the trend whereby categories of same-sex sexual practice are almost always excluded from research of HIV and AIDS, as well as from care and intervention programmes. They further proceed to draw attention to the risk behaviours and treatment needs of people who engage in homosexual sex, and explain why same-sex sexuality has to be seen as key within South African efforts to study, test and prevent HIV infection. Msosa et al. (2019) argue that discrimination creates an atmosphere in which LGBTI citizens are afraid to seek life-saving medical care in Malawi. Therefore, this demonstrates that religious homophobia contributes to health inequality for LGBTI people, especially in compromising their access to health and quality life.

The Evangelical Association of Malawi (EAM) condemns homosexuality

Mawerenga (2018) records that the EAM made a twofold denunciation of homosexuality in Malawi. First, it condemned what it said was the promotion of same-sex marriages by saying that it is a violation of the gender complementarity of a man and a woman (Gen. 1:27-28; 2:18, 24; Matthew 19:1-7; 1 Corinthians 7:2). However, EAM's heteronormative attitudes have been criticized by LGBTI rights activists. For instance, argues that they are oppressive, stigmatizing, marginalizing of perceived deviant forms of sexuality and gender, and make self-expression more challenging when that expression does not conform to the norm. Meyer (2015) relates that heteronormative culture privileges heterosexuality as normal and natural and fosters a climate where LGBTI individuals are discriminated against in marriage, adoption rights, tax codes and employment.

Second, the EAM urged the executive and the legislature not to repeal the anti-gay laws. Tuck (2012) argues that religion-based viewpoints on homosexuality are based on the sacred texts; hence, they are intransigent because adherents consider them to be more unchangeable than legal constitutions. Also, the commingling of religion and politics often creates a form of identity politics that perpetuates LGBTI people's inequality in the following spheres: marriage, adoption, healthcare, equality before the law, employment, etc.

Having presented a discussion on the ecclesiastical bodies' engagement with homosexuality, I proceed to discuss religious homophobia as exemplified in the 'Citizen March for Life and Family'.

The Citizen March for Life and Family

Sangala (2017) argues that the EAM and ECM organized the 'Citizen March for Life' on 6 December 2016 and that the march exemplifies religious homophobia. For instance, Rev. Matilda Matabwa, the Secretary General of the Malawi Assemblies of God, argued that sex and marriage are natural between man and woman, and that the man and woman union is an ideal that forms the basic unit of a society.

Muheya (2016) argues that some rights activists accused the religious fraternity of promoting discrimination and human rights violations against sexual minorities. They argued that the faith community did not have the mandate to call for nationwide protests against homosexuality since Malawi is a secular state, and as such, all views should be considered equally. Moreover, it would be against Malawi's Constitution which protects both minority and secular views.

Mawerenga (2018) argues that the 'Citizen March for Life and Family' has four main implications. First, the ECM and the EAM used militant rhetoric: 'Malawi as a country is under siege', 'under attack', 'under immense danger', 'all Christians and people of goodwill should stand up and defend life and family …' This suggests that the religious community in Malawi had declared war against the LGBTI community. Second, it insinuated that human rights are not applicable to LGBTI people and that they should be excluded from society. In this way, the faith community demonstrated exclusion rather than inclusion of the LGBTI community in both the church and society. Third, the negative projection of homosexuality as an intrusion into Malawi's values, beliefs and faiths further marginalized the LGBTI community. Fourth, the mobilization of religious bigots in fighting against homosexuality endangered the lives of LGBTI people in the country.

Therefore, the 'Citizen March for Family and Life' encapsulates religious homophobia by generating ecclesiastical, socioeconomic, cultural and political inequality for the LGBTI community in Malawi. Having presented a discussion on the 'Citizen March for Family and Life', I proceed to present another manifestation of religious homophobia which comprises calls for the execution of gays in Malawi.

Calls for the execution of LGBTI people in Malawi

On three different occasions, the religious community in Malawi has called for the execution of LGBTI people. Malamba (2012) opines that the calls for the execution of LGBTI people contradict Article 3 of the Universal Declaration of Human Rights (UDHR) which states that everyone has the right to life, liberty and security of person and also violates the Constitution of the Republic of Malawi which provides for the right to life in Section 16(1) and states that such life shall not be arbitrarily deprived.

Mawerenga (2018) observes that Apostle Samuel Chilenje of the Jesus Pentecostal Church called for the execution of gays in Malawi. The blatant inequality displayed in this call implies that only heterosexual Malawians have the right to life while all homosexual Malawians should be executed. Therefore, this is the highest form of inequality expressed by a religious minister in Malawi calling for the annihilation of the LGBTI community.

Chilunga (2014) reports that Sheikh Dr. Salmin Omar Idrussi, the former Secretary General of the Muslim Association of Malawi (MAM), called for the execution of gays in February 2014. Idrussi argued for the continued criminalization of homosexuality and for the stiffening of the sentence from a fourteen-year jail term to a maximum death sentence. Nevertheless, Malawi's anti-homosexuality laws contravene various human rights treaties like the African Charter on Human and Peoples' Rights (African Charter), the International Covenant on Civil and Political Rights (ICCPR) and the International Covenant on Economic, Social and Cultural Rights (ICESCR). The laws also fail to conform to the right to non-discrimination, the right to equality before the law and equal protection of the law, and the right to privacy. Finally, they contribute to violations of the right to liberty and security of the person, the right to the highest attainable standard of health, and the right to freedom of association.

Phimbi (2017) recounts that Sheikh Dinala Chabulika, the spokesperson of the MAM, reiterated the call for the execution of gays in September 2017.

Chabulika argued that homosexuality is against not only the Islamic teachings and religion but also an abomination. Therefore, those practising it must be executed. However, as pointed out earlier, calls for the execution of gays contravene the right to life.

These representative statements from Christianity and Islam demonstrate the highest levels of religious inequality in Malawi which called for the annihilation of the LGBTI community. Unfortunately, if not challenged, these forms of religious bigotry and homophobia may eventually lead to violent verbal and physical attacks, and deaths of LGBTI people.

Other events in Malawi also highlight the inequality that the LGBTI community has to negotiate daily.

Ken Msonda's 'Kill the Gays' remarks

Ken Msonda, a Malawian politician, posted inflammatory remarks against the LGBTI community on his Facebook page. The post was entitled 'Kill the Gays.' Nkawihe (2016) reports that Msonda made seven homophobic comments. First, he described gays and lesbians as sons and daughters of the devil who were worse than dogs. Second, he faulted the Malawi Police for arresting gays and later giving them bail. He suggested that the best solution was just to kill them. Third, he criticized the media houses for parading 'the dogs' on TV and newschapters hiding behind human rights. For Msonda, 'the devil' has no rights. Fourth, he challenged to meet the human rights campaigners in court over what he called a satanic, doggish and demonic act of homosexuality. Fifth, he accused sexual minority activists of profiteering from homosexuality by using innocent young girls and boys. Sixth, he called upon the Police to immediately arrest homosexuals because they are inciting citizens to break the law. Finally, he refused to withdraw his Facebook post, maintaining that gay practices remained sinful and God could condemn the nation if they were to be legalized and all those advocating for gay rights should go to hell.

Mawerenga (2018) argues that Ken Msonda's remarks are significant in exposing religious homophobia in Malawi for seven reasons. First, he equates same-sex practice with the devil, calling it satanic and demonic. In so doing, he indirectly singles out same-sex practice as anti-God, thereby mobilizing religious bigots to fight against what would then be the evil of homosexuality. Second, his remarks dehumanize the LGBTI community by insinuating that they are worse than dogs. Third, his remark that gays should be killed serves as a threat to the 'right to life' of the LGBTI community. Fourth, his remarks resonated well with religious bigots from both the Christian and Islamic faiths who started fundraising initiatives to finance Msonda's court case. Fifth, he uses a highly sensitive religious lexicon in crafting his anti-homosexual rhetoric: 'God', 'devil', 'demonic', 'Satanic', 'sinful' and 'hell'. This suggests the commingling of politics and religion in the fight against homosexuality. Sixth, his claim that the devil has no rights implies that LGBTI people also have no rights. Seventh, his attack on rights activists as 'satanic agents and fortune seekers' is very misleading.

Having presented the calls for the execution of gays, I proceed to present a discussion on the national interdenominational prayers for the rains as a manifestation of religious homophobia in Malawi.

National interdenominational prayers for the rains

Gwede (2016b) reports that the clergy argued that God was not giving sufficient rains to Malawi because of the nation's tolerating of same-sex liaisons. This was said during an interdenominational prayer meeting for the rains in Lilongwe. In so doing, the clergy contributed to religious inequality by singling out same-sex practice as a cause of drought. Thus, the people's anger was provoked against the LGBTI community for hindering rainfall in an agrarian society. However, this should be understood in two ways. First, it acts as a scapegoat – blaming the LGBTI community as being responsible for natural disasters. Second, it incites violations against LGBTI people in the context of conflict, post-conflict and post-disaster situations. The Human Rights Council (HRC) (2014) argues that stigmatization and discrimination on the basis of sexual orientation increase gender-based violence in post-conflict and post-disaster situations, negatively affecting LGBTI persons in the provision of food assistance, shelters and humanitarian aid.

Having presented a discussion on the national interdenominational prayers for the rains, I proceed to discuss the religious communities' fight against the repeal of anti-gay laws as a manifestation of religious homophobia in Malawi.

The religious community fights against the repeal of anti-gay laws

Two religious groups, namely, the Public Affairs Committee (PAC) and the Young Pastors Coalition of Malawi (YPCM), fought against the repeal of anti-gay laws in Malawi.

The Public Affairs Committee against repeal of anti-gay laws

Bee (2012) reports that the PAC, an influential inter-religious body, cautioned former President Joyce Banda to tread carefully in her desire to legalize homosexuality in Malawi. She had pledged in her first State of the Nation Address (SONA) on 18 May 2012 to repeal the anti-homosexual laws: Sections 137 A and 153–156 of the Penal Code. However, she backtracked from her pledge to repeal the anti-homosexuality laws in September 2012 after fierce criticism from the religious fraternity. The PAC's intervention negatively contributes to legal inequality for LGBTI people in Malawi.

Khamula (2015) reports that the PAC also reacted to the government's concession that it had suspended homosexual laws because of pressure from donors. The PAC argued that the government's mandate was to serve Malawians and not donors such as Germany, Britain and the United States.

The PAC's initiatives exemplify religious homophobia by hindering the LGBTI community in Malawi from enjoying their rights and realizing equality before the law. The glaring inequalities of LGBTI people in Malawi were highlighted in a 2018 Human Rights Watch study. Two major findings of the study are pertinent for this discussion. First, the study discovered that the continued criminalization of same-sex conduct in Malawi negatively impacts the daily life of LGBTI people in several ways. For instance, they face routine violence and discrimination in almost all aspects of their daily lives. Police often physically assault, arbitrarily arrest and detain them, sometimes without due process or a legal basis, at other times as punishment for simply exercising basic rights, including seeking treatment in health institutions. Second, the study established that the combination of criminalization of adult consensual same-sex conduct and social stigma has had an insidious effect on their LGBTI individual's self-expression, forcing them to adopt self-censoring behaviour because any suspicion of non-conformity may lead to violence or arrest.

Therefore, the PAC's insistence on the continued criminalization of homosexuality is a clear example of religious homophobia resulting in a multifaceted discrimination of LGBTI people.

The Young Pastors Coalition of Malawi (YPCM) fights against a moratorium on anti-gay laws

Mawerenga (2018) relates that in February 2016, the YPCM sought an injunction at the Mzuzu High Court to suspend the anti-gay laws moratorium in Malawi. Judge

Dingiswayo Madise of the Mzuzu High Court granted the injunction on 9 February 2016. Moyo (2016) notes that in May 2016, Judge Dingiswayo Madise of the Mzuzu High Court sustained an injunction obtained against anti-gay laws moratorium until a constitutional court review of the anti-homosexual laws is made.

Human Rights Watch opines that the challenges facing LGBTI people in Malawi have been further exacerbated by a lack of clarity and divergent opinions regarding the legality of a 2012 moratorium on arrests and prosecutions for consensual homosexual acts. In 2016, a High Court order suspended the moratorium pending judicial review by the Constitutional Court. This uncertainty seemed to have encouraged private individuals to attack LGBTI people with impunity, while health providers frequently discriminate against them on the grounds of sexual orientation and gender identity.

Having presented a discussion on the religious communities' fight against the repeal of anti-gay laws, the last section of the chapter presents a discussion on the impact of religious homophobia on the well-being of the LGBTIQ community in Malawi, particularly in the areas of HIV and health and civil rights.

The impact of religious homophobia on the well-being of the LGBTI community in Malawi

Implications on HIV and health

Mawerenga (2018) argues that human rights violations increase the vulnerability of HIV infection among the LGBTI community in Malawi. Discriminatory policies and practices can also result in people being denied access to the information, support and services necessary to make informed decisions and to reduce their vulnerability and risk of HIV infection. Moreover, many homosexuals in Malawi operate underground due to stigmatization and discrimination, coupled with the country's incriminating laws against homosexuality.

Albuquerque et al. (2016) state that members of the LGBTI community are more susceptible to health problems, such as anal cancer, cervical and breast cancer, chlamydia trachomatis, cryptosporidium, giardia lamblia, herpes simplex virus, human immunodeficiency virus, human papilloma virus, isospora belli, microsporidia, gonorrhea, viral hepatitis types B & C, and syphilis. Also, they are more susceptible to the abuse of alcohol, tobacco and illicit drugs, obesity, unprotected sex, and mental disorders. Although this is a multifactorial scenario, it may be further complicated because of the poor access to healthcare and the discriminatory practices of involved professionals stemming from homophobia. The fact is that experiences of discrimination and prejudice against sexual minorities can directly contribute to a poorer health status which reduces their ability to work and affects their productivity at the workplace.

The experiences of LGBTI people in Tanzania help to shed light on those in Malawi. For example, a Human Rights Watch (2020) report documents how since 2016 the government of Tanzania has cracked down on LGBTI people and the community-based organizations that serve them. The Health Ministry in mainland Tanzania has prohibited community-based organizations from conducting outreach on HIV prevention to men who have sex with men and other key populations vulnerable to HIV. It closed drop-in centres that provided HIV testing and other targeted and inclusive services, and banned the distribution of lubricants, essential for effective condom use for HIV prevention among key populations and much of the wider public.

A Human Rights Watch (2018) report states that punitive legal environments, stigma and discrimination based on sexual orientation together with high levels of violence against key populations impedes sustainable national responses to HIV. Evidence shows that when discrimination in public heathcare centres and hospitals is routine, it leads to a climate of fear that fuels human rights violations and deters transgender women, gay men and other men who have sex with men (MSM) from seeking and adhering to HIV prevention, treatment, care and support services.

Implications on civil rights

Badgett et al. (2014) intimate that criminalization of same-sex behaviour violates the civil rights of LGBTI people. Police often physically assault, arbitrarily arrest, detain and extort LGBTI people, thereby taking them out of productive employment. Malamba (2012) argues that the homosexuality discourse in Malawi has implications on civil rights. For instance, Steven Monjeza and Tiwonge Chimbalanga's arbitrary arrest in 2009 and imprisonment on multiple charges of unnatural practices and gross indecency were tantamount to discrimination in the criminal justice system. The state also violated the gay couple's human dignity in two ways: first, by subjecting them to public homophobic hate speech during their trial; second, by subjecting them to forcible anal medical examination aimed at proving that they had sexual relations. Finally, the state violated the gay couples' right to privacy. In particular, Tiwonge Chimbalanga was subjected to very dehumanizing treatment because the authorities wanted to establish his gender identity. Hence, they undressed him and observed his genitals which led them to conclude that he was a man. Gloppen et al. (2020) observe that despite the Malawi government's yielding to international pressure in a high-profile case by unconditionally releasing Steven Monjeza and Tiwonge Chimbalanga, the laws criminalizing homosexuality remain in place, with dire consequences for LGBTI Malawians.

Badgett et al. (2014) observe that the restriction of civil rights against LGBTI people has socioeconomic implications such as lost labour time, lost productivity, underinvestment in human capital and the inefficient allocation of human resources through discrimination in education and hiring practices. The decreased investment in human capital and suboptimal use of human resources, in turn, drags the broad socioeconomic output of a country.

Political homophobia which is embedded in religious beliefs has also been prominent in Africa resulting into the curtailing of civil rights for LGBTI individuals. Gloppen et al. (2020) argue that the former president of Zimbabwe, the late Robert Mugabe, was a catalyst of political homophobia in Africa when he first denounced the gay community in 1993. His example was later followed by African politicians in Botswana, Burundi, Egypt, Ghana, Cameroun, Kenya, Malawi, Nigeria, Tanzania, Senegal, Uganda and Zambia who similarly attacked the LGBTI community. LGBTI persons in Africa are deliberately targeted as a sexual minority group by various politicians to divert attention away from pressing issues of corruption, economic decline or development challenges. The assumed mechanism is that as a regime's faith is at play in elections, or due to public opposition or internal power struggles, homophobia is employed by political actors to divert attention.

However, this leads to a violation of LGBTI people's rights, including arbitrary arrests and prison sentences for loving people of the same sex, murder, corrective rape, assault, exclusion from health services, employment discrimination, discrimination from public service delivery, and the often state-sanctioned dissolution of LGBTI organizations and intimidation of LGBTI rights activists.

Incidences of 'corrective rape' in some parts of Africa reflect a violation of LGBTI rights. Mawerenga (2018) argues that 'corrective rape' is the use of rape against people who do not conform to perceived social norms regarding human sexuality and gender roles with a goal of punishing abnormal behaviour and reinforcing social societal norms. For instance,

Noxolo Nogwaza, 24, a lesbian activist, was gang raped and killed in Kwa Thema, South Africa, in April 2011 in a 'corrective rape' attack. Her body was mutilated; her eyes were gouged out of their sockets; her brain was split open; and her teeth were scattered around her body. Hence, several rights were violated in this case i.e. the right to life, bodily integrity, and freedom from torture and inhuman or degrading treatment, and security of a person. Religious homophobia feeds such violence and inequality by suggesting that LGBTI people have less rights and stand condemned in the eyes of God. (Hamburu 2018: 191)

Conclusion

The chapter has presented the dynamics of religious homophobia and inequality in Malawi. It has noted at least two implications of religious homophobia which lead to the inequality of LGBTI people. First, some LGBTI individuals abandon religion altogether due to the seemingly irreconcilable tension between religious faith and sexuality. Second, religious homophobia infiltrates the public sphere and influences inequality against the LGBTI community; thereby violating their civil rights in five ways: (i) workplace discrimination causes LGBTI people to be unemployed or underemployed; (ii) LGBTI students face discrimination in schools from both teachers and fellow students which affects their right to education; (iii) some LGBTI people become victims of physical, psychological and structural violence, which affects their ability to work due to physical injuries and psychological trauma; (iv) LGBTI people face arbitrary arrests, imprisonment, extortions, beatings and humiliations by Police officers, thereby affecting their daily lives; and (vi) calls for the execution of LGBTI people threaten their right to life.

Therefore, the chapter contends that when LGBTI people are denied full participation in the church and society because of their perceived or real sexual orientation and gender identity, their human rights are violated, subsequently leading to a negative effect on a country's level of socioeconomic development. Religions need to uphold the human rights of all, fight stigma and discrimination against LGBTI people and invest in tolerance for them to contribute towards removing different forms of inequality in society.

Part Three

Encountering religion, disability, age and inequality in Africa

Gender inequality and disability among the Ndebele religio-cultural communities

African women theologies of disabilities praxis

Sinenhlanhla S. Chisale and Kesiwe Phuthi

Introduction

Religion and African culture are 'double trouble' in addressing issues of gender inequality and the politics of disability. African women and men with disabilities face different kinds of discriminations, stigma and isolations that are associated with their differently abled bodies. There are religio-cultural beliefs and stereotypes in African communities that guide the attitudes and behaviours of communities towards people with disabilities. These attitudes and behaviours manifest themselves differently among women and men with disabilities. Written from an African women theology and disability approach, the aim of this chapter is to highlight the extent to which religion and culture promote and challenge gender inequality as experienced by women with disabilities among the Ndebele of Zimbabwe. The aim is to conceptualize African women theologies of disabilities praxis that contribute towards achieving equality, justice and human flourishing where everyone is normal and equal in their different bodies.

Setting the scene

According to John S. Mbiti, Africans are a notoriously religious people (1969: 1). This statement is still a reality for the contemporary African because religion is the umbilical code that connects him or her to his or her story of existence. Mbiti (1969) argues that African communities' morality and ethical life is guided by a religious system that has a set of beliefs and practices that permeates into all the departments of life so fully that it is not easy or possible always to isolate. Disability existed in Africa in the precolonial period and Africans had their own ways of understanding disability before the dawn of colonialism. Their perceptions and attitudes towards disability were informed by their African traditional worldview. Disability in this chapter combines all forms of visible impairments and is discussed from a Ndebele religio-cultural perspective.

The African worldview is always suspicious of issues that are beyond explanation and it searches for meaning from the supernatural powers or ancestors. According to Oladipo (1998: 201–2) Africans interpret their religion from an attitudinal point of view. They believe that the answer to a puzzling reality lies in the transcendental realm, from supernatural powers. A religio-cultural perspective in this chapter refers to African traditional religion (ATR) and Christianity. ATR in African contexts is informed by a blend of African spirituality and culture. Some African cultural traits that inform the African customs, ideas, values and norms emerge from African spirituality. African spirituality and African culture are different; however, they are at times used in a parallel manner to explain the African worldview (Kanyoro 2002). At the dawn of colonialism, missionaries brought different religions to the African continent, creating a friction between African spirituality, culture and other religions, mainly Abrahamic religions (Christianity, Islam and Judaism). This then caused a hermeneutical challenge between African spirituality and African culture. This chapter acknowledges this hermeneutical challenge and, as a result, treats the two as different on the one hand and as consolidating on the other.

African spirituality and African culture are all visible in ATR. ATR perceptions of disability are twofold. On the one hand, disability is seen as a curse by ancestors and, on the other, it is a blessing by the ancestors (Ndlovu 2016: 32). When viewed as a curse, those living with disabilities are often perceived as a form of suffering sent by the ancestors to punish the family. Whereas when viewed as blessing, those living with a disability are assumed to be having special and unique powers. We shall discuss these later in the chapter. Similarly, Abrahamic religions, particularly Christianity, have complex perspectives towards disability. On the one hand, they perceive disability as a curse or suffering for a sin committed by the family and on the other disability is a blessing and a gift from God (Bunning et al. 2017). Ancestors in African spirituality are the departed who lived an ethical life and these are believed to be mediators of the living to God.

From the foregoing, we can argue that disability perceptions in both Christianity and ATR are both liberative and oppressive. This binary is critiqued by African women theologians for oppressing women by reinforcing patriarchy as a norm. Thus, African women theologians campaigned for the liberative religious and cultural teachings to be filtered from the oppressive (Oduyoye 2001). According to Oduyoye (2001) and Kanyoro (2002), oppressive religo-cultural teachings should be reinterpreted through theories such as African feminist cultural hermeneutics, *bosadi* theology and other African women theologies that address the binary religio-cultural teachings. In African worldview the hermeneutics of African culture and spirituality reveal an interplay of *isiko* (customs or culture) and *inkolo* (faith). Christian pastoral praxis acknowledges this interplay; hence, scholars like Stuart Bate (1998) encourage urgent inculturation of Christian praxis. Inculturation is defined by Agbo as 'a process of bringing the people's culture systematically into church' (2017: 7). Thus, Bate (1998) says inculturation should not be taken as cryptic or special but it should be taken as part of the ordinary way of being church.

African culture is diverse (Mbiti 1969); it is therefore important to note that this chapter discusses culture from the Nguni, particularly the Ndebele from Zimbabwe. Culture among the Nguni is also diverse depending on the location of such people. The Ndebele from Zimbabwe, formerly known as the Matabele, originated from Natal in South Africa in the nineteenth century under the leadership of Mzilikazi who ran away from Tshaka's wrath when they came into conflict in 1823 and were forced to flee. The culture of the Ndebele is a blend of Zulu, Xhosa, Swati and Ndebele from Mpumalanga in South Africa. Perceptions of disability among the Ndebele of Zimbabwe are shaped by their culture and religion and they are connected to their spirituality.

Thus, although this is a non-empirical study, it uses some snapshots of empirical data from a project coordinated by one of the authors titled: *Gender-Based Violence among Women and Girls with Disabilities in Relation to Sustainable Development Goals in South Africa* from 2016 to date. That project draws from qualitative data derived from life history narratives conducted in Johannesburg with refugee women with visual impairments. The chapter is written from African women theologies of disabilities approach to highlight the extent to which Christian religion and culture promote and challenge gender inequality experienced by people with disabilities among the Ndebele. The aim is to conceptualize African women theologies of disabilities praxis that embrace equality, justice and human flourishing where everyone is normal and equal in their different bodies. The chapter is divided into four sections: first, is an introduction of African women theologies of disabilities and gender inequality in Africa. Second, is a presentation and discussion of dominant cultural gendered perceptions of disabilities that perpetuate inequality and are emancipatory among the Ndebele of Zimbabwe. Third, is a discussion of Christian-gendered perceptions of disability that perpetuate inequality and those that are emancipatory, that is, leading to equality and inclusion. Fourth, is the discussion of African women theologies of disabilities praxis that informs acts of equality leading to human flourishing. Last, are the concluding remarks.

African women theologies of disabilities and gender inequality

Gender inequality is a thorn in African communities. It affects all women due to patriarchy and religion that enforce women's submission and silence. Women with disabilities experience inequality against all members of society; they are at the bottom of the ladder or hierarchy. Written from an integration of African women theology and theologies of disabilities approach, this chapter seeks to highlight the extent to which Christian religion and African culture promote and challenge gender inequality experienced by people with disabilities among the Ndebele of Zimbabwe. African women theologies of disabilities approach is an integration of African women theologies and theologies of disabilities.

African women theologies were introduced by the Circle of Concerned African Women Theologians (hereafter Circle) under the leadership of Mercy Oduyoye, who argued that feminist theology does not address the lived realities of African women (Oduyoye 2001). She then, with other African women theologians, conceptualized African women theologies that focus on cultural hermeneutics (Oduyoye 2001; Kanyoro 2002); narrative theology/story telling (Njoroge 1997); communal theology (Kanyoro 2001); Bible and African culture (Dube 2000; Masenya (ngwan'a Mphahlele) 2003) and others. African women theologies tackle gender equality by starting from the lived experiences of African women. They reimagine gender equality as honouring human dignity. African culture is perceived as both liberative and oppressive; however, rather than condemning culture they propose that liberative culture should be separated from oppressive culture. They acknowledge that all culture has weaknesses and is not immune to external changes (Kamaara and Wangila 2009: 132; cf. Kanyoro 2001). Thus, they emphasize the significance of time, space and context in theologizing, where both culture and religion evolve and reform with time. This, according to Dreyer (2011), challenges exegesis to be alert to the dehumanizing texts of culture, religion and the Bible through hermeneutics of suspicion.

African women theologians promote solidarity with those who suffer oppression and marginalization of all kinds by calling for the transformation of the hierarchy perpetuated by patriarchy (Phiri and Nadar 2010: 93). Patriarchy informs the system of domination that leads to the abuse of power. Thus, Ackermann argues that solidarity informs resistance of the exploitative systems and ideologies (2008: 272). They construct resistance of oppression and marginalization of women from a theology of equality that is informed by the image of God. Kanyoro confirms this as she argues that 'women's humanity and as beings are also created in the image of God' (2001: 162). Reynolds (2008) explains that the image of God is universal to all human beings and is expressed in variety and difference. All humanity is accorded dignity due to the special connection that humans have with God; thus, due to this dignity, no one should be excluded or marginalized in the community of God. Solidarity and the image of God in all humanity challenge everyone to be responsive to the pains of others. As a result, theologies of disabilities begin from people with disabilities' lived experiences and highlight that people with disabilities are marginalized due to their different bodies. Disability theologians argue that theologies of disabilities focus on the frailty and dependence of the body by reimagining it from inclusion, access and dignity (Eiesland 2004; Reynolds 2008).

Disability is diverse and that is why there are theologies of disabilities rather than one theology of disability. The diversities of disabilities cannot be addressed by a singular theology of disability, but by plural theologies of disabilities. This is because disability is not only about the body of a person, but it can also be about the mental health of a person that does not have anything to do with the body. Theologies of disabilities are able to address this diversity. Phiri highlights this as she explains that her motivation of calling for theologies rather than theology is that 'African women theologians want to acknowledge that even within Africa, there is diversity of women's experiences due to differences in race, culture, politics, economy and religion' (2004: 16). Likewise, women with disabilities' experiences of disability differ due to race, culture, economy, religion, class and the form of disability. Some forms of disabilities are corrected through assistive technologies and devices, while others cannot and may need expensive assistive care giving. Participants in a project directed and conducted by one of the authors[1] explained:

> Disability assistive devices are expensive; some of us can hardly afford to purchase such devices if no one is willing to donate. Because of this, for those born without a disability, there is life or life continues beyond the disability thus if they are from a rich family. While for a poor person born without a disability

there is suffering and agony beyond the disability. (In depth interviews with a participant from a project on GBV among women and girls with disabilities 13 February 2017)

Like all forms of liberation theologies, theologies of disabilities are context and culture bound. The way people from first world countries perceive disabilities is different from those residing in poor third world countries due to different race, culture, politics, economy and religion. Participants from the GBV and disability project highlighted that people with disabilities with citizenship of economically stable countries do not experience violation of their rights compared to those with citizenship of poor countries and families. An example of a person with a disability from South Africa and Zimbabwe was given as follows:

For example, you see someone with a disability from South Africa crying for inclusion and access while us from Zimbabwe still cry for the most basic human need such as food and shelter, that is why we wake up daily going to our work spaces ... issues of inclusion and access are basic needs for everyone but for us from poor countries food and shelter are the most important basic needs.

(In depth interviews with a participant from a project on GBV among women and girls with disabilities 13 February 2017)

This statement highlights the diversity of the lived experiences of disability. As a result, disability is not homogeneous; thus, Chisale's (one of the authors) work on conceptualizing African women theologies of disabilities that challenge the lived realities of African women with disabilities while being sensitive to their diverse contexts of culture and religion is long overdue. On the one hand, African women with disabilities are oppressed by patriarchy enforced by culture and religion and, on the other, they are oppressed by able-bodied women 'who want to be in control of their bodies' (Wilhelm 1994: 106). Theologies of disabilities are, therefore, sensitive to bodily limitations and lived experiences. Swinton argues that the departure point of theologies of disabilities is 'the recognition that people with disabilities have been at best a minority voice in the development of Christian theology and practice and at worst have been completely silenced within the conversation' (2011: 274–5). Thus, in the call for inclusion and acknowledgement of people with disabilities, feminist scholars of disabilities conceptualized disability theologies from a perception of how people with disabilities experience their relationship with God.

Eiesland (1994) presents God as disabled in an effort to present the frailty of God and that this weakness confirms that God is in solidarity with the weak and suffering. This theology is categorized under liberation theologies where theologizing begins from the lived experiences of humanity. Eiesland's approach of disability is supported by Reynolds who argues that 'God not only acts in solidarity with weakness, God acts through weakness' (2008: 231). In this weakness God becomes weak and vulnerable in order to reconcile with humanity. Reynolds highlights that dependence that is caused by disabilities is normal and accepted. This weakness and vulnerability reminds us that we depend and interdepend on each other and above all, we all depend on God.

African culture and gender inequality for women with disabilities among the Ndebele

Patriarchy in African culture has normalized gender inequality where women and men are treated differently. Men and boys are given the superior and leadership status, while women and girls are given the inferior and lower status. All women are expected to be submissive to men and are treated as second-class citizens. African culture informs African traditional religious norms and values. Culture, as argued by African women theologians, is twofold; it can oppress and liberate (Oduyoye 2001). In some cultures, the oppressive take precedence over the liberative due to patriarchy. Women with disabilities are often discriminated against and excluded in society and religious spaces due to their different bodies which are assumed to be contrary to the perfect body. Reynolds argues that perceiving bodies and disability is often shaped by the 'cult of normalcy' (2008: 60), where society perceives the normative as what all bodies are supposed to be. As a result, the disabled bodies are perceived as corrupt and a deprivation of good and normative (2008: 62). Women as the stigmatized and discriminated in society experience this discrimination and stigmatization in threefold when they have visible disabilities due to purity theology and purity culture.

Purity theology and culture is based on the biblical and cultural view of purity. Purity theology analyses practices, images, symbols, concepts that are associated with purity in both the Bible and culture. Disability is one of the images and symbols that is associated with impurity in both the Bible and African culture. As a result, people with disabilities, particularly women, are discriminated against because of their disability (visible bodily impairment), sexuality (menstruating) and their gender (female). Thus, women with disabilities experience gender inequality in comparison to other women due to their visible disability; in comparison to men with disabilities due to their sexuality and in comparison to all men due to their sexuality and gender.

Gender inequality in African traditional religion among the Ndebele

African women with disabilities experience gender inequality due to the stigma and discrimination linked to disability and sexuality. The Ndebele perceive disability in line with the impurity of the body. This then religiously and inevitably excludes such bodies from the sacred and religious spaces. According to this line of thinking, African traditional religious spaces are sacred spaces that can only be accessed by the pure and clean bodies. The African spiritual realm is the space of ancestors. It is only accessed by the chosen, while certain people – particularly menstruating women, disabled women, women who just had sexual intercourse and women who just gave birth – are not allowed to access such spaces. It is held that they will pollute the sacred space and anger ancestors. African traditional religion perceives disability as a message from ancestors, although the disabled person is not allowed to access the space of the ancestors. Chisale confirms this as she explains that for some Africans disability is an 'ancestor's project' or ancestors' message to the family (Chisale 2018a: 1).

Bunning et al. argue that perceptions of disability generally implicate the mother of the disabled child as the cause of her child's disability. It is asserted that the disability is because of her deeds that angered 'ancestors by breach of moral code or failing to honour their memory. Improper family relations, including extra-marital affairs and incestuous relationships have been cited as perceived causes of disability with the mothers generally implicated' (2017: 2). Although the mother is implicated, the child who is disabled lives with this negative stereotype for the rest of his or her life. This is because the significant others decide how the person should live her or his life in connection to society (Helander 1993). The way significant others perceive their family members with disabilities informs and feeds the society's perceptions.

Such perceptions contribute to the discrimination and exclusion of people with disabilities on the one hand, while, on the other, they encourage the inclusion and respect of people with disabilities. Among the Ndebele who live in deep and traditional rural areas of Zimbabwe, a woman with a disability is not allowed to brew beer for ancestral functions (*ukuthethela*) or to serve in the function because they are considered *izilima* (deformed). It is believed that allowing them to perform such functions may anger ancestors, who will punish the whole family. *Isilima* is a derogatory name meaning deformed or *isigoga* meaning a broken person. A broken body is a cursed body among the Ndebele and is not worth and fit to be in the presence of the ancestors.

Sexually, women with disabilities experience discrimination and exclusion more than men with disabilities, because they are not supposed to have sex, fall pregnant and mother children (Kamga 2011). Among the Ndebele, if they fall pregnant, they are forced to terminate their pregnancies because it is believed that they are angering ancestors, or that they will not be able to perform mothering duties (Chisale 2018a). Contrary to this, men with disabilities are not forbidden from enjoying sex and fathering children, because their bodies do not have the reproductive responsibility of carrying, delivering and mothering a child. Men with disabilities' fertility are celebrated because the birth of a disabled child is commonly implicated to the mother (Bunning et al. 2017: 2). Additionally men with disabilities are often treated better than women with disabilities. According to Lintvelt,

> The son with a disability will still have some use – maybe as a goat herder or beggar, but the disabled girl is of no use. In the minds of many parents, being disabled means a girl cannot have any children and cannot work. A female child with a disability will mean nothing to the family and is seen as nothing more than a burden – even something to get rid of as soon as possible.
>
> (2015: 288)

This indicates that the frailty or disability of the body is socially gendered. Disability does not limit the masculinity of men with disabilities in African communities. A man is honoured for his masculinity and the frailty of his body is overlooked. In many African (and global) communities, it is the penis that defines masculinity (Ngubane-Mokiwa and Chisale 2019). The functioning of the penis to plant a seed in a woman's womb and have children is the most significant masculine highlight for some African men.

The fragility of the body is feminine; thus, women and girls with disabilities are assumed to be the most vulnerable members of the community. The Ndebele assume that disability is inherited from the mother; thus, women with disabilities are monitored; if they fall pregnant the family often forces them to abort (Chisale 2018a: 5). Treating women with disabilities as asexual has been challenged by feminist scholars for exposing women and girls with disabilities to rape due to the myth that having sex with a virgin cures HIV. The assumption is that since they are supposed to be asexual, it means that they are virgins (Nyangweso 2018: 8).

The inequality between women and men with disabilities is associated with the assumed inability of the body to perform gendered domestic roles rather than sexuality. Similarly, the inequality between abled women and women with disabilities is linked to the performativity of bodies rather than sexuality. Besides sex and reproductive roles, the Ndebele assume that women with disability cannot perform gendered domestic chores, particularly cooking, washing and cleaning for the husband. Above all, it is assumed that they cannot perform daughter-in-law chores; thus, they cannot be wife material. As a result, they are stigmatized when it comes to *lobola* (bride price). Those who want to get married are often undervalued because it is assumed that they will not be of much use to their in-laws physically. This is a real challenge, as marriage is highly regarded in the community.

The Ndebele community is highly patriarchal and religious, and this puts women with disabilities in a vulnerable position. This is so because their disability is associated with the defilement of African morality since disability is assumed to be a curse from ancestors. The burial rites of people with disabilities differ from those who do not live with disabilities among the Ndebele. Certain rituals are performed when a person with a disability dies and is buried. Ndlovu argues that disability inequality follows a person living with a disability to their death, because they are denied a decent burial (Ndlovu 2016: 34). A person with a disability is not regarded as an ancestor; ancestral roles are given only to able-bodied people who lived a moral and ethical life in African communities (Kruger, Lifshitz and Baloyi 2007). Because they are generally denied and discouraged from having biological children or to getting married, any women with disabilities, thus, do not qualify to be ancestors. Even when some women with disabilities decide to have their own biological children, they are still stigmatized when it comes to ancestral roles. This is because they are believed to be a curse from ancestors. The question then is: How then can a curse be an ancestor? Literature on disability in African contexts reveals that perceptions of disability highlight that disability is a curse of affliction caused by ancestors (Ndlovu 2016: 32), but it mutes the role of people with disabilities in ancestral roles and if they are allowed to be ancestors after they pass on.

Emancipatory views on gender and disability in African traditional religion among the Ndebele

Paradoxically, the Ndebele also believe that people with disabilities are closer to God and ancestors than any other human being. They are believed to possess divine powers on earth. Some families use a family member with a disability to plant in the farm, because it is believed that what is planted by that person will produce rich and multiplied yield. Participants in the project on gender-based violence among women and girls with disabilities confirmed this when one of them said:

> The family valued me towards the planting season, because they believed that I had special connection to nature, so what I planted produced multiplied and rich yields. When it came to the farming season, I was meant to plant seeds of the most important farm produce, my disability was valued during the farming season … and sometimes I enjoyed that attention and special treatment, but sometimes it frustrated me because I felt overworked.
>
> (In depth interviews with a participant from a project on GBV among women and girls with disabilities 20 February 2017)

This suggests that disability is not only stigmatized and associated with shame among the Ndebele; there are some positive, life-affirming beliefs that protect people with disabilities. This is confirmed by the Ndebele saying: *'isilima sikamlimu'*, meaning a disabled child of God. This saying positions a person with a disability closer to God than any other creation. No one wants to consciously invite the wrath of God by harming or oppressing God's special children. Such sayings elevate the human dignity of people with disabilities and enhance their inclusion. The African cultural-religio worldview and philosophy does have many positives and is not all about being destructive, as is at times insinuated by outsiders.

The widely known communitarian principle promoted by *Ubuntu* in Africa is a deep root that provides all nutrients needed by a community. It highlights the norms of African people, particularly how Africans ought to live and exist among themselves. According to Nussbaum, 'the concept of *ubuntu* presents the capacity in African culture to express compassion, reciprocity, dignity, harmony, and humanity in the interests of building a community where justice and mutual caring is maintained' (2003: 21). *Ubuntu* invokes equality, where there is interdependence and interrelationships. The Ndebele use *ubuntu* to instil the spirit of interdependence and interrelationships in childhood stages through folktales, proverbs, sayings, symbols, song and dance to cultivate and promote the respect of the different other's dignity and worth. Ndlovu (2016) presents some saying, idioms and proverbs among the Swati of Swaziland that discourage the discrimination against people with disabilities and promoting the African principles of *Ubuntu*. For example, sayings like:

1. *Wahleka sichwala nawe uyawuchwala ngemuso*, or, should you laugh at a disabled person, you will also be disabled in future.

2. *Wahleka inkawu utayitala*, or, should you laugh at a person with albinism, you will also have a child with albinism.
3. *Linceba lendvodza alihlekwa*, or, one should never make fun of another person's wound (Ndlovu 2016: 35–6).

Like the Swazi, the Ndebele discourage the discrimination of different others, particularly people with disabilities through proverbs:

1. *Akusilima sindlebende kwabo*, loosely and literally translated as, a person with a disability is valued by his or her family.
2. *Inxeba lendoda kalihlekwa*, loosely and literally translated as, never laugh another person's wound or do not laugh or make fun of another person's misfortune.

And sayings such as:

3. *Isilima asihlekwa* or *hleka isilima sufile*, loosely and literally translated as, do not laugh at a person with a disability because you never know your future or laugh at person with a disability after you die.
4. *Isilima esihle ngesilomnganu*, loosely and literally translated as, living with a disability is better than dying. This is often said when a family member is involved in an accident that leaves him or her disabled, the family will then be comforted through this saying.
5. *Isilima ngesenkosi*, loosely and literally translated as, a person with a disability belongs to God.

It is important to highlight the clash of terms between Ndebele and Zulu. In Ndebele *isilima* is a person living with a disability or differently abled and in Zulu *isilima* is a stupid or foolish person. The above proverbs and sayings are Ndebele proverbs used by the Ndebele from Zimbabwe to challenge discrimination by promoting equality and human flourishing. According to Ndlovu (2013: 1001), '[t]he Ndebele are aware that disability can affect anyone, it knows no boundaries'. It is a taboo among the Ndebele to laugh or ill-treat a person with a disability. A human is defined through his or her humanity rather than disability. Sayings, idioms, symbols and proverbs are used to inform acts of kindness, generosity, inclusiveness and hospitality promoted by *ubuntu*. The above sayings respect the dignity of humanity by promoting morality and fairness within Ndebele communities.

Ubuntu, which is a crux of African relations and existence, is a solution to inequalities that exist in African communities. However, *ubuntu* has of late been found to have weaknesses when it comes to issues of inclusion and equality. The philosophy of *ubuntu* has been found to be elevating patriarchy over equality (Mangena 2009; Du Toit 2011; Manyonganise 2015). Chisale (2018b) argues that *ubuntu* that promotes inequality is corrupted due to the fluidity of this philosophy, but the original and traditional philosophy of *ubuntu* is inclusive and promotes equality between men and women. This resonates with Chitando (2015) who argues that *ubuntu* is a solution to patriarchy. Patriarchy is a source of different inequalities in African communities, particularly the Ndebele where men's status gives them priority over women in all spheres of life. The Ndebele proverbs, idioms and sayings were developed to promote *ubuntu* and respect of human dignity. These are used to inform attitudes of society towards inclusion and exclusion of community members. Some of the Ndebele people in Zimbabwe are Christians and they blend their culture with Christianity. Therefore, it is important to also reflect on how Christianity either promotes or challenges inequality for people with disabilities, with special focus on women with disabilities.

Christian religion and inequality for people with disabilities among the Ndebele

There is an explicit overlap between African culture and religions found in Africa, particularly Abrahamic faiths, namely, Christianity, Islam and Judaism on the one hand, and ATRs on the other. Thus, all religion in Africa has some African cultural traits in it. This has enabled religious ideas to be embraced seamlessly. The Hebrew Bible is used by Christians as their holy book and it perceives disability as a punishment from God. The Bible is used to discriminate against and stigmatize those who do not conform to purity theology or culture. In the Bible disability is linked to the issue of divine control (Exod 4:11; Lev. 21:16-23). The Hebrew Bible somehow also contributes to the stigmatization of people with disabilities because disability is linked to purity theology or culture. Some hermeneutics of the Hebrew Bible perceive disability as a purity issue where God used it to exclude the 'deformed' and imperfect bodies. It seems as if 'God found most pleasure in a perfect and normal body' (Bengtsson 2014: 284).

Fundamentalist Christianity, which includes conservatives and traditionalist, often positions people with disabilities as outcasts and weak members of their communities using loose and naive interpretations of the Leviticus code that says '[n]one of your descendants who has a defect may come near to offer the food of his God ... no man who is blind or lame, disfigured or deformed; no man with a crippled foot or hand, or who is a hunchback or dwarfed, or who has any eye, defect, or who has festering or running sores or damaged testicles' (Lev 21:16-21). The Hebrew Bible also highlights that sacrificing animals with impairments was not accepted by God (Lev. 22:20-21; Mal 1:8). According to Bengtsson sacrificing such animals was disrespect to God, because even 'the rules regulating the sacrifice similarly express God's quest for normality and perfection' (2014: 284). Ableism and the perfection of the body seemed to be important to God in the Old Testament narratives and cuts across human bodies and animal bodies. This view of disability emerges from the purity and morality theology which informs the religious model of disability. Henderson and Bryan argue that the religious model of disability is based upon the assumption that some disabilities are the result of punishment from an all-powerful entity. Furthermore, the belief is that the punishment is for an act or acts of transgression against prevailing moral and/or religious edicts (2011: 7). The view of disability by the religious model is oppressive to people with disabilities as it perceives them as symbols of shame, pity and 'holy' stigma. This emerges from the hermeneutics of purity, where an 'imperfect' and non-conforming body is impure and dirty.

Disability and gender inequality in Christian religion

The Hebrew Bible's Leviticus code seems to include all people with disabilities in the exclusion from the sacred space; yet, hermeneutics of purity reveal that women with disabilities are more excluded from the Christian sacred space, due to their disability, menstrual blood and reproductive feminine body. Feminist theologians of disabilities argue that politics of the body, particularly sexuality, affect women with disabilities more than their abled counterparts. According to Freeman (2002), investigations into gender analysis, sexuality, power relations in ecclesial spheres, explorations on theology from experience, women's lived experiences and embodied reality are all relevant for women with disabilities. The theological politics of the body are explored by Bennet who argues that the woman-disability interplay emerges because feminists' politics highlight ways where women struggle with the limitations and frustrations of the feminine body that are caused by naive Christian hermeneutics and these have contributed to poor theologies that often oppress the different bodies (2012: 427). In African contexts, Christians blend the Christian religion with their African culture, where the female body is intrinsically stigmatised and discriminated against due to purity and morality theology. Disability intensifies this discrimination because naive Christian hermeneutics perceive disability as a distortion of God's purpose for human creation, a destruction of the image of God (Reynolds 2008: 177).

Since some churches unconsciously enculturate their cultural customs into their Christian faith, the Ndebele culture emphasizes the otherness of people with disabilities as a result, inevitably discriminating and stigmatizing them in Christian spaces. Due to the purity theology, women with disabilities are often excluded from serving in the liturgy, first, because of their disability and second because of their gender and sexuality. In some instances, they are excluded from serving in the liturgy due to their disability because serving the liturgy requires that the servers or liturgist stand or kneel for long hours; the disabled body is inevitably excluded. In addition, they are excluded from liturgy due to their sexuality and gender because of menstrual blood. African Independent Churches (AICs) have strict laws on purity of the body; thus, women with disabilities are excluded, not only because of sexual purity theology, but also because of the purity theology that focuses on the perfect body. In some instances, AIC worship spaces are in mountainous areas that require physical strength and ability to climb the mountain; this excludes people with disabilities because they need assistance to reach the top of the mountain.

The Church excludes people with disabilities through the use of some damning teachings from the Bible, which perpetuate the prejudice, inequality, discrimination and stigmatization of people with disabilities. According to Eiesland (1994: 73–4), a theological analysis of disability in Christianity firstly conflates disability to sin; secondly conflates disability to virtuous suffering and thirdly conflates disability to charity. These themes, according to Eiesland (1994: 70), are 'disabling theology'. Theologically, Christianity through the Bible has contributed to the exclusion of people with disabilities through teachings of moral impurity which perceives disability an unusual relationship with God and that the person with disabilities is either divinely blessed or damned (Eiesland 1994: 70).

Emancipatory views on gender and disability in Christian religion

Contrary to discriminating oppressive texts and hermeneutics used by some fundamentalist Christians, there are emancipatory texts and hermeneutics on disability in the Hebrew Bible and these promote solidarity. Morality theology emerges as key in responding to people with disabilities. Morality theology on disabilities emphasizes how communities should respond to people with disabilities as weak and vulnerable members of the communities. This emerges from Job as he pleads his case with God when he said: he defends his righteousness and advocate of justice by arguing that he always stood for the blind and lame (Job 29:14-15). The Levitical code, although giving negative and exclusionary standpoint on disability, also highlights that it is the role of everyone to protect and be in solidarity with those with disabilities. Thus, Lev 19:14, 'do not curse the deaf or put a stumbling block in front of the blind but fear your God' and, Deut 27:18, 'cursed is the man who leads the blind astray on the road'. God protects the weak and takes the side of the weak and marginalized. In the New Testament Jesus became a practical theologian in his ministry, where his pastoral praxis is directly engaged in caring, healing and liberating people with disabilities.

The Catholic social teaching principle, 'preferential option for the poor', explains this relationship between God and the marginalized. Preferential option of the poor is a Roman Catholic social teaching that was embraced and popularized by Latin American Catholic theologians, particularly pioneers of liberation theology such as the Peruvian theologian Gustavo Gutierrez who argued that God in Christ is on the side of the poor, marginalized and oppressed (Gutierrez 1973). The preferential option of the poor is linked to Matthew 25:40 where Jesus confirms that 'whatever you did for the least of these, you did for me'. Who could be the least of these, other than the poor, weak, oppressed and marginalized such as children, populations who do not conform to the normative and people with disabilities. Zephania 3:19 and Micah 4:6-7 explicitly reveal God's preferential option of the poor, weak, oppressed and marginalized, by promising to liberate them from their marginalization. Thus, 'at that time, I will deal with all who oppressed you. I will rescue the lame; I will gather the exiles. I will give them praise and honor in every land where they have suffered shame' (Zep 3:19; Mic 4:6-7). There are several scriptures that are liberative to the people who live with visible disabilities.

Like African traditional religion and culture, Christianity emphasizes the equality of humanity affirmed by Paul as he says, 'In Christ: There is neither Jew nor Gentile, neither slave nor free, nor is there male and female, *disabled or abled* (added), for you are all one in Christ Jesus' (Gal 3:28). The binary categorization does not exist in the Gospels for Christ unconditionally loves everyone. The emancipatory hermeneutics in the African traditional religion and culture of the Ndebele and Christianity can be used to reimagine equality from faith and cultural approach, as we highlight below.

Reimagining pastoral praxis of equality from African women theologies of disabilities

African traditional religion, culture and Christianity function together among the Ndebele. All have double interpretations about disability and equality, the liberative and oppressive. Thus, this chapter chooses the liberative to inform pastoral praxis from African women theologies of disabilities. African women theologies of disabilities promote mutuality among humanity while highlighting that women and men with disabilities do not experience disability inequality, exclusion and inclusion in a uniform way. In African contexts the Hebrew Bible and ATR are combined in interpreting disability. The analysis that the Bible and African culture are used together to perpetuate gender inequality in society and church are highlighted by African women theologians in narrating their lived experiences of oppression (Phiri and Nadar 2010: 224). African women theologians confirm that there is no single story in African women's lived experiences. African women have different stories that on the one hand cause despair and on the other provide hope. The same Bible and culture are also used together to promote gender equality and provide fresh hope for the marginalized, particularly women with disabilities.

Since the Bible and culture are used together, it is important that life affirming biblical and cultural texts that promote equality, justice, fairness, inclusion, responsiveness, love should be identified and taught to African children, so that there shall be a generation that is ethical and inclusive. Ndlovu resonates with African women theologians when saying that African worldviews that are life affirming and promote positive attitudes about people with disabilities should be merged to Christian and philosophical ethical principles that advocate for social equity (2016: 37). Africa is rich in proverbs, sayings and idioms that promote humanness, inclusion, reciprocity, respect, care and compassion. These proverbs, sayings and idioms should be used to inform pastoral praxis, because they evoke solidarity. African women theologies of disabilities affirm solidarity, because they believe that all bodies are vulnerable and fragile; as a result, they can experience a calamity leading to disability anytime. This is highlighted by Eiesland (1994) who argues that disability and ability are only temporary and that a human body is a 'body in trouble'. This is parallel to a Ndebele saying, *isilima asihlekwa*, meaning 'do not laugh at a person with a disability because you never know your future'.

Equality ethics, African women theologies of disabilities and pastoral praxis

In the hierarchy of community, African women with disabilities' fight for equality are doubled if not tripled. On the one hand, they compete for equality with men with disabilities; on the other, they compete for equality with able-bodied women, and in countries where the racial struggle is 'violent' like in South Africa, Black women with disabilities compete for equality with white women with disabilities. The struggle continues if the women with disabilities are refugees; on the one hand, they fight for equality with other refugee women and, on the other, they fight for equality with the women with disabilities who have citizenship in the receiving country. In all these struggles, religion, culture and colonialism are implicated. African women theologies of disabilities offer a pastoral praxis model that is sensitive to these inequalities, by promoting mutual relationships through the African ethic of equality conceptualized as *ubuntu* and Christian ethic of equality affirmed by Paul in Gal. 3:28. The African and Christian equality ethics are used together by the Ndebele because they are closely related. They are used by the Ndebele in promoting equality, solidarity, responsiveness, love, fairness and all positive principles that promote equality. Both African and Christian ethics of equality define humanness through the common dignity, rather than one's limitation.

The juxtaposition of African culture and Christianity is visible where Christian theologians use an African philosophy of *ubuntu* alongside Christianity (Chirongoma, Manda and Myeni 2008; Louw 2010; Chitando 2015). A combination of *ubuntu* and Christianity is able to instil good values in communities and stimulate justice, equality, interdependence and interconnectedness of humanity, communities and churches. *Ubuntu* is an alternative expression of the sayings that promote inclusion and equality of everyone including people with disabilities. Emerging research in theology uses *ubuntu* to advocate for the inclusion of people with disabilities (Amanze 2014; Ndlovu 2016), as they share the same dignity as all other human beings. The equality principles reject binarism where there is 'us' and 'them', 'women' and 'men', 'abled' and 'disabled', 'black' and 'white', which Paul condemns in Gal 3:28.

Binarism creates a hierarchy where there is dominance of the less privileged. Although the Ndebele are hierarchical and patriarchal, the equality ethics challenge them to be inclusive, fair and welcoming. Communities are taught on the significance of fairness and justice, because communities are a group of equal people. African women theologies of disabilities highlight that we are all disabled in diverse ways; thus, pastoral praxis should not categorize humanity in binaries. For this reason, some programmes that suggest that people with disabilities are different from other humans such as 'special education' contribute to these binaries, enforcing or deepening inequality and exclusion. Thus, African proverbs, idioms and sayings that present the equality of humanity should be revived and taught at schools, communities and churches. This will abolish the exclusion or making fun of other people's misfortune.

The Ndebele teach children that it is a taboo to laugh or make fun of a person with a disability, if one does so they are likely to face the wrath of God or ancestors through a misfortune. There is a common saying among the Ndebele, *okwenza omunye lawe kuyakwenza,* meaning what happens to one human will happen to another. This saying reminds people that no one is immune to suffering or misfortune. Although this is helpful, it sometimes instils fear of disability to children and other community members, who, rather than embracing a person with a disability, tend to fear the disability. Fear of one another disrupts human flourishing in society and the purpose of human existence. Rather than fearing another human being, pastoral praxis should emphasize God's image that is inscribed in all human beings. Thus, the diversity of human bodies should not be feared or perceived as difference, but bodily diversity should be perceived as God's mystery of creation. No one has an answer on how and why God created humanity in diverse ways. Human diversity remains a mystery and reflects the diversity of the Kingdom of God, where everyone is equal at all levels.

This then challenges pastoral praxis to be inclusive and accommodating to a body with a disability by reimagining the Kingdom of God as diverse and inclusive. Thus, liturgies and worship services that are inclusive should be introduced, acknowledging that all humans are made equal and from the image of God. The purity and morality theology should be reinterpreted to accommodate the feminine and disabled body. Thus, liberation theologies of disability and feminism should, in their focus of politics of the body, highlight the visibility of God in the feminine and disabled body.

Conclusion

This chapter highlights the wealth of religio-cultural perceptions that can be used by pastoral praxis to break down the hierarchies of inequality that rob people of their dignity in African religio-cultural spaces. Both culture and religion have emancipatory views about disability that enhance the dignity and worth of humanity and their diversity. Positive African proverbs, idioms and sayings remind communities of solidarity. Unfortunately, the new generation hardly knows any of these. This has broken and corrupted African communities which used to be communal and welcoming to different people. The chapter suggests that if the positive proverbs, sayings and idioms that emphasize equality are revived and merged with Christian and cultural teachings that emphasize equality, no one will feel excluded or discriminated. African women theologies of disabilities are able to revive these through reimagining the image of God through the eyes of people with disabilities, particularly women and girls.

Born free? Born free for what? Exploring the lived experiences of Christian young adults in South Africa regarding inequality and social justice

Nadine Bowers Du Toit, Dione Forster, Shantelle Weber and
Elisabet Le Roux

Introduction

South Africa is one of the world's most unequal nations. The legacy of Apartheid remains dire, as the sharp divide between the rich whites and poor Blacks remains. This chapter examines inequality in South Africa. By focusing on the experiences of religious youth in Stellebosch, a town in the Western Cape, the chapter lays bare the impact of religion on inequality. It highlights the extent to which young adults feel alienated by current political processes and draws attention to the need for churches to be actively involved in developing theologies that will be liberating for young people. The chapter expresses the hope that churches might play an important role in addressing inequality in South Africa. However, they will need to be more deliberate and creative if they are to achieve this goal.

Background

South Africa is currently ranked as the most unequal nation in the world by the World Bank, with high rates of racially skewed poverty and inequality still largely a legacy of the past (Baker 2019: 1–11). For many young South Africans born either just before or after the demise of apartheid, termed 'Born Frees', the ongoing realities of poverty and inequality bring to light the question of whether they are truly 'free' in a post-apartheid era (Mattes 2012: 133; Malila 2013: 4–7; cf. Nwadeyi 2019). Their lived experiences of inequality, views on issues such as reconciliation and restitution, as well as their own understanding of their role in societal change are, therefore, important to understand against this backdrop. Furthermore, how do Christian 'Born Frees' understand and interpret these issues in light of scripture and their lived experiences within community and church?

The research findings presented in this chapter, therefore, seek to engage the lived theologies of inequality among young South African Christians (between the ages of eighteen and thirty-five). The focus of this study is the community of Stellenbosch, a town in the Western Cape, as this community is considered as one of the most unequal places in South Africa and remains largely geographically segregated along its former racial lines. It is also a youthful community, as it is estimated that 64 per cent of the population in this Wineland district is under the age of thirty-five (Cubizolles 2011: 33–55; Waal 2014: 1–6).

The context(s) of the study

South Africa, reconciliation and the church

South Africa remains a deeply religious nation. The most recent survey of the South African population conducted by StatsSA was done in 2013. This survey shows that 84.2 per cent of South Africa's citizens self-identified as Christians (*General Household Survey 2013*, 2014; Schoeman 2017: 3). This is an increase of 4.4 per cent from 79.8 per cent in 2001 (Hendriks and Erasmus 2005; Schoeman 2017: 3). The largest percentage of Christians belong to a diverse conglomeration of churches and Christian groupings which are collectively categorized as 'African independent' (40.82 per cent) and 'Other Christian' (11.96 per cent). The traditionally 'mainline' Christian Churches remain prominent, with the Methodist Church of Southern African as the largest mainline Christian denomination (9.24 per cent), followed by the collective grouping of Reformed Christian churches (Uniting Reformed Church, Dutch Reformed Church, Presbyterian Church, etc.) at 9.04 per cent. This last grouping is particularly prominent in Stellenbosch, with deep historical roots throughout the community. A 2010 Pew report found that 74 per cent of South Africans 'indicated that religion plays an important role in their lives' (Lugo and Cooperman 2010: 3; Schoeman 2017: 3–4). The Global Values Survey helps us to understand an aspect of this 'important role' – this survey shows that religious organizations remain among the most trusted institutions in society, enjoying higher levels of public trust and confidence than either the state or the private sector (Winter and Burchert 2015: 1). The report notes that there was increasing dissatisfaction with the state of democracy ' … while trust in political institutions recedes. In contrast, civil society organisations enjoy growing trust' (Winter and Burchert 2015: 1–2). In this report, the church is classified within the 'civil society' grouping. Hennie Kotzé, the lead researcher on the Global Values Survey for South Africa, clarifies the situation when he comments, 'Religion in general, and churches in particular, plays an important political socialization role [for South Africans]' (Kotzé 2016: 439–40; Kotzé and Garcia-Rivero 2017: 33).

Reconciliation and forgiveness become central concepts in such a heavily polarized society as South Africa's. However, within the South African social, political, economic and religious context, reconciliation and forgiveness are contested issues. The 2015 Institute for Justice and Reconciliation (IJR) report found the following:

> While most South Africans agree that the creation of a united, reconciled nation remains a worthy objective to pursue, the country remains afflicted by its historical divisions. The majority feels that race relations have either stayed the same or deteriorated since the country's political transition in 1994 and the bulk of respondents have noted income inequality as a major source of social division. Most believe that it is impossible to achieve a reconciled society for as long as those who were disadvantaged under apartheid remain poor within the 'new South Africa'.
>
> (Hofmeyr and Govender 2015: 1)

Recent events in South Africa, such as the #Feesmustfall protests (which impacted the community of Stellenbosch as well) against economic inequalities and economic injustice in higher education, the spate of racial slurs and denials of Black pain on social media and the re-racialization of society through identity politics (Mbembe 2015), seem to support the IJR's findings.

The lived experiences of inequality among South Africans have a significant influence on their views of 'the other' and their willingness, or unwillingness, to engage in processes that may contribute towards forgiveness. It has been widely argued that forgiveness is a necessary condition for moving forward to a better future for all South Africans (Mandela 1995: 617; 2012: 44; Thesnaar 2008: 53–73; 2013: 1–13; Tutu 2012: 47–8, 74, 218). Yet, some of the entrenched theological, social, racial, economic and political challenges that South Africa faces seem to suggest that forgiveness and reconciliation are almost impossible.

A survey of research in this field shows that Black and white South African Christians hold very different views on the concepts and processes of forgiveness (Byrne 2007; Chapman and Spong 2003: 169; Daye 2012: 8–18; Elkington 2011: 5–35, 135–55; cf., Forster 2019a; 2018: 1–13; 2019b: 70–88; Gobodo-Madikizela and Van der Merwe 2009: vii–xi; Krog 2010; Thesnaar 2008: 53–73; 2013: 1–13; Tutu 2012: 10–36, 47–60, 92–124; Villa-Vicencio and du Toit 2006: 75–87; Vosloo 2012; 2015: 360–78). Vosloo notes with regard to the unfinished business of forgiveness in South Africa that 'forgiveness and related concepts regarding engagement with the past continue to be influential, albeit also highly contested, in public discourse' (Vosloo 2015: 363). This is particularly true for the public life and witness of Christian communities and Christian individuals in South Africa.

One significant problem that has been identified is that these un-reconciled persons seldom have contact with each other because of the legacy of the apartheid system which entrenched inequality by separating persons racially, according to economic class, and geographically (Hofmeyr and Govender 2015: 1). The result is that, as the inter-group contact theory suggests, each group's own social views and religious beliefs (in-group identity) become entrenched, and the views and beliefs of the 'other' (out-group identity) are rejected or ignored because they are not understood or engaged across the aforementioned separating boundaries (Brewer and Kramer 1985: 219–23; Bornman 1999: 411–14; 2011; Duncan 2003: 2, 5).

In at least one sense this makes processes of reconciliation very difficult. Not only is it difficult for persons to forgive one another since they have no proximate or authentic social engagement, forgiveness (as aforementioned) is also theologically contested because of deeply held and entrenched faith convictions about the nature and processes of forgiveness. Moreover, the lack of restitution and enacting of justice on behalf of the beneficiaries of apartheid (white South Africans), seeking the well-being and dignity of those persons harmed under apartheid and beyond (Black South Africans), has created deep wounds, a great deal of distrust and understandable anger (Bowers du Toit and Nkomo 2014: 1–8; Forster 2018: 1–13). In other words, there are both a hermeneutic and a social barrier to forgiveness that is complicated by the lived reality of inequality in South Africa. In fact, in recent years the discourse of reconciliation in South Africa has shifted to include that of restitution in order for the injustices wrought by the apartheid system to be addressed by socioeconomic means, such as land, but also through social restitution. South Africa, therefore, faces significant challenges with regard to dealing with the 'sins' of its past and the complexity of our present life (Hofmeyr and Govender 2015: 1–3).

Born free? Youth and inequality

This study focuses on young adults (eighteen to thirty-five years) within Christian congregational contexts. Young people turning twenty-six years old in 2020, and the majority of South Africa's young population who were born after them, have been labelled as the 'born free' generation.[1] The term 'born free' is deeply contested (John et al. 2015). It most often refers to young South Africans born after the so-called end of political apartheid in 1994. Unfortunately, many of these youth face the same daily reality of poverty, racism, violence and spatial injustice that their parents and grandparents faced (Mattes 2012: 133–55; Kotze and Prevost 2015: 142–68). Therefore, while this generation has experienced the 'right to have rights', the enactment of those rights has not been realized in any significant and transformative manner (Benhabib 2004; 2013). Jansen (2015) notes that one of the most devastating aspects of poverty is that if you were born poor and struggle to secure food, there is a good chance that you will become a young child, adolescent and young adult still poor and uncertain of where you will find your next meal. Young people are the biggest cohort of new job seekers and are, therefore, the most vulnerable group with regard to unemployment, which is one the pressing concerns in relation to inequality impacting South Africa (Cloete 2015).

Some social commentators, such as Manamela (2015: 8), have described today's youth as depoliticized and apathetic. Nevertheless, youth culture across the globe has placed emphasis on institutional questioning, public accountability, and the need for direction and honest communication between people. According to Mawuko-Yevgah and Ugor (2015: 7) a social crisis is brewing due to a majority of youth and their families having increasing difficulty accessing good education, land and housing, food, security, medical care, drinking water and other socioeconomic services due to the private interests and gain of a tiny class of global elite. Weber (2014) makes the point that there is, therefore, a need for intentional engagement with the realities these youth face, and that this requires creating safe spaces where they could ask questions concerning their faith, morality and identity. In their reflections on African Youth and global resistance to neoliberalism through exploring the dialectics between cosmopolitan and identity politics, Abembia Ayelazuno (in Jurgens 2018: 38–40) confirms that the agency of South African youth is clearly visible in the struggles waged for example by the Shack Dwellers Movement, *Abahlali base Mjondolo* and many other protests by the poor. In fact, the #Feesmustfall protests in South Africa (2015–17) at tertiary institutions with regard to issues of equal access to tertiary education, institutional racism and a decolonized curriculum indicate that youth agency exists within South Africa (cf. Grassow and Le Bruyns 2017: 1–9; Costandius et al. 2018: 65–85). Unfortunately, these protests also remind us that race still divides its citizens and that class consciousness has still not dominated race consciousness, making it problematic to forge solidarity between Black and white youth.

Weber (2020: 10) makes the important point that some of this generation's parents and grandparents are so traumatized by the past that any mention of engaging with such matters within church spaces is frowned upon. Nevertheless, engagement with youth around issues related to their country's histories, their familial or tribal positions within those histories and also social justice issues that impact their faith daily is imperative in South Africa today (Weber 2017: 8). Christian youth today need to be able to live out and experience their identity in Christ alongside morally engaging in society and growing in their faith (Weber 2017: 8). Sadly, according to Lee, the Christian young adults and activism during #Feesmustfall were a cause for young people to experience 'disappointment and alienation in their church settings, which they [found] to be dismissive at best and oppressive at worst toward their activism' (2018: 4). Lee's findings highlight that the church could become a space from which young activists drew courage, spiritual support and were bolstered by theological teaching (such as Liberation Theology), which gave voice to their plight (Lee 2018: 81–7). This research, therefore, seeks to explore how South African young people understand and discern this tension between their Christian faith and the unjust realities they live through every day.

In the town of Stellenbosch, inequalities are most visible in the marked differences of where young people live, the schools they go to, their parental income groupings, language and race (Swilling et al. 2012). This is further reflected in things like sport, afterschool activities and leisure time activities. Some poor youth do not have as many opportunities, resulting in boredom, which in turn leads to various criminal and irresponsible sexual activities, which eventually impact this local community. Where these youth live would also give one an idea of the municipal services (water, sanitation, electricity, safety and security) they have access to; these have also been described as unequally distributed in Stellenbosch and aligned to previous racial segregation (Swilling et al. 2012). Various university students (Krige 1998; Robyn 1998; Hendrich 2006; Simmons 2008; Robertson 2015; Meiring 2017) have focused research on different aspects of inequality among youth in Stellenbosch.

The empirical study discussed in this chapter, therefore, seeks to contribute towards texturing, troubling and thickening of the understandings of what it will take for this generation to become truly free. The town of Stellenbosch is used as a case study to do so.

Research methodology

Our key research question was the following: 'In what ways do the lived realities of the continued and intensified realities of inequality in post-apartheid South Africa, impact on the lived theologizing and political agency of the "born free" generation of South Africans (18–35 years) concerning issues of social justice, inequality and reconciliation?'

The project addressed the following aims:

1. to discuss the current socioeconomic milieu of South Africa and Stellenbosch[2] in particular;
2. to explore and contrast perceptions in relation to race, class and inequality in the eighteen to thirty-five age group of church-attending young adults;
3. to explore theological and ethical constructs that may shape these perceptions and
4. to investigate the notion of political agency and how it related to issues of social justice, inequality and reconciliation.

In investigating the lived theologies of inequality, the research followed a qualitative, inductive methodology. A qualitative approach is considered more suited to this study as it allows the researchers to investigate issues that require explanation or understanding of phenomena in specific contexts (Snape and Spencer 2003: 54). An inductive and interpretivist approach is needed when it is not fully understood why certain actions and events occur, or how these are being dealt with and understood (Bryman 2008: 3665; Babbie and Mouton 2010).

A multi-case case study which allows contemporary phenomenon to be investigated in depth and within a real-life context, while considering multiple factors and sources of evidence approach, was employed (Yin 2009: 187). The collection and integration of multiple perspectives and accounts enable the development of a detailed, in-depth understanding of the research issue, which in a multi-case case study approach strengthens the generalizability of the findings. A multi-case case study approach, therefore, provides a more holistic, comprehensive and contextualized understanding of the issues being studied (Lewis 2003: 528).

Our three case studies were of congregations of the same confessional background within Stellenbosch, a town known for its extreme socioeconomic disparities characterized by a racial element. These three congregations each represent one of the three main racial groups in Stellenbosch[3]: a church from the so-called coloured community[4]; a church from the black (Xhosa) community and a church from the white community. It is important to note that due to the legacy of apartheid spatial planning, the communities in which these churches are situated remain racially homogeneous and separated, which is why to a large extent the churches can still be categorized according to race. We focused our study on youth between the ages of eighteen and thirty-five years, conducting twelve in-depth interviews within each congregation. A gender balance was attempted and was largely successful. A list of thirty potential participants was compiled by a leader from each church, with the research team doing final selection of the twelve participants from each congregation. The issue of whether to use racial designations within the study was a contested one; however, as race and inequality remain directly aligned, we chose to maintain these designations. Ethical clearance was obtained via Stellenbosch University.

The core research team was responsible for liaising with the churches and arranging access for the researchers. One of the collaborators and two research assistants interviewed the respondents and interviews were conducted in the participants' language of choice (English, isiXhosa or Afrikaans). Interviews were then recorded and transcribed (and also translated, in the case of isiXhosa interviews). Transcribed interviews were then analysed thematically, using Atlas.ti.[5] A provisional coding sheet was designed by the research team, which was updated and adapted based on the content of the data. Each case study was firstly analysed individually and then, based on the individual case study findings, a synthesis report was produced, reflecting on the lived theologies of inequality of Stellenbosch youth. The team that both interviewed and analysed were diverse in terms of race and gender.

It should be noted that studies of this nature have limitations. As the study aimed to give voice to the lived experience and lived religion of Christian young adults in Stellenbosch as recounted by them, it does not necessarily document their actual engagement with these issues – only their perspectives. It also cannot be generalized to the whole of South Africa. However, this type of grounded, qualitative research does provide a 'thick' description of the kind of perspectives emerging from Christian young adults on these issues. The key findings discussed below are the main findings discussed in the synthesis report.

Key findings

Inequality is a lived reality for young adults and it remains aligned to race

All respondents recognize the reality of poverty and inequality in South Africa and, more especially, the inequality within the context of the town of Stellenbosch. This finding, indeed, echoes the perception of Stellenbosch as one of the most unequal places in South Africa. White respondents all agreed that South Africa has high levels of inequality and all agreed that Stellenbosch is a very unequal town – save one younger participant who does not live in the town. Furthermore, it is clear that race and inequality are aligned. Those white respondents who had crossed racial or economic borders and had been confronted with 'the other' noted they were less likely to be able to ignore the reality of poverty and inequality. For the Black and coloured respondents, inequality is a very real lived experience, which often provoked raw emotions. Several coloured respondents noted feelings such as feeling heartsore, angry, frustrated or even numb. Black respondents also had undercurrents of anger in the tone of their responses. Black and coloured respondents both made much of the ways in which the legacy of apartheid and spatial inequalities and social divisions continued to be replicated in Stellenbosch:

> I think that there's an established boundary I would say like, rich is somewhere, and poor is somewhere, like even within the community of Stellenbosch if you go to certain areas you can clearly see okay this is a rich area or this is a poor area. And people don't actually associate, I mean there are those exceptional ones that associate with different classes like rich and poor, but most times it's the rich and the poor. (Coloured respondent)

Both these groups noted the way in which their communities faced challenges relating to safety, access to basic services, access to opportunities and education, infrastructure and transport. This, of course, illustrates the nature of generational inequality and once again highlights the question as to whether these young people are truly 'Born Free'. All three groups were asked regarding their understanding of the notion of 'white privilege' and all recognized that privilege remains aligned to race in a post-apartheid context. While some white respondents acknowledged the privileges accrued from the past system, a number of white respondents felt that policies such as affirmative action could be seen as minimizing these apartheid gains and even for some it was viewed as reverse oppression.

Churches in the town mirror the inequality young adults see in society

In what could be viewed as an indictment of the churches in the town, the research found that all respondents noted that the churches in Stellenbosch still reflected the inequalities and racial divisions in broader society and that there appeared to be little 'border crossing'. Whether or not this is true at the leadership/pastoral level is not verified by this study; however, young adults from this study's perceptions were that there is little ecumenical engagement across race and colour lines in the town. From the perspective of Black and coloured respondents, there was evidence also of distrust towards white churches in central Stellenbosch, who they felt were elitist and also possessed an unequal amount of resources (such as buildings and equipment):

> Um, the churches within this town specifically in town, central town, make a lot of money. Because if you think about the elites of the elites actually going to these churches.

It is clear that there is not only little trust, but little proximate engagement between groups.

Relative privilege was also evident between Black and coloured churches, and Black respondents noted that the coloured churches were more privileged relative to the Black churches. All three congregations were almost completely racially homogenous. This is of course in turn a reflection of the geographical divisions, which remain aligned to race in this town. These findings are particularly worrying if one considers that churches are key civil society role-players who have an important role to play in the transformation of society and yet it appears that rather than leading in the crossing of racial and socioeconomic boundaries churches appear to merely replicate the inequalities aligned to these factors.

Forgiveness, reconciliation and restitution remain contested issues

The fact that issues of forgiveness, reconciliation and restitution were clearly 'hot button' issues which elicited a large number of different perspectives and elicited conflicted and nuanced responses within the groups is unsurprising in light of the 'unfinished business of forgiveness' and the contestations already noted. While some white respondents felt that reconciliation would only be possible with forgiveness, others felt that as they had not participated in apartheid and, therefore, despite admitting that they had benefitted in some ways, maintained that these decisions were taken by another generation and they, therefore, did not require forgiveness as it had not been enacted by their generation.

> I don't feel like I have to apologise to someone or ask for forgiveness. For me it is that many of these things (are the result of) decisions taken by many people on my behalf and many years (before I was born). (White respondent)

Coloured respondents on the other hand felt that while it was important to forgive, it was harder to forget the pain and it was clear that this pain had been transmitted across generations.

> And with the young people, like we didn't really see what went on, but our parents felt pain. So now the parent carries the pain that they felt onto you, now you also 'sommer' feel angry, because you parents suffered under it or something.

It is interesting, therefore, that reflections on this issue have generational dimensions to it.

Respondents in this church appeared to be conflicted as to whether reconciliation and restitution were different or the same; however, all respondents appeared to indicate that actions to right the wrongs of the past were needed to address the injustices of Apartheid and the ongoing unjust legacy. Nevertheless, it appeared that respondents in this church were also conflicted concerning restitution and some felt it may amount to 'revenge seeking', with restitution perceived a kind of necessary evil, but not necessarily the answer to relational brokenness. Black respondents, however, were clear that there is no reconciliation and forgiveness without justice:

> ... yes, you know reconciliation is a process; you can't have reconciliation without justice and for that matter people in South Africa and everywhere you get, in Stellenbosch, people are talking about reconciliation but justice is the issue, let's get things fair on the table, let's try to correct the past then we talk about reconciliation, you know the whole issue of forgiveness, you can't forgive people; I mean or reconcile with people without really having the process of, reconciliation is kind of the end result, there will always be tension between races, especially between black and white people if there is no justice and we really need to work towards that justice in order to reconcile and even to consider forgiveness its really impossible to just reconcile if these issues are not corrected. (Black respondent)

A fascinating perspective from Black respondents is that they felt that the expectation for forgiveness is placed on them rather than it being something that white persons should take responsibility for and work towards. In comparison to coloured respondents, Black respondents spoke plainly about restitution. Both the general issue of wealth sharing and economic transformation and that of land redistribution (with consent and compensation and without compensation) were raised many times by participants. Restitution and righting the injustices of the past, which continue to be features of inequality today, also included for these respondents issues related to the economic sphere, education, transportation, safety, employment, job security, etc.

White respondents were also conflicted when it came to issues of restitution and what this entailed. Most agreed that land reform and affirmative action were understandable in light of the past (despite some respondents feeling that they should not take responsibility for the actions of previous generations) and recognized that it was nuanced, but several respondents noted that there should be conditions under which these took place:

> But I can understand when people feel that it isn't right, but I don't know, there are so many different opinions. It doesn't feel right, because it feels as though it just throws the injustice over to the other side. But, I mean white people had so many privileges, that I guess you need to correct it in some way. I would just say that it needs to be corrected by competent people, competent people employed in the right positions, not employing someone who doesn't deserve to be there. (White respondent)

Respondents were also fearful of land reform in terms of land grabs (which Stellenbosch was experiencing at that time), which some said did not make economic sense or if not managed properly or tainted by corruption could affect property prices.[6] Some also felt that it made little economic sense, but had important symbolic value:

> I think about it in two ways. The one is – first the hard one – I don't think it makes economic sense. As in it does not make sense to try and give land back to people who originally owned it, especially not if that land is being used for farming and those kinds of activities. But, on the other hand, I also know that there is a thing such as human dignity and it is important and it makes sense. So people have a very strong emotional reaction to land and sometimes it would be better for the country to not think about it economically, but to think about the people. So there is this trade-off between economics and humanity. (WC respondent)

These reflections by respondents highlight the pressing need to address the well-being and dignity of those harmed by Apartheid and for young Christians like these to dialogue regarding the notion of justice in order to challenge entrenched beliefs which are often aligned with race and class.

Lived theologizing is focused largely on the Golden Rule

In terms of what participants believed the Bible helped them to think about poverty and inequality, the overarching agreement across groups was that the love of neighbour and the fact that 'God is love' should motivate one to both act in compassion regarding poverty and inequality and cross-borders. From this ethic, once again, respondents across the board felt that this challenged them to treat others with respect, love, tolerance and understanding. The issue of human dignity was a strong theme in the coloured group:

> *Because everyone is created in His image, everyone is equal in His eyes and so if you are now the richest man or the poorest person on the street, we are all maar equal.*

This was also tied to Jesus as being seen as being *'for the marginalized, was for the people that were basically, were seen as nothing, were dehumanized'*. The Black respondents interpreted love in light of the concept of Ubuntu and believed that this should be a guiding value. This indigenous framing also problematized the notion of love saying that this was not evident in the ways in which inequality in the town still existed and were concerned that while the majority of South Africans reside in faith communities, there was still inequality and, therefore, still a lack of love. Therefore, Christian and indigenous values should guide us in our engagement with these issues.

White respondents also problematized certain parts of the Bible, because they felt that their faith calls them to treat everyone with dignity and saw Jesus as an example of being with the marginalized as reflected here. This is a possibly encouraging point of contact for intergroup contact. A concerning, but marginal, view was that some also spoke about the fact that Jesus also said that 'the poor will always be with us' or never condemned slavery. The latter implies that there might be a need for hermeneutics around issues of justice and inequality and reflects the very different views of white and Black Christians concerning such issues.

Lack of clarity regarding the ways in which the church can act for change

The question regarding the church's role regarding issues of inequality elicited a range of responses, many of which were vague. This perhaps indicates that respondents struggled, despite being able to articulate the issues around poverty and inequality, its racialized nature etc., still difficult to point to what churches should actually do.

Black and coloured respondents did not appear to be clear on the ways in which their own churches were currently responding to poverty especially – despite the fact that there were some direct initiatives which they were not aware of. In contrast, the white group all appeared to be aware of their church's involvement in surrounding areas through a faith-based organization (FBO) and its encouragement to be engaged. They were positive about this involvement and also understood it as allowing them the opportunity to cross racial and class boundaries, although two respondents did reflect on whether this was an outflow of white guilt and some noted that perhaps the church could do more to encourage engagement.

The coloured congregation is involved in community work (coaching, life skills, youth ministry), but perhaps due to the transient nature of their attendance, quite a few respondents were not aware of the initiatives. This group appeared to suggest that the key role of the church is spiritual formation and that churches should equip young people in particular to engage with societal issues better and to be empowered to be self-reliant:

> And so I will say the church is lacking in education on these issues, they're really lacking in terms of, that they don't tell you that when you're outside, this is going to happen to you. They just tell you that trust God, pray and that's where the problem comes in.

Coloured respondents also noted that the church could become a place where job opportunities are shared or resources mobilized, or people educated for civic participation, but it was also clear that some thought that there was not much a 'poor' church could do. Black respondents, interestingly enough, largely suggested cognitive strategies as starting points to address the problem such as workshops, inviting speakers and hosting discussions in order to understand the problem. However, they did not seem to view the Church as a space in which concrete and practical action could be taken. Perhaps this is because they felt that the church was not proactive enough in encouraging societal transformation and they appeared to indicate that political parties and action might be more effective. The church was not, therefore, seen as being able to take concrete action (mobilization for advocacy, development, etc.). This in an important point for church leaders and members to note and is worrying considering the public role the church is expected to play in civil society and the considerable influence it has on society. It means that the church is not adequately equipped, or able to serve its members, in bringing about actual structural change. Black members, however, noted that one of the ways that inequality could be bridged was by communities sharing resources and that churches should lead the way in this as there still remained too much inequality between churches in the area; yet, the shared Christian faith obligates people to act in love towards their neighbour. They were also clear, however, that this should not come in the form of paternalistic 'hand outs' from white churches.

The latter reflects the ongoing racial divide and growing mistrust between racial groups and sadly, also between confessing Christians from different races – as well as the need for church leaders in the town to take note and continue to take bold steps towards ecumenical engagement on issues of social justice such as inequality, reconciliation and restitution.

Responses regarding youth agency for change were surprising

There is often a great deal of inertia and hopelessness in responding to what appears to be an enormous task, and this could be one of the reasons why young people responded in the ways that they did. While the university #Feesmustfall protests were led by students of similar age, who mobilized largely Black and coloured students concerning advocacy for change, it is interesting that none of the respondents appeared to mention advocacy, protest or community mobilization as a personal strategy in addressing these issues. These responses also reflect the dialogical tension between apathy and action found in the literature review.

The most prominent means suggested for change across all race groups was that of creating dialogue across race, class and geographical lines (which of course intersect in the town). All three groups talked about the need to facilitate dialogue between communities as a starting point. This suggestion certainly affirms inter-group contact theory's approach.

The most prominent way in which white respondents spoke about their own role in change was to treat others with human dignity – to treat all South Africans fairly and with respect. This would be enacted through reaching across borders of class and race in friendship and getting to know others' stories. Respect should be a given; however, it is implied by one persons' example of teaching her children to treat the Black domestic worker with respect as one of the ways in which she can address the human indignities resulting from inequality that it becomes clear that this is not a given. This is a very basic – and perhaps even problematic – starting point and reveals the racial and economic fissure lines in our society that are still not healed. Another common way towards change suggested more especially by Black and coloured respondents was on coaching of youth and children to build self-reliance and self-respect in an unequal and still racist society: 'Given a chance, personally I would actually concentrate on the children … if we ever focus on the youth because they have like youth power to change the outcomes of the future.' While white respondents focused on volunteerism and creating employment opportunities, very few respondents in the other two congregations barely touched on this. This finding is not surprising, in that due to the socioeconomic circumstances of the two groups such action could either be seen as part of their everyday culture (i.e. volunteerism) or that unlike the white respondents they are less likely to own businesses through which to create employment.

For the large part, however, while Black respondents were politicized and articulate when it came to the political means necessary for change, they appeared to look towards authority figures to take leadership in societal change. Most of the Black cohort are fulfilling several ministerial roles within church but did not expressly mention their role in societal renewal – one noted that they are

> … striving to do the righteousness of God always but I don't want to use my power to do that I just need the Lord's spirit to lead me in doing that for instance the simple things, not to preach too much, not to sing too much, not to pray too much, … to take care and show the love of God to other people and take care of the people … poor people, disadvantaged people, you are taking the real Gospel to the people by doing that not by standing on the pulpit and shouting too much.

The latter provides a hopeful departure point for societal engagement and reveals that young adults are open for dialogical engagement across racial lines, but it becomes clear from the findings that there is a need for training perhaps in community advocacy and mobilization, which addresses the root causes of poverty and inequality in this divided town rather than only deal with the symptoms through projects or dialogical engagement.

Conclusion

This study focused on the intersection between Christian young adults, inequality, reconciliation and restitution in South Africa. Sadly, what emerges from this study is in many ways a deep challenge to the churches and it, therefore, uncovers pointers that need to be taken into consideration by congregations in this context. Congregations in Stellenbosch clearly still echo the socioeconomic and racial divisions of the town, and its apartheid history. While young people saw it as important for the church to engage and even be part of restitutionary action, they struggled to point to what churches should actually do, despite the fact that they note that there are inequalities and a need for restitution. The reason for this could be a result of the conflicted feelings many had regarding the notion of restitution and its relationship to reconciliation. Most respondents, therefore, focused on dialogical engagement across racial lines, non-governmental organization (NGO) interventions or on the equipping of children and younger people to overcome these inequalities through empowerment and self-reliance. While these are certainly good places to start to engage issues of racial and socioeconomic division and empower communities, churches were not, for instance, noted as places from which economic activities could be engaged. Nor where they noted as sites of advocacy for community change and mobilization. As noted in the introductory sections, this is not surprising if young adults have experienced 'disappointment and alienation in their church settings, which they find to be dismissive at best and oppressive at worst toward their activism'.

The lived theologizing of young people was also interesting as they focused on the 'Golden Rule' of love of neighbour, but seldom engaged the prophetic and social justice texts within the Pentateuch or Prophets as theological resources. The latter is neither right nor wrong, but it is interesting in light of the fact that South Africa's prophetic tradition of Liberation Theology and Black Theology could be seen as rooted in these texts rather than the Golden Rule (Mtshiselwa 2015: 1–9; Boesak 2016) and that these texts speak more prominently into issues such as socioeconomic injustices, many of which were raised by respondents as needing to be addressed. The latter implies that there might be a need for hermeneutics around issues of justice and inequality. It is interesting to note, however, that indigenous values (such as *Ubuntu*) reinforce or align with values in scripture, but also assist in critiquing praxis. Ultimately, respondents across racial lines were hopeful, and this hope was rooted in their faith. Churches in towns such as Stellenbosch, therefore, have a great deal of work to do in seeking the welfare of their communities. Young adults could be at the forefront of this work if equipped with theologies that allow them to develop their prophetic imagination, and spaces are created for them to not only dialogue across lines of race and class, but actively engage the economic and social injustices that lie at its roots.

Religion and income inequality among retirees in Botswana

A communal contextual theological approach

Tshenolo J. Madigele and Ronald Tshelametse

Introduction

In this chapter we identify income inequality as prevalent in Botswana. The inequality is observed primarily amongst the employed and the retirees (the elderly). Our research reveals that religion is accountable for this inequality as it formed part of the cartel that developed laws and policies that force the elderly into retirement. Thus, the church can be held accountable for the income inequality here observed. Christian-based laws, values and policies have brought with them challenges that may be categorized into physical, economic, spiritual and psychosocial. Meanwhile, we also established that religion is adequately resourced to mitigate against the inequality. The resources here identified include communal contextual pastoral theological intervention and the current status of the church as a potential policy influencer. The church's independence from the state can be utilized as a powerful agent of change to transform policies and laws pertaining the retirement age. It is thus by the values upon which the laws are based and by inaction that the church is identified with income inequality amongst the employed and the elderly retirees. The chapter used data, arguments and discussions drawn from books, articles, magazines and relevant websites.

Background

One of the visibly dominant forms of inequality in Botswana is income inequality. This inequality mostly presents itself amongst the employed and the retired. The retired experience income challenges resulting in physical, economic, spiritual and psychosocial deficiencies. These retired are usually forced into retirement. The forced retirement age in Botswana is 60+. At sixty years of age retirement is mandatory irrespective of health, physical ability, psychological readiness/ ability, spiritual orientation and economic status (Tlou 1994; BPOPF 2017). The economic life is short, from thirty-three years to sixty years. Twenty-seven years' achievements at a modest salary of an average person are inadequate to sustain a pensioner for twenty-five years (sixty to eighty-five) (BPOPF 2017; UNFPA 2018).

Meanwhile, the United Nations Population Fund (UNFPA 2018) shows that there is a gap between labour income and consumption across different age populations that is worth considering. However, the elderly are forced to retire early and awarded low or no pension provisions (BPOPF 2017). The government pension that amounts to 430 pula per month (approximately US$41 at the time of writing) is available to Batswana citizens from the age of sixty-five years (Clausen et al. 2000; UNICEF Botswana 2018). This means that there is a five-year retirement-pension gap. This five-year gap could be impoverishing for some who are reliant solely on the government pension. With no pension income, some older people are often forced to work in low-paid or demeaning jobs to provide for themselves and their dependants (Stanley 2008).

Shaibu and Wallhagen (2002) assert that Botswana does not have any form of assistance for the elderly other than the old pension scheme. There is also a destitute programme that gives out food hampers amounting 500–600 pula (US$50–US$60) a month and a cash allowance of 250 pula (US$25) for those that do not need food (UNICEF Botswana 2018; Onen et al. 2019). The stigma of being classified as destitute has dissuaded some of them from utilizing the programme, which is also the case in Nigeria. The destitute programme is perceived as humiliating and compromises people's dignity and self-esteem. This presents a challenge for intersectional collaboration of various departments to devise appropriate resources for the elderly without the humiliating consequences (Shaibu and Wallhagen 2002: 140).

The United Nations Population Fund policy brief highlights on maximizing the demographic dividend in Botswana until 2050. Thus, the working-age population will have an opportunity to enhance their socioeconomic lives (UNFPA 2018). It is imperative for this opportunity to extend to the ageing population. Thus, changes in economic policy are needed to prepare for the ageing population.

The World Bank on Global Poverty Line Update (2015) reveals that the elderly in Botswana are at a high risk of poverty. According to this report, someone who lives on less than US$1.90 (19 pula) is categorically poor. Therefore, the elderly with a pension as the sole source of income and for an average month of thirty days live below the Poverty Datum Line. Poverty, narrowly defined as a lack of material means, may on its own form a severe impediment to older people. Davis (2003) understands poverty as the consequent inability to participate effectively in economic, social and political life that profoundly disadvantages older people.

Some of the barriers to developing good economic policy on elderly retirees are pervasive misconceptions, attitudes and assumptions about older people especially (Cook 2011). According to Butler (1980), ageist attitudes have a potential to limit the way problems are conceptualized, and the capacity to seize innovative opportunities. Misconceptions about the elderly are baseless, social constructs that have no physiological basis.

Moreover, the loss of ability associated with the elderly is only loosely related to a person's chronological age. However, studies show that some elderly people at the age of eighty have levels of both physical and mental capacities similar to that of many twenty year olds (Lee et al. 2005). This does not ignore the fact that other people experience significant declines in capacity at younger ages. Some sixty year olds are not in a good position to be in a formal work environment. In that regard, the economic policy must be designed to maximize the number of people who experience these positive trajectories of ageing. It must also address the needs of those who lose their capacity at earlier ages. It is from this background that this article argues that differences in physical functioning should not be correlated with income.

This chapter, therefore, appeals for the deployment of *communal contextual pastoral theological approach* by the Christian community in order to address inequality in Botswana. The fight for the recognition of the rights of the elderly should be a fight for all, and as a privileged community, the church is in a position to make sure that the elderly people are not subjected to income inequality. The church should devote attention to matters of justice, development and transformation. The Christian community, therefore, is challenged to collectively bring together their skills and focus on the holistic or contextual dimensions of elderly people. This means that their pastoral approach should touch all the aspects of human existence such as the social, economic, political and psycho-emotional aspects (Patton 1993).

Income inequality among retirees in Botswana: A religious crisis

Religion is generally understood to be a set of beliefs and practices that are common within a group of people. It is characterized by worship, law, traditions, faith and mystic experience (Gunn 2003). Botswana is home to a number of religions which include Christianity, African traditional religion (ATR), Islam, the Baha'i Faith, Buddhism, Hinduism, Sikhism and Judaism. The oldest religion in the context of Botswana is ATRs (Amanze 1994). ATRs have no specific founders, no sacred scriptures, no written theologies and no missionaries. They are said to be embodied in the bloodstream of the people themselves (Amanze 1994: 229). According to statistics, Christianity stands at 79.1 per cent of the population, hence qualifying as the majority religion (Republic of Botswana 2019; Botswana: International Religious Freedom Report, 2007).

This chapter aims at discussing how religion impacts income inequality among retirees in Botswana. As a majority religion, and as a religion that has a long history and has enjoyed its monopoly in the politics of the country during the missionary period which predates colonial rule in 1885, Christianity is best placed to be a subject of discussion; hence, the word 'religion' will be used synonymously with the word, 'Christianity' in this chapter.

Whereas at independence the mainline churches (of missionary origin) constituted the religious majority, we learn of three categories into which Christian churches are often classified (West 1975). These are mainline churches, African independent churches (AICs) and Pentecostal/Charismatic churches (Amanze 1994).

History teaches that Christianity, commerce, colonialism and civilization were introduced at the same time. There was no way colonial subjugation of the indigenous people and the emergence of the modern state could be separated from Christianity (Ogunbado 2012; Nkomazana 2015). On the other hand, we learn that some of the Protestant missionaries who moved to Africa were not supported by a missionary organization. They formed a number of missionary agencies such as Church Missionary Society (CMS- 1799), Universities' Mission to Central Africa (UMCA-1860–1918) upon their arrival (Sundkler and Steed 2000: 84). UMCA was intentional about putting the Bible in the centre and was focused on places that were deeply affected by famine, warfare, slave trade, superstition and illnesses in the Eastern side of Africa (Jennings 2002). CMS on the other hand settled in Southern Africa in places that were very remote and health hazardous with an attempt to spread the Gospel. They felt that southern Africa had an urgent need of salvation (Endfield and Nash 2007). They also saw it imperative to promote education in order to facilitate direct understanding of the Scripture even though they were blamed for their *tabula rasa* approach in terms of the interaction between the gospel and local cultures. Their display of cultural and religious superiority is relegated to lack of knowledge in anthropology and working among people of different cultures. Furthermore, the missionaries confronted the then social ills such as genital mutilation and gender-based violence. They were also actively involved in anti-slavery movements. British evangelical missionaries are remembered for their passion to correct evil practices that were done by British officials who spread false religion for their own selfish gain (Prill 2019).

According to Walls (1987), David Livingstone had a strong view that Christianity, commerce and civilization had interests in common, hence unashamedly support one another. In his contention, Christianity has principles and values for moral guidance, while commerce and education facilitate production of goods from fertile soil to trade with Europeans. All this, coupled with a good system of governance, will ensure civil rights for the people. According to Livingstone, the true salvation for Africa could be found in her fertile soil. Africa's natural resources could provide much more profitable access to the Western manufactured goods that Africans desired (Nkomazana 1998).

However, Livingstone's ambition was short lived as the emergence of the revolution came with higher demand of raw materials. The local agriculture was not capable of meeting those demands. Meanwhile factory markets in Western countries multiplied. The more they multiplied, the more people in Botswana migrated to cities to satisfy the swelling growth of factory markets of European countries (Nkomazana 1998). Urbanization and a shift to natural resources such as gold and diamonds contributed significantly to decrease in rural and agricultural production (Shaibu 2013). It can be argued that there are two aspects of modernization: the shift from subsistence agriculture to wage employment and the participation in Western education are more influential aspects of modernization affecting the older population in Botswana and other African countries.

This chapter is primarily concerned about the economic well-being of the retirees in Botswana, particularly the income inequality that occurred and continues to manifest under the unwatchful or watchful eyes of Christianity. The discussions above show that modernization and industrialization have created the gap that leads to the disrespect and economic abuse of elders due to income inequality in Botswana today. The impact of modernization on the forcefully retired elderly in Botswana has been to create poverty due to marginalization, loss of social and economic support from economically active members of the family and the weakening of institutions that functioned as sources of social and economic support. It can be argued that there is an inverse relationship between the status of treatment of the aged and the degree of modernization. Rural to urban migration and the emphasis on a monetary economy also tend to weaken the extended family as a support system for the retired elderly dependent group (Shaibu 2002). A change in family structures exacerbates the situation. The retired elderly are gradually pushed into isolation. Meanwhile, the critical and important roles of the aged, wise and experienced, as promoted by African culture, are undermined.

Agricultural life was replaced by a monetary economy; the values of communalism were replaced with individualism. The elderly who depended on familial support and agriculture were left with nothing and no one to lean on. Their situation got worse with the advent of HIV and AIDS. They are obliged to care for orphans who lost their parents. However, there are no policies to ensure their long-term and sustainable economic life. Some religious ideologies of personal salvation undermine responsibility towards the marginalized, including the retired elderly. To be fair, however, some Christian teachings call for social responsibility. These need to be utilized to support the retired elderly in the country.

Botswana gained independence in 1966 and embraced religious pluralism. Section 11(2) of the country's Constitution provides for freedom of religion. Furthermore, the Constitution creates a separation of religion and state and provides the enabling environment for the exercise of freedom of religion as well as social harmony (Republic of Botswana 1966). The declaration of religious freedom created a space for non-preference of any particular religion over others; hence, it declared that there is no state religion (Clarke, 1983). However, some aspects of religion could be used as an ethical framework for the sake of protecting the freedoms of others and in the interest of defence and public morality (Fombad 2004).

Generally, government functions begin with a Christian prayer although members of other religious groups are not excluded from offering non-Christian prayers at such occasions. Public Holidays Act (Cap 03:07) and Government Notice 506 show that the following Christian days will be observed as public holidays: Good Friday 21 March; Easter Monday 24 March and Ascension Day 1 May. The Bible is used when Presidents and Members of Parliament are sworn into office; it is mandatory that they take the Oath of Office in which they pledge allegiance to the nation and Constitution, in addition to protecting and defending it. Thus, religion is used to promote political interests, even when religious values such as freedom, honesty, integrity, openness, tolerance, justice, the sanctity of life and peace contradict that (Kalu 2010:36; Tsele 2001:210–211).

Ruele (2016) explains that Christianity in the current form is faced with serious socioeconomic and political challenges in the form of landlessness, homelessness, subjection to undemocratic systems, violation of human rights and the 'captivity of the Church'. According to Ruele, through its ethical or moral values, the church is supposed to promote social justice but it has been held hostage by its leadership. The church has lost its primary role of being prophetic and has rather embraced the 'prosperity gospel' at the expense of its moral duty (Ruele 2009). The doctrine of prosperity made popular by these churches is used to enhance individual's economic lives. In that regard, the church is failing to respond to the issues relating to social justice as it seems to serve the interests of its leaders. The political leadership has held the church at ransom, hence prohibiting it from being active in the socioeconomic and political order in Botswana. According to Ruele, the ruling party politicians declared that the church should leave politics to the politicians during public officers' strike (2016: 244).

It could be argued, therefore, that the church in Botswana fails to pursue social justice and combat income inequalities because it is still under captivity of the current political leadership. Its focus remains on spiritual matters and it rather stands for the ideology of the elites, instead of being an institution of liberation of the disadvantaged people (Ruele 2016). Togarasei (2017) agrees with Ruele on the idea that religion is more focused on spiritual matters than on socioeconomic and political matters of the people. Togarasei's article was on Modern Pentecostal Churches (MPCs) in Botswana from their beginning in the post-independence era to the present day. He maintains that the form of Christianity introduced by MPCs is making some contributions to the socioeconomic and political life of Batswana and its influence within the Christian faith is increasing.

Christianity, therefore, increases inequality through its displaced focus, when its focus is on serving the interest of the ruling regime than on its people. It has further ignored the socioeconomic and political needs in favour of individual materialistic gain. David Livingstone, a missionary in the colonial era, embraced the ideology that salvation comes from the soil, hence combining spirituality with material things. In the process, the more powerful Britain gained at the expense of Batswana. Similarly, the gospel of prosperity emphasizes that prosperity is the fruit of faith and manifestation of God's blessings (Togarasei 2011; 2013). This is the same individualistic, hedonistic ideology that keeps on ignoring the needs of the other.

Moreover, because of their urban inclination (Togarasei 2005), their teachings on hard work, employment creation and self-employment are not reaching out to the retired elderly who are based in rural areas. Therefore, this biased teaching could be a source of economic inequalities. When the church makes its impact on urban setting, its impact would be felt more by the working class than by those that need more economic empowerment in rural areas. This is an indirect effect of religion on income inequality in Botswana.

However, religion has always been a catalyst of change (Little 1993; Mbiti 1999: 1; Rodgers et al. 2018). Africans resort to religion unconsciously wherever they are because they are deeply religious. As much as religion is accountable for this inequality, there are several ideologies that can be invoked to reverse the scenario. The church in Botswana can use its position to influence the reversal of the mandatory retirement at sixty-five years of age. In order to relate the gospel to socioeconomic and political matters in the post-independence Botswana, a communal contextual pastoral theological approach becomes relevant.

A communal contextual pastoral theological approach

John Patton (1993) introduces the *communal contextual pastoral theological approach* that highlights the task of pastoral care as a mission of the whole Christian community and focusing on the holistic or contextual dimensions of human beings. This means that pastoral ministry should touch all the aspects of human existence such as the social, economic, political and psycho-emotional aspects. He emphasizes that pastoral care and counselling is not only a minister's or counsellor's role but a role of the whole church community. Patton's approach has its main focus on the Christian community, and it operates within the confines of the church. This approach, however, ignores the existence of humanity outside the walls of the church.

Jesus' ministry was not confined within the walls of the church or a worship place; the approach of his ministry was characterized by dynamism. Paul employs the same expression when he talks about the church being visible in a particular family (Romans 16:3-5) and a particular city, i.e. Corinth (1 Corinthians 1:2). Similarly, there have been warnings against individualism. Such critics argue that Africans are community oriented. In using the New Testament, Lartey recalls the way in which Jesus interacted with persons of other faiths. He used four biblical texts to show that Jesus interacted with people of other faiths (Lartey 2006: 137). Lartey encourages the principle of dynamism rather than exclusively focusing on one area and one people (2006: 136). Even though this approach lacks a sense of inter-denominations and ecumenism, its communal nature is based on how and whom should pastoral care be extended to others. Firstly, Patton sees the Christian Church as a new community which has a shared vision and which commits to be responsible towards one another. This approach is based on the biblical tradition's presentation of a God who cares and who forms those who have been claimed as God's own into a community celebrating that care and extending it to others (Paton 1993: 5). Patton believes that healing comes through hearing. According to Patton (1993), pastoral care is based on members of caring communities expressing their care by hearing and remembering others as reciprocity of God's hearing and remembering created beings. He asserts,

> A ministry of the Christian community that takes place through remembering God's action for us, remembering who we are as God's own people, and hearing and remembering those to whom we minister.

(Patton 1993: 15)

This means that God created human beings for a relationship with God and with one another. God continues in relationship with his creation by hearing us, remembering us and bringing us into a relationship with one another. Discussions above show that the retired are the forgotten community in Botswana. They need to be remembered, heard and understood for them to gain their strength and liberation. Patton argues that pastoral care and counselling are open to questions, experimentation, modifications and re-adjustments as new facts and more in-depth insight into various situations are attained. This means that different problems and situations help with the formulation of new knowledge. The essence of counselling is communication. It is when understanding takes place between those who are communicating with one another (Patton 2005). Pastoral care involves communicating painful experiences, suffering, or various emotional pains and deep hurts (Patton 1993: 15).

In essence, Patton appeals for a community-centred approach to replace the fast-weakening structures of traditional social relationships and support in the face of modernization and urbanization. Secondly, he emphasizes how particular contexts inform the method and goal of care. Pastoral caregivers should understand the context of care. Thus, pastoral care should take notice of people's cultures, experiences and worldview. What pastoral caregivers ought to do is to respond by remembering and reflecting on God's dealings with the community. Patton calls attention to contextual factors affecting both the message of care and the persons giving and receiving care.

Communal contextual pastoral theology, therefore, puts more emphasis on the development of the human person from the context of community. Thus within the Christian community, worship and celebration, preaching, teaching and evangelism, care and counselling, human development and enhancement together with pastoral formation are intertwined to give a communal and holistic approach to growth in all areas of communal and individual lives. We are concerned with the well-being of the retirees in Botswana. Since social structures of caregiving had been weakened by modernism, urbanization, civilization and church mutation, our major question is, 'who cares for the elderly?' There is a need of a community of care; a community that is not confined by space, location or time; a dynamic community that reaches out to the people in need wherever they are. There is a need of a community that acknowledges pluralism and thus ecumenical in approach – a community that will not undermine people's cultures but will use culture to liberate people if not reasoning on cultures (Patton 1993: 70; Lartey 2006).

Therefore, this new community should be moved by love and be touched by the suffering of the people. It should be 'humanity oriented'. This chapter concurs with Patton on the idea that this community of care should be composed of both the clergy as facilitators and the laity. Professionalism can be a problem because the need for professional competence can hinder voluntary effort and the qualities which function best in fellowship. Professional care will be needed when caring activity is limited to professional treatment (Patton 2005).

Pastoral caregivers are also expected to have the capacity to mobilize and utilize resources within the community to provide care. They should be able to revive the spirit of usefulness within the retirees so that they can assume their roles and identity. Pastoral caregivers should be able to come up with community programmes that are based on the needs and contexts of the retirees. Pastoral ministry to the retirees also involves identifying common or individual needs of the retirees. Another important dimension is to recognize the support system that is already in place. What skills and gifts can members of the church community offer? The support system within a congregation may consist of social workers, nurses and lawyers. If they are not there, it would be better to engage professional carers who are funded by government bodies but other roles such as advocacy, spiritual care and practical support such as transport can be carried out by the church (Patton 2005).

As emphasized by Patton (2005: 27), the church minister or pastor should be the facilitator. The role of the facilitator is to bring the people together and mobilize the required support. The facilitator should help his or her congregants to cultivate love, respect and a sense of mutual responsibility among all ages. He or she should also make sure that older people are visited in their homes so that their needs can be communicated with the church minister and other members of the church. If some elderly people are not able to communicate their needs, the facilitator shall contribute or involve someone skilled in making people come forward for assistance (Clinebell 1984: 310–22; Patton 1993: 224).

Pastoral caregivers in the field should keep on reporting their progress back to the church, where they could be assisted on how best they can handle their cases and for debriefing. The whole church will have ownership of the programme. The facilitator's role also entails engaging professionals to journey with the elderly and their families on the process of ageing. He or she should also assist them to go through the process of grieving and when they experience a change in living arrangements and challenges of caregiving. The facilitator should also facilitate the training of the pastoral caregivers in order to make their services more effective. This study maintains that the local church should form relationships with local welfare departments, health facilities and businesses for the betterment of the care of the elderly.

Pastoral caregivers should also have the capacity to listen. Even though the approach of pastoral ministry proposed in this study is on the sharing of experience, pastoral caregivers are facilitators of healing. They are expected to be empathetic and to be able to understand the meaning-making world of the elderly retirees. This study observes that people are their best judge of what their needs are. Therefore, it is essential to listen and learn from them (Lartey 2003: 69; Patton 2005: 3).

For Lartey, listening skills will enable pastoral caregivers to enter into the real-life experiences of oppression that exist in all communities in the world in their struggle to recover their humanity (2003: 102). He asserts that listening to the confidant's story over and over again with interest to help their healing process can accelerate their feelings towards the acceptance of their grievances (Lartey 2003: 69). This acceptance will help them to deal with their problems by themselves or with the help of relevant people. Moreover, pastoral caregivers should be inspired by scripture and human experience. The dignity of those who are suffering can be restored by those who are privileged.

The church: A privileged institution

The church is challenged to regain its position through engaging its resources for social change. The church is in a privileged position not only because of its material resources but also because it is the community that had been empowered by God. After Jesus got baptized at the River Jordan, he went through tests and after that Jesus preached,

> The Spirit of the Lord is upon me, because he hath anointed me to preach the Gospel to the poor; he hath sent me to heal the broken-hearted, to preach deliverance to the captives, and recovering of sight to the blind, to set at liberty them that are bruised.
>
> (Luke 4:18)

Reflecting on above assertions, it could be argued that Christians, therefore, have been given the prophetic role to liberate retirees from any form of deprivation. We learn from Luke 4:18 that a church is a therapeutic community of healing and is a herald of peace. It should be in a position to voice out the concerns of the people to the powers that be (Maluleke 2010). Christianity therefore sustains life in its fullness through community.

Just like other religions, Christianity has virtues and moral values. These values include justice, equality, dignity, sanctity of life and social harmony. Some of these values are promoted within the African traditional setting (Agi 2008). When Christian communities live in the consciousness of these values, there will be transformation of the community of Botswana. The church has a sacred responsibility to engage with the values and resources of Christianity through the concept of community towards creating a new social order.

Experience is another source and resource that can be used by the church for social transformation. According to Pears (2010), critical questions such as what is God doing in a particular situation at a given time is to be asked by the church. Contextual issues are deeply connected to the religious and cultural heritage of a people (Pears 2010). They are also socially situated in various networks of activity of practice. The Bible is another source for social justice and transformation. A historical reading of the Bible mainly calls for individual and communal salvation. The message of the Bible is on redemption from poverty and oppression (Gillett 2005). This means that the church would be a liberating institution if it uses the Bible in a liberating way and if it is capable of being attentive to contextual issues such as economic inequality and of transforming oppressive situations. This means acknowledging various contexts and being sensitive to the relevant issues in the context (Lartey 2006: 42–50; Msomi 2008: 206). Here we are talking about the church and the retired elderly meeting together in the context of Christian faith, church environment and community of faith, and their ethnic and cultural contexts, with a focus in working through living problems.

Conclusion

This chapter is concerned about the economic well-being of the retirees in Botswana, particularly the income inequality that occurred and continues to manifest under the unwatchful or watchful lens of religion. It has been argued above that modernization and industrialization linked to religion have created the gap that leads to the disrespect and economic abuse of elders due to income inequality in Botswana today. Botswana hosts several religions: Christianity, African traditional religion, Islam, Baha'i Faith, Buddhism, Hinduism, Sikhism and Judaism – the oldest one being African traditional religions (ATRs). Meanwhile, 70 per cent of the population are Christians; hence, Christianity qualifies as the majority religion in Botswana. In its different forms, Christianity as a religion has influenced politics and the socioeconomic platform of the country. Commerce, colonialism and civilization are the brainchild of Christianity. Until recently, it was not easy to separate the state from Christianity.

Christianity is perceived as a custodian of principles for moral guidance, while commerce and education facilitate production of goods. The hallmarks of modernization brought about by Christianity are: the shift from subsistence agriculture to wage employment and the participation in Western education. With increasing urbanization and migration in Botswana and an increasing number of children born to unwed mothers, the retiree has become a key figure in many households. The retiree is often the main care provider for children of absent daughters. Despite this burden the wage system developed albeit by the religion of Christianity imposes a retirement age. This leads to a visible income inequality amongst the employed and the retirees.

The church, which is supposed to promote social justice, has lost its primary role of being prophetic and has rather embraced the 'prosperity gospel' at the expense of its moral duty and is failing to pursue social justice and combat income inequalities. Modern Pentecostal Churches (MPCs) in Botswana are the implicated in this regard. Christianity, therefore, increases inequality through its displaced focus. This is the same individualistic, hedonistic ideology that keeps on ignoring the needs of the other. Moreover, because of the urban inclination of these charismatic churches the retired elderly who are relegated to rural areas lose out on the theology of prosperity and this could also be a source of economic inequalities. When the church makes its impact on urban setting, its impact would be felt by the working class than by those that need more economic empowerment in rural areas. This is an indirect effect of religion on income inequality in Botswana.

To mitigate, we propose the use the communal contextual pastoral theological approaches in relating the gospel to the socioeconomic and political issues in the current Botswana. The approach emphasizes the integrated wholeness of both individual and community existence and increased dependency on others. Therefore, both ordained ministers and the church engaged in caring services are to acquire systematic, effective and skilful practice in order for them to improve the quality of life of the elderly people and their families. It also places emphasis on meeting persons in their contexts (ethnic, cultural, communal and environmental). This approach has its emphasis on experience, which is personal in the context of community. The approach is also theological in its emphasis on contextual issues of existence. We also call on the church to utilize its independent position to influence laws and policies governing retirement age.

Recommendations

Our recommendations are as presented below:

1. *Interdisciplinary cooperation*: The church should engage other service providers. This multidisciplinary cooperation could promote coherence of care, which increases the quality of care and life of the elderly people.
    i. *Training for pastoral caregivers*: Theological colleges and institutions in Botswana are challenged to introduce and incorporate the study of the elderly and their challenges so that the church could be able to deal with this particular context of suffering.
    ii. *Establishment of protocols for referrals*: The church and other service providers should have a protocol for referral among themselves.
    iii. *Policymaking that gives dignity to the retired elderly*: This chapter recommends that the policymakers in the Ministry of Finance, Government, and the Ministry of Housing and Rural Development should consider the unique identities of the retired elderly in their

interventions. This calls for a person-centred policy in order to enhance the dignity of every retired elderly person. The church and the government are, therefore, to work together to ensure that the elderly receive appropriate attention and care.

   iv. *Collaboration in equipping the retired elderly in the following area*

The retired elderly should be incorporated into job settings that cater for their age groups so that they can supplement their government grants and lessen financial burdens. The elderly people at the community level should be trained and empowered to lobby for their own better access to treatment, government grants and other services. There should be programmes in place to assist those who qualify to obtain the necessary documentation, and then to get grants. Churches must play both an advocacy role in promoting the rights of the retired elderly in pursuit of social justice, and a supportive role in mitigating the suffering of the retired elderly as fulfilling their pastoral mandate.

Part Four

Religious movements and inequality

Dis/continuity of economic inequality and new prophetic churches in post-1994 South Africa

Mookgo Solomon Kgatle

Introduction

The concentration of wealth is still in the hands of the white minority, while the Black majority continues to be poverty stricken in post-1994 South Africa. Hence, many scholars argue that the legacy of Apartheid that divided people according to class, race and gender is still prevalent in South Africa. Other scholars have made a call to the religious sector to change the status of economic inequality in a democratic South Africa. Most of these studies have shown that instead of solving the problem, the religious sector is actually continuing the legacy of economic inequality in South Africa. This chapter seeks to illustrate through the theoretical framework of dis/continuity that although there is some level of continuity with economic inequality by some New Prophetic Churches (NPC) in South Africa, there is a need to also explore their discontinuity with the same. Thus, by dealing with factors that lead to continuity with economic inequality, NPC have potential to address other socioeconomic challenges that face South Africa, such as poverty and unemployment. This shall be done by briefly introducing the NPC in the context of South African Pentecostalism as a case study in this chapter. The theme of economic inequality shall be explored in a South African context with the aim of illustrating continuity and discontinuity of NPC with such economic inequality.

Outlining the context

This chapter borrows the theme of 'dis/continuity' from Allan Anderson (2018)'s book on 'spirit-filled world religious dis/continuity in African Pentecostalism' where he demonstrates African Pentecostalism's 'continuity with African cultural beliefs and confrontation of such beliefs in discontinuity.' Similarly, this chapter seeks to illustrate NPC's continuity with inequality and confrontation of such inequality in discontinuity. A number of scholars have come up to illustrate the continuity of South African Pentecostalism with inequality. Some even suggest that Pentecostal theology in some churches propagates gender inequality by emphasizing male leadership over women leadership (Gabaitse 2015: 3). Others opine that Pentecostalism survives in the harsh realities of capitalist state and neoliberal policies but perpetuates economic inequality. This chapter argues that the relationship between South African Pentecostalism and economic inequality is a complex one that requires a balance between continuity and discontinuity. While it is acknowledged here that there is some level of continuity on the one hand, the chapter also seeks to demonstrate the gap that highlights its discontinuity with economic inequality. This shall be done by showing the South African picture of economic inequality and a brief introduction of NPC in order to use them as a case study for dis/continuity.

Methodology and theoretical framework

This chapter uses literary analysis (see Kusch 2016) to analyse literature on economic inequality in South Africa. The same method is used to analyse the interaction between the economic inequality and NPC in South Africa. Thus, the chapter will rely on previous studies that have addressed the issue of economic inequality. However, economic inequality should be understood in the context of other social inequalities that took place prior to democracy in South Africa; hence, reference is made here to racial segregation. The chapter studies the broader South African Pentecostal movement with a particular reference to the NPC and their relation to economic inequality. This chapter uses the theory of dis/continuity to understand the basis for continuity and discontinuity in a specific discourse (Zimbardo 1999: 345).

Economic inequality in South Africa

The root cause of economic inequality in South Africa prior to the democratic dispensation in 1994 is racial segregation that has divided people according to their racial groups; Black, white, Indian and coloureds[1] (Lephakga 2017). The system made sure that the quality of life was not the same among the racial groups; the white minority enjoyed more privileges than their Black counterparts did. Some jobs and rights to own property were reserved for the few while the majority of the Black people were forced to live in townships and homelands away from their working places. In addition, the Black people were dispossessed of their land which they could have used for economic activities like farming. This historical exclusion of Black people during apartheid from the main activities of the economy like owning properties, working, agriculture and others is the main cause of inequality (Ncube et al. 2014). Consequently, the system created two nations within the same country: the first nation belongs to a white minority; it prospers and has access to the best health, education and other economic facilities. The second nation is the direct opposite that lives in harsh conditions of undeveloped infrastructure, dilapidated houses, dysfunctional health and education systems (Gelb 2003: 1). The system has produced two classes of people, one that is extremely rich and the other that is extremely poor that depends on menial jobs in the informal sector.

In post-1994 South Africa, economic inequality remains the same, white people continue to earn much higher salaries than their Black counterparts. White people continue to own the strategic streams of the economy and their companies are listed on the Johannesburg Stock Exchange (JSE). This is despite the government intervention of introducing many pro-poor activities like social grants; the reality is that people need to be active in the mainstream economy than just to receive grants. In addition, instead of changing the lives of the people, South African politicians have become greedy and serve their own interest than the people (Masango 2014: 2). Hence, South Africa remains one of the countries with high levels of inequality in the world with white people at the top and the Black people at the bottom of the economy, even when political leadership is held by Black people (see Du toit and Nkomo 2014: 2). In the words of Molobi (2016: 2), 'the most productive 10% of the population receives almost half of the income'. This situation is more likely to continue as long as there is no political will to drive economic equality among all the citizen of the country.

The recent statistics by Stats South Africa (2019) regarding economic inequality show:

> The white population group had the highest annual mean and median expenditure compared to other population groups across all four years; while black Africans had the least. Black Africans had an annual median expenditure of only R6 009 in 2006 and R9 186 in 2015. Meanwhile, the white population group had their annual median expenditure sitting at R77 308 in 2006 which increased to R100 205 in 2015. The annual median expenditure for whites was

more than ten times higher than that of black Africans across all four years. Furthermore, the white population group had more than nine times the annual mean expenditure of black Africans in 2006; although, this ratio declined to more than seven times in 2015.[2]

The annual median expenditure is used to determine the average annual expenditure by the white racial group per year. When looking at the statistics above, it means that most Black people in South Africa live on R25 per day while white people live on R275 per day. The above statistics can only be a true reflection when collected across all the regions of South Africa; if for example we look at the rural provinces like Eastern Cape and Limpopo, the graphs will obviously change as majority of people there live below the bread line. This is shocking in a country where the majority of people are Black.

The new prophetic churches in South Africa

South African Pentecostalism include three main streams (Anderson 1992; see Mashau 2013: 10) or sub-traditions such as Pentecostal Charismatic Christianity (Anderson 2002: 167) or what Frahm-Arp (2010: 153) calls classical Pentecostalism, African Independent Pentecostal Churches (AIC) (Anderson 2005: 66) and Charismatic Churches (Anderson 2005: 70). However, NPC are different from the three streams in approach, but one still classifies them as Pentecostals because the prophetic is considered as one of the characteristics of Pentecostalism. There is a new development within Pentecostalism recently that has seen the rising of Pentecostal churches that are more inclined in prophetic tradition (Kgatle 2019 cf. Kgatle 2020: 1). These churches exist elsewhere; for example, in Zimbabwe, Chitando and Biri (2016) called them the Pentecostal prophetic sector. These are prominent in West African countries such as Ghana (see Omenyo 2013; Quayesi-Amakye 2015).

These churches are known for four main reasons: first, they practise what most of their leaders call forensic prophecy or 'one on one prophecy' where believers receive direct prophecy that involves their daily living, including personal information like cell phone number, car registration number and so forth (Revelator 2017). Second, their deliverance ministry, unlike in other streams, is based on consultations where they charge around R7000 or more per consultation. Thus, members can consult a prophet to receive counselling or direction for their lives but they will need to pay a certain fee depending on the level of their problems (Tsekpoe 2019). Third, one of the common miracles that they perform while ministering on the podium is 'miracle money' that appears in people's accounts without working for it (Vengeyi 2013: 29). Last, they are known for their love of prophetic titles like 'Major 1' or 'Seer 1', 'Mzansi Prophet' and other fashionable prophetic titles (Ramantswana 2019: 8).

In South Africa, prominent NPC prophets include, among others, Shepherd Bushiri, founder of Enlightened Christian Gathering (ECG), that was founded in 2010 with its headquarters at the heart of Pretoria (Dube 2020: 42). ECG is one of the fastest growing NPC in South Africa, with some of the members coming outside South Africa. The second NPC prophet is Alph Lukau, born on 25 October 1975, is the founder and senior pastor of Alleluia Ministries International, founded in 2002, which, according to their website, is based on the Bible and rooted on the word of God (Timeslive 2019: 1). Lukau rose to fame when he performed a resurrection miracle in his church but the miracle received criticism from other sectors of society. In a South African township, north of Pretoria, there is Pastor Daniel Lesego of Rabboni Centre Ministries, also founded in 2002 (Rabboni Centre Ministries 2017). Lesego, together with his spiritual sons, were involved in series of controversies that marked the abuse of religion in South Africa, including eating of snakes, drinking of petrol, spraying insecticide on congregants and so forth. Finally, there is Pastor Paseka Motsoeneng, also known as Pastor Mboro. He was born on 8 April 1968 and he is the founder and senior pastor of Incredible Happenings, situated in Katlehong near Germiston, east of Johannesburg.

New prophetic churches continuity with economic inequality

The NPC prophets in South Africa are continuing the legacy of apartheid when they charge exorbitant fees for members of their own congregations to see them. Banda (2020: 3) says that Prophet Shepherd Bushiri organizes gala dinners and charges R25,000 per table or R1,000 per individual. Other than the gala dinners, prophets have tendency of charging consultation fees for counselling and prophecy which can amount to R7,000 per person (Tsekpoe 2019). This means that without money one cannot be closer to a prophet, while those who have a lot of money can sit closer to the prophet. In other words, prophets are using money to bring service to the people by taking advantage of the people's, which is the highest form of the commercialization of religion or what Dube (2020: 5) calls 'Prophetpreneurship'. Dube continues to say when prophets do this they are subjecting their members to greater levels of poverty instead of uplifting them from the same poverty. The nation cannot succeed if the prophets are preaching the gospel by taking advantage of the poor people in communities (2020: 5). Society cannot prosper if NPC are mismanaging the financial resources of the church and not educating the young people (Dube 2019).

When the prophets offer prayers for healing, deliverance and prosperity to the people of God, they in turn benefit financially as people are going to return their favour by offering gifts to men of God. In addition, when the prophets sell materials like stickers, bangles, flyers, anointing oil, anointing water, calendars and so forth to the congregants, they benefit financially while the members are impoverished (Ramantswana 2019: 6). Consequently, the prophets, instead of praying for the people as Jesus has commanded them, are preying on their pockets. The incidents of NPC prophets where they are involved in fake miracles, false prophecy and fake healings are a sign of preying on people than praying for them (Ramantswana 2019: 6). However, congregants are so unsuspecting because they have been told that when the water or oil has been prayed for by the prophet, it will serve as protection against various forms of sicknesses and diseases. The element of prayer places a higher demand for these items as many people are suffering of many diseases and other social ills (Tsekpoe 2019: 285). The followers are told that to see the prophet has more value than just to hear him or her preach on the podium. Thus being in contact with the man of God affords one an opportunity to receive a direct message or prophetic word which others have not received in the audience.

In addition, most NPC prophets in South Africa drive luxury cars while their congregants are suffering in poverty. According to Mashau and Kgatle (2019), 'Prophets of prosperity gospel continue to live conspicuous materialistic lifestyles in affluent suburbs and drive the most expensive cars on the market, whilst their congregants are drowning in the triple unholy alliance of poverty, unemployment and inequality.' Prophet Shepherd Bushiri, for example, owns a fleet of luxury cars, lives in an expensive mansion and owns a private jet that flies him from one country to the other (EntertainmentSA 2017). Bushiri shocked the world when he bought (now late) daughter a luxury Maserati car for her fifth birthday (IOL 2017). However, Bushiri is not alone in displaying some form of luxury and higher life; Pastor Alph Lukau lives in a rich suburb in Morningside closer to Sandton city. Like Bushiri, Lukau owns several luxury cars like Bentley and Lamborghini Aventador, all costing millions of rands (Timeslive 2019). The common thing between the prophets is that they live a life that is far removed from what the congregants are living, as many of their followers live in townships and villages.

It is discouraging to think that prophets buy these expensive cars and live in luxury houses while they have employees such as personal assistants, musicians, ushers, body guards and so forth who equally deserve decent salaries. Is this not presenting a gap between the pastor and his employees in another form of economic inequality? Is the relationship between the pastor and employees not presenting another scenario of the rich at the top and the poor at the bottom? While it may be argued that the employees would be unemployed if they were not helped by the pastor, it should not be a motivation for exploitation. While pondering on these questions, there is another challenge, whereby prophets continue in these lifestyles while they are actually renting for fellowship. The ECG of Prophet Shepherd Bushiri was paying rent for their gathering space on monthly basis in thousands of rands, whereas they could have been using money for luxuries to build a church. Meanwhile reports by the Citizen 2016 show that members of the church have been pledging and paying huge amounts of money towards the building of the church but have not seen any building to date. Of course, the prophets would argue, for example, that when buying luxuries, they are using their own money, not the offerings, and the tithes of the church. However, the challenge remains that their of wealth, whether from the church finances or own pocket, demonstrates an ecclesial economic inequality.

New prophetic churches' discontinuity with economic inequality

When we concentrate on the actions of the prophets, we run the risk of missing the point that the message of the prophets shows that it challenges inequality. According to Kangwa (2016: 20), the message of the NPC prophets of miracles, healing and deliverance is satisfying the social needs of many African people. In addition, it is the same message that is causing many people to be attracted to these churches such that so many of them do not even see the wrongdoings of the prophets but care only about their healing and deliverance. De Witte (2018: 3) adds that it was the societal challenges in Africa that gave birth to churches like NPC in a quest to bring solutions. Thus, where people do not have proper healthcare systems, education, housing and other needs, they run to NPC for help. In a way, they see NPC as having the necessary tools to solve the socioeconomic challenges that they face on daily basis (Akanbi and Beyers 2017: 2). By listening to an NPC prophet, people have hope that they too can become rich and live a quality life in all aspects.

In the context of a poverty-stricken country where only few people are rich, NPC have become the only hope for the people to come out of their desperate situation (Banda 2019: 2). Banda (2019: 8) continues to say, 'while there are indeed abusive churches, there are also many South African churches that function as fountains of human flourishing, promote the well-being of the poor and protect the marginalised and the abused in society'. Therefore, it is inaccurate to only point out the continuity of the NPC with inequality, highlighting some of the successes of this type of churches. Some of the NPC have become place whereby those who were economically excluded have gathered courage to take part in the mainstream economy. Some NPC go to the lengths of creating opportunities for their members to start businesses in the church and thus creating an entrepreneurial activity that uplift the poor (Kaunda 2015: 128). Every member attending the NPC church, including those who are working, will be encouraged to sell something whenever they get an opportunity. They are taught that a salary is not enough to keep a person out of poverty, hence the need to be entrepreneurial.

NPC are confronting the root causes of economic inequality, namely, racial segregation. As stated in previous sections, racial segregation has isolated people to ensure that they live according to racial groups such as white, Black, coloured and Indians. The NPC have a way of bringing people of all the racial groups together, thus potentially discontinuing inequality. The worship services are conducted outside the racial divides that dominated most of missional mainline churches in South Africa. When one looks at some of the Pentecostal churches like the Apostolic Faith Mission (AFM) of South Africa (although the church united in 1996), there are still some elements of Black and white in such churches (Resane 2018). The unity in churches like AFM is a forced one as some of the white congregants do not want to be associated with Blackness. In the AFM, many white pastors have joined non-geographic regions in order to disassociate themselves from fellow Black ministers. It is different with churches like ECG in Pretoria; people of different ages, races and classes come together to fellowship in one place. Therefore, in having multi-racial services, NPC are moving the society in the right direction where opportunities are available for all people regardless of race, age and gender.

Mediating continuity with economic inequality

First, in order to mediate on the continuity with economic inequality, the NPC prophets need to bridge the gap between the poor and the rich by sharing. By sharing in this chapter, one refers to a concept where people come together to share food and other material possessions (Acts 2:42-47). When people share equally among themselves, there is no difference between the rich and the poor; they all appear the same. Thus, when the rich prophets make an effort to come down to where the marginalized and the down trodden are, they are slowly bridging the gap between themselves and the poor. This is exactly what happened in the early church in the book of Acts; the rich sold their possessions and shared equally with the poor. The wealth in the world is enough to cater for every human being on earth; therefore, when that wealth is concentrated in one group, they need to share with others. Similarly, the prophets who got rich because of the many sacrifices that their followers have made need to share in their prosperity. In this way, NPC will exist as equal societies where there is no difference between the prophet and congregant.

Second, the NPC prophets need to create a communal identity with an understanding that a person does not exist in isolation or as an individual but with others. In Africa, we talk about 'ubuntu', which literally means that an individual exists in the company or because of others. In this context, it means pastors exist because there are congregants; he or she is prosperous because of congregants. Therefore, it is upon NPC prophets to value the same people who made them to prosper. They cannot continue to drive big and live in big mansions while their own congregants are suffering and lacking basic needs. Common identity makes it possible for a person who earns more than others to remember that whatever they have achieved needs to be shared with others. Communal identity will always thrive above individual identity and achievements. The prophets should realize that they have common, identity even with people outside their churches. Therefore, common identity should not be limited to church or religious people or the followers of specific denomination. Actually, it should bridge the gap between the religious and the nonreligious because the common factor is humanity, not religion.

Third, the NPC prophets need to reach out to the communities around them, like the townships, informal settlements and villages in rural areas. At the end, these communities illustrate the gap between the poor and the rich, hence a need to reach out to these vulnerable people. The NPC prophets should leave their comfort zones in cities and suburbs and reach out to the whole community than just preaching to their congregants. There are other advantages to reaching out to communities than just solving inequalities; it solves other problems like crimes, drug abuse and so forth. Thus by reaching out to communities, the NPC prophets will be creating an atmosphere for social cohesion among the people, which is important in a polarized country like South Africa. Where there is social cohesion, there will be no room for racial segregation, hatred and other social ills as people learn to tolerate each other. The prophets will use such moments to share food parcels and other necessities with the people that are in need of such most and ensure that people never run hungry. In addition, these will be moments where families come together to support each other.

Last, the NPC prophets should adopt a model of inclusive development where everyone is part of the development regardless of their economic class, gender, sex, disability and religious affiliation. Inclusive development ensures that people engage in productive projects rather than merely sharing food parcels in the church that solve temporary hunger problems. The excluded groups should be uplifted by involving such groups in the mainstream economy, which involves training in basic skills. Sharing food parcels has potential but is limited in creating long-lasting solution to inequality, hence the need for NPC prophets to develop their people. The prophets should not be the only ones with high skills and qualification but should believe in the development of others as well. Those who have made it in life should transfer their skills and knowledge to the rest of the society that need to be developed and trained in important skills. The NPC prophets should look at their followers not only as subjects of sermons but as people with potential and future leaders. The unequal South African society can change when there is willingness by the leaders, specifically NPC prophets, to invest in others.

Conclusion

The South African picture of economic inequality shows that many Black South Africans, who are in the majority, continue to live in poverty, even after the democratic, dispensation while their white counterparts continue to lead affluent lives. It is a picture of an unequal society, which shows that the legacy of social injustices that happened during racial segregation has not disappeared as people are still divided by their economic status. The contribution of this chapter is the NPC's discontinuity with the economic inequality, without dismissing its continuity. Therefore the NPC, by dissociating themselves with economic inequality, have a role to play in solving the economic challenges of a democratic South Africa. The NPC prophets can do so by sharing their wealth with the poor, not only as a philanthropic exercise, but also an expression of the willingness to empower other people, especially the marginalized. They can do so by stopping to buy luxury cars, houses and private jets while their members are struggling to even buy bread. They need to apply Acts 2:44-47, which demonstrates that the people in the early church were together in unity and did things together and shared material possessions equally among themselves. In doing so, NPC prophets will be able to bridge the gap between the rich and poor, to ensure a communal identity among believers and be able to reach out to other poor people in the communities.

Prosperity, philanthropy and social differentiation

Neo-Pentecostalism and socioeconomic inequality in Harare

Simbarashe Gukurume

Introduction

The impact of new Pentecostal charismatic churches (PCCs) on African communities remains highly controversial. On the one hand, there are scholars who maintain that these churches are making a positive impact on the lives of their adherents. On the other hand, there are scholars who maintain that these churches only serve to perpetuate inequalities in society. This chapter contributes to the discourse by analysing how PCCs in Harare, Zimbabwe, are marked by ambivalence in relation to inequality. It draws attention to the extent to which the PCCs utilize a range of rituals that can be regarded as liberative and addressing inequality. However, there are also some beliefs and practices that deepen inequality. It is within this ambivalence that PCCs in Harare continue to attract many followers.

Background

A few weeks after I started fieldwork on new PCCs in Harare, I met Patrick. I was introduced to Patrick by a colleague who went to the same church as him. My relationship with him evolved from attending church events and meetings until he became one of my key informants. Patrick would regularly inform me of special events lined up at his church, the United Family International Church (UFIC). He always invited me to attend such events. One Sunday afternoon,

I attended a service at the City Sports Centre in Harare, a venue used by UFIC for its Sunday and Tuesday services. When I arrived, thousands of people were already in attendance, with a couple of overflow tents almost full. This sight confirmed claims Patrick made to me that UFIC was arguably the fastest-growing and most popular PCC in Harare. The church is led by a youthful and charismatic prophet – Prophet Emmanuel Makandiwa. In no time, Prophet Makandiwa made a grand entry into the church and made his way to the neatly decorated pulpit. After a few songs, he ordered the praise and worship choir to take to their seats and he started to make prophetic declarations. 'Today I want to tell you that you will not go back the same, something is going to change in your life-your business will begin to prosper, your marriage will work, your finances-you are going to drive that dream car, that ten digit salary, you were not born to be poor, but to prosper and conquer.' Declarations like these were always invoked by many of my interlocutors whenever we had discussions on poverty and inequality.

The vignette with which I begin this chapter was drawn from my fieldwork at UFIC, one of the new PCCs that my study focuses on. It encapsulates how PCCs try to (re)configure the material subjectivities of their membership through various strategies, including the prophetic. In this chapter, I look at Pentecostal practices and rituals as a window through which to explore how Pentecostalism simultaneously creates, maintains and also attempts to address social inequalities among its membership and the community at large. The chapter focuses on the ways in which new PCCs simultaneously address and reproduce socioeconomic inequality in Harare. By drawing on empirical data from longitudinal ethnographic fieldwork, participant observation and in-depth interviews with PCCs members, this chapter argues that although PCCs are playing an important role in reducing inequalities through their entrepreneurship training and charity work, they also tend to exacerbate socioeconomic inequalities through their everyday practices such as seeding, partnering and tithing. This chapter also argues that the nexus between neo-Pentecostalism and inequality is complex and ambivalent. There is a growing interest on research pertaining to the nexus between religion and inequality in Africa and beyond (Wilde 2018; Schnabel 2020). However, most of such researches have focused on mainline churches, especially those based in Europe or America. Some scholars have also begun to focus on religion outside the context of the church. For instance, there is a growing body of research on religion and development (Chitando, Gunda and Togarasei 2020; Öhlmann, Gräb and Frost 2020), as well as religion and sexualities (Chitando and van

Klinken 2016). However, there is hardly any research on Pentecostalism and how this relates to socioeconomic inequality in African countries like Zimbabwe. As such, this chapter fills this knowledge gap through an ethnographic exploration of Pentecostalism in Harare.

This chapter is divided into five sections. In what follows, I review literature on and about inequalities and the church in Zimbabwe. From there, I examine and engage literature and debates about Pentecostalism, prosperity discourses and spiritual warfare. After that, I look at the ways through which PCCs help to bridge inequalities among their membership and the community at large. I do this by drawing on the modalities of philanthropy and charity activities done by and through PCCs and their wealthy members. I argue that Pentecostal philanthropy and charity enable members to navigate the vagaries and precarities of a stratified society, yet simultaneously reproducing socioeconomic differentiation within and beyond the church. In the following section, I discuss the role of entrepreneurship, financial literacy and penny capitalism in reducing socioeconomic inequalities and then conclude the chapter by reflecting on key issues and arguments made in the chapter.

My argument in this chapter is informed by and based on twenty-four months of ethnographic fieldwork among new PCCs in Harare. I collected data in three PCCs, namely, the United Family International Church (UFIC), Spirit Embassy, now renamed the Good News Church (GNC), and the Prophetic Healing and Deliverance (PHD) Ministries. I spent several months doing participant observation and in-depth interviews with congregants from these three churches. All the three PCCs are led by youthful charismatic prophets and grew rapidly during Zimbabwe's post-2000 economic and political crisis. Apart from participant observation, and semi-structured interviews, I also relied on secondary sources such as church publications and newspaper articles. Interviews were conducted with eighty-five participants from the three churches. However, for this chapter I make use of data from thirty-five participants drawn mainly from one of the PCCs. My participant observation involved regular church attendance during church services, cell group meetings, social outing and other activities such as workshops and conferences. This enabled me to harvest rich ethnographic data through observations, conversations and participation in church rituals and activities. The study was qualitative in nature and this enabled me to develop rich descriptions of how Pentecostalism intersects with inequalities. I decided to focus on UFIC and PHD because they are arguably the country's fastest growing PCCs and host thousands of congregants during their Sunday services.

Inequalities and the church in Zimbabwe

Over the years, income inequalities in Zimbabwe have been widening due to a plethora of factors such as the protracted socioeconomic crisis (Gukurume 2017). In fact, Zimbabwe is now regarded as one of the most unequal countries globally, with a Gini index value of about 60 (Manero 2017). A Gini coefficient is a measure that is used to ascertain the gap between the rich and the poor. It measures the extent to which the distribution of wealth within a group deviates from a perfectly equal distribution, with values from 0 to 1 (Manero 2017; World Bank 2011). Economic disparities in Zimbabwe are, however, not in any way new. They do have a long history that was rooted in a racialized colonial order that characterized the Rhodesian state. Indeed, inequalities during the colonial era were predominantly racial in nature, with white Rhodesians occupying the apex of the social order (Dashwood 2002). In post-independent Zimbabwe, economic disparities were worsened by the country's adoption of neoliberal structural adjustment programmes in the early 1990s and shifted from racial to predominantly class inequalities (Kanji 1993; Dashwood 2002). The last two decades of economic crisis and decline have only helped to exacerbate the inequalities in the country. This widening of inequalities occurred simultaneously with a rapid growth of new Pentecostal Charismatic Churches (PCCs) in the country's urban spaces (Gukurume 2018). Some scholars have argued that religious groups like PCCs have emerged to 'heal' the afflictions of inequality and poverty which has become a key feature of the postcolonial crisis in sub-Saharan Africa (Pfeiffer 2002). In fact, Pfeiffer (2002) asserted that the rapid expansion of these churches in Mozambique was driven by the intensification of social and economic inequalities wrought by structural adjustment programmes.

Similarly, Smith (2001: 558) argues that the rapid growth of Pentecostalism in Nigeria and other countries in Africa is linked to people's disenchantment with poverty and inequality and the quest for wealth and prosperity. This observation corroborates classical sociological and anthropological works on religiosity and inequality. There is a huge body of anthropological research which constructs religion as a source of real and perceived comfort for people who are socially marginalized and deprived of economic opportunities and resources. For instance, prominent scholars like Karl Marx saw religion the sigh of an oppressed creature, the heart of a heartless world, and the soul of soulless conditions and the opium of the people. For Marx, what exacerbates inequalities are contemporary transformations driven by the rapid spread and growth of capitalism and attendant disparities in accessing income and resources.

Amid intensifying inequalities and increased social vulnerability to poverty, many people are compelled to convert to PCCs as a way of safeguarding their personhood because Pentecostalism promises its adherents real and perceived wealth and success as well as protection from evil forces, witchcraft and the economic burden of familial ties (Gukurume 2017). Indeed, some scholars have argued that there is a strong correlation between being impoverished and conversion to Pentecostalism (Norris and Inglehart 2004). For them, greater income inequality significantly increases the religiosity of the poor and vulnerable members of the society.

Pentecostalism, prosperity and spiritual warfare

Many new PCCs in Zimbabwe and beyond emphasize the centrality of spiritual warfare as a prerequisite for prosperity and upward mobility. PCC members believe that poverty and inequalities are a consequence of the works of demons which block the flow of material blessings from God (van Wyk 2015). Consequently, PCC members are encouraged to constantly fast, pray and make huge financial sacrifices to the church to fight off demons that cause bad luck, misfortunes and poverty. In PCCs, the prosperity gospel is a Pentecostal discourse based on the belief that it is the will of God for born-again Christians to prosper and accumulate wealth. In fact, wealth and being rich is imaged as a divine right for all believers (Gukurume 2018). In a context marked by uncertainties wrought by the neoliberal order in Zimbabwe and Africa more broadly, PCCs' twin theology of prosperity and spiritual warfare becomes compelling to many struggling citizens. Comaroff and Comaroff (2000) asserted that the recent remarkable popularity and growth of Pentecostalism is due to its inherent capacity to provide people with tools to make sense of the vagaries of neoliberal capitalism. Similarly, Joel Robbins (2009) argues that Pentecostalism appeals particularly to the disenfranchised members of the society and relates it to the ways in which Pentecostalism fosters a sense of 'ontological security' and social cohesion which is often absent in capitalist societies dominated by the individuality of the neoliberal order. For many scholars, Pentecostalism is an intractable part of the occult economies (Comaroff and Comaroff 2000) where wealth is miraculously created from nothing. Therefore, PCCs' prosperity theology becomes a version of emergent rejoinders to the transnational growth of what Comaroff and Comaroff (2000) referred to as 'spectral capital' which is largely ascribed to supernatural and occult sources. However, it should be underscored that such spectral capital is not always evenly distributed. Consequently, hierarchies of inequality are incipient within Pentecostal congregations, as the promised prosperity does not reach all equally (Smith 2002; Haynes 2012). Indeed, Comaroff and Comaroff (2000: 314) argue that while Pentecostalism interfaces with the neoliberal order through Pentecostal adherents' pursuance of wealth that is seemingly visible everywhere, yet consistently elusive to many of them (Haynes 2012). This elusiveness and disparity in wealth is often linked to and understood through the workings of the supernatural forces (Geschiere 1997).

Therefore, while Pentecostalism creates and recreates subjectivities that enable the people to navigate and negotiate multiple forms of uncertainties, it is also inextricably entangled with inequality. In her study of Zambian Pentecostals in the Copperbelt, Haynes (2012) asserts that the local definitions of prosperity are not characterized by homogeneous individualized forms of material wealth, but rather by progress along a gradient of material accumulation through relational forms that span differences in economic status. For Haynes, therefore, this reconfigured type of prosperity theology serves to integrate born-again Christians into the broader social world by foregrounding material inequality and encouraging ostentatious displays of riches.

In his study of Argentinian Pentecostal churches, Koehrsen (2018) noted that Pentecostalism tends to cultivate class differences through appropriation of specific religious styles and consumption tastes. Of note is that within Pentecostal circles conspicuous consumption is not only an embodiment of prosperity, but also a symbol of being blessed (Gukurume 2017). As such, PCC members are compelled to appropriate the spiritual technologies that enable them to engage in ostentatious consumption and make upward mobility possible. Thus, access to, and consumption of, global material commodities for PCCs members becomes a space through which particular forms of subjectivities and identities are forged and constituted. However, not every member of these PCCs has the capacity to access and purchase the global commodities or connect to global circuits that mark them as 'blessed' or affluent born-again Christians. Consequently, critics argue that while PCCs help people to make money miraculously and bridge inequalities, some of their rituals simultaneously expose and exacerbate socioeconomic inequalities within their membership. Indeed, members are stratified in PCCs based on how much money they pay to the church on a monthly basis, a practice known as partnering (Biri 2012; Gukurume 2018).

For instance, in one of the popular PCC based in Harare partners are categorized as gold, silver and bronze partners (Taru and Settler 2015; Gukurume

2018). Social inequalities and stratification often manifest when members make gifts to the church and their pastors. Moreso, given the strong emphasis placed on tithing and seeding by new PCCs, many critics have labelled these as self-enrichment projects, where the church leader gets progressively richer while their congregants get poorer. Therefore, for these critics Pentecostalism was not only producing inequalities, but also exacerbating them in their churches and in the community at large. This belief was widespread among old Pentecostals and mainline church officials who accused new PCC prophets of enriching themselves at the expense of their followers. Stories of the prophets' meteoric rise to riches were widespread in the newspapers and in everyday conversations. In spite of this criticism, PCC prophets were not shy to flaunt their wealth publicly amid mounting poverty.

Indeed, most of the prominent Pentecostal prophets live lavish lifestyles that many people, including their congregants, aspire towards and can only dream of; yet, they have to regularly sacrifice money to stand a chance of accumulating wealth. The belief of making huge financial and material sacrifices in the church is anchored by what is called 'seeding' in Pentecostal parlance. Haynes (2012) asserts that the significance of making gifts to church leaders through seeding or tithing, and the financial needs of pastors all bring material issues into religious life. Asamoah-Gyadu (2013) argues that Pentecostal 'gifting' is not only reciprocal, but also transactional because members are taught to expect appropriate redemptive uplifts like wealth, marriage, employment, promotions, good health and financial or business breakthroughs from God when giving obligations are faithfully fulfilled. Of note is that in the PCC 'gift economy', the less materially endowed members are more likely to become invisible. Consequently, this invisibility and its attendant material concerns in part explain the high membership turnover in some PCCs. In their study of religious inequalities inside Spanish prisons, Griera and Clot-Garrel (2015) assert that it is in the invisibility of some actors and practices in terms of not being perceived and categorized as religious where the basis for power inequalities lies.

Some scholars have argued that given the chronicity of crisis that characterizes the postcolonial era in most sub-Saharan Africa, Pentecostalism has become a critical source of hierarchy and social stratification (Haynes 2013). She further noted that prosperity is not characterized by a homogeneous individual accumulation of material wealth; rather, it is imagined as progress along a gradient of material accumulation through relational forms that span differences in socioeconomic status.

Pentecostal philanthropy and inequality

Many new PCCs try to make an impact in addressing inequalities through active engagement in charity work in and outside the church. PCCs such as the United Family International Church (UFIC) and the Prophetic Healing and Deliverance (PHD) Ministries have full-fledged charity departments and engage in extensive philanthropic and altruistic activities. UFIC's Agape Family Care offers scholarships to less privileged students at primary, secondary and university levels. Indeed, during my fieldwork, a number of participants told me that the church was funding the education of several orphaned and poor students. In UFIC these activities are spearheaded by Prophet Makandiwa's wife, Ruth Makandiwa through the church's charity arm: the Agape Family Care. As such, through this charity arm, UFIC has become an important source of material support for the poor members of the society. One of the members working in the charity department told me:

> The AGAPE Family Care offers scholarships to poor and orphaned children ... Pay rent and donate food handouts to the elders and widowed people. Through our charity work we have made an impact on the lives of many poor people in the country.

> (Interview, Owen)

UFIC's engagement in transforming the personhood of its members and the community should be understood within the context of Pentecostal discourses of spiritual warfare and holistic personal transformation of born-again Christians. Miller and Yamamori (2007) argued that through charity activities, PCCs have helped to transform the 'bare life' of the marginalized members of the society. To understand how some PCCs such as the UFIC and Spirit Embassy reconfigure their poor congregants' bare life into a meaningful one, George's story is illustrative. George lost his parents through an accident when he was doing Form 3. 'After the death of my parents, life became a daily struggle and things were never the same-I dropped out of school to look for money to support my other siblings', George told me in an interview. George sought menial jobs to raise money for food and rentals, but continued to study on his own at night. George wrote his Ordinary Level examinations and passed. One of the people who offered him menial jobs, a senior member of a PCC, then recommended him to the church's charity department.

After hearing George's story, the charity department agreed to finance George's education, as well as that of his two siblings. During my fieldwork,

George was completing a Bachelor of Accounting degree at the University of Zimbabwe and had already been offered a job in the church's accounting department. Interestingly, George and his two siblings had since converted to the church which assisted them and vowed to remain there for life. In his own words, 'this is my family now, I could not have been what I am without them so I can only repay papa (Prophet) by being a loyal and committed son'. George's admission pertaining to loyalty resonates strongly with the 'big men' logics, where hierarchical socialities are entrenched through redistribution. In this case, the nouveaux rich prophets redistribute their wealth to their followers to buy loyalty and earn prestige (Smith 2001; McCauley 2012).

George's story is not peculiar to him; it resonated with many similar stories that were told by some interlocutors during my fieldwork. Formulaic stories and testimonies shared revealed the ways in which 'bare lives' like that of George were transformed, not only spiritually, but also materially. Moreso, George's conversion and membership to UFIC have provided him and his siblings a fictive kin and natal community, an alternative family, one which has grown to become a source of support from them and a springboard for upward mobility. George told me that his connection to UFIC has repositioned him in a different class and or status positionality which would not have been possible without the church's assistance.

Many PCCs in Zimbabwe believed that it is their responsibility to deliver people from the spirits of poverty and inequality (Maxwell 1998). Indeed, in most Pentecostal churches, social vices such as poverty and inequality are spiritualized and believed to be a consequence of the demonic and other evil spirits. Following this, Gifford (2009) revealed that Pentecostalism should be viewed as a spiritual enchantment directly related to the socioeconomic and political crisis of the African postcolonial state.

Significantly, a meticulous analysis of the modalities of Pentecostal philanthropy and exchange exposes the hierarchical relationships that are forged through religious rituals such as gifting and receiving (McCauley 2012; Haynes 2013; Gukurume 2020). Indeed, in the church's political economy of philanthropy, the well-to-do and the wealthy prophets emerge as or become what McCauley (2012) referred to as the 'new big man' rule. These modalities of charity therefore create hierarchical relationships between the givers and the receivers of the church's largesse. Such hierarchical relationships are organized around the charisma and wealth of the philanthropic big man, but also around the amounts of material sacrifices made to the church and its pastors. This was confirmed by Amos, one of my interlocutors who told me:

> Gold partners and others who make huge donations to the church have a special place in the structures of the church. They have one-on-one meetings with the prophet. It is unlike poor members who only see the prophet close during church services.

> (Interview, Amos)

Intimate associations with the Prophet and his wife are revered in most PCCs, and church members who are privileged to sit close to the Prophet and have one-on-one meetings with him are elevated to an elite or nobility class of the church. For ordinary church members, it was rare, if not impossible, to have a face-to-face conversation with the Prophet and other senior pastors. In the three years that I did fieldwork in the three churches in Harare, most of my interlocutors never had a chance to have close contact with the Prophet, except during church services. Thus, church partners who donate huge amounts of money to the church are elevated to a position of respectability within the church. Indeed, by giving gifts, members not only cement their links with the spiritual patrons, but also initiate an exchange relationship with God. Rituals of giving created layered hierarchies of sociality within the church. Of note is that the Pentecostal gift economy is mediated by and engender a very specific patronage network (McCauley 2012). Similarly, in her work on Zambian Pentecostal churches, Haynes (2012) noted that Pentecostal churches are a terrain of patron-client relationships between church leaders and congregants. For Smith (2002), the relationship of Pentecostalism to structures of inequality is deeply rooted in the patron-client setup. Following the same argument, Marshall (1995) noted that while Pentecostal charismatics fiercely attack kin and ethnic-based patron-clientism (Bayart 1993; Chabal and Daloz 1999), they seek to replace this with patronage networks which are based on born-again persona. By doing, they actively accentuate patron-client hierarchies, albeit with a Pentecostal outlook.

Pentecostal charismatic churches and penny capitalism

Many new PCCs in Harare actively encourage and promote members to engage in what Maxwell (1998) called '*penny capitalism*'. Penny capitalism refers to small-scale trading and various forms of businesses dealings, largely in the informal sector of the economy (Maxwell 1998: 355; Gukurume 2018). Maxwell described penny capitalism as the trading of cheap commodities such as sweets, fruits and foodstuff within and outside the church to fund religious activities, but also one's existential needs. Such activities enable members of the PCCs to accumulate wealth and sometime reconfigure their personhood and that of others through donating to the church's charity activities. As such, penny capitalism has both personal and collective impact on socioeconomic inequalities. It should be seen as one of the ways through which PCCs try to improve the lives of their members in the here and now. This strongly resonates with observations made by Van Dijk (2009) who, in his study of Ghanaian migrant Pentecostal's in Botswana, argues that these churches integrate their church members into the social and economic networks and circuits of consumption.

Many of my participants who engaged in circuits of exchange and petty trade encouraged by the church noted that they had transformed their lives for the better through engaging in micro-enterprise trading. For instance, Jordan, one of my interlocutors, told me that the church assisted him to register a small company. Jordan started selling car tyres in Harare. Jordan told me that his initial clients were church members and after a few months his business grew rapidly. The growth of his business also enabled Jordan to change his lifestyle and also to donate to the church and other less-privileged members of his church. Jordan noted:

> The church helped me to start my business. This was after I had attended the Billionaires' Mindset Business Summit and other entrepreneurship workshops organised by the church. I am grateful to the church for transforming my life, for giving me an opportunity to network and get clients. My life is now much better and now I have to change the lives of others by donating to the poor and the church.
>
> (Interview, Jordan)

Jordan's story is interesting because it reveals the complex impact that Pentecostal petty trading makes in transforming the life and livelihoods of members. Similar stories like the one told by Jordan were also echoed by a number of my participants from the PCCs that were part of this study. Many of my interlocutors believed that sacrificing money and other resources to the church and the poor was a prerequisite for further prosperity and success in business and life. The frequency with which PCCs such as the UFIC and Spirit Embassy taught entrepreneurship skills and organized business seminars during my fieldwork reveals the importance these churches placed on petty trading in the everyday life and upward mobility of their membership. 'Do not expect God to bless when you are doing nothing, start something that will allow God to notice your effort maybe a small business - God blesses the works of your hands!' pastor Godfrey emphasized during one of the many business seminars I attended.

The church's role in promoting entrepreneurship (van Dijk 2009; van de Kamp 2011; Biri 2012) relates to the Weberian notion of Protestant Calvinist ethic and spirit of capitalism (Weber 2001; Berger 2008). Given PCCs' strong emphasis on entrepreneurship, Berger (2008) referred to them as intentional Weberians whose prosperity ideologies motivate them to succeed in the marketplace (Haynes 2012). Pentecostalism, therefore, becomes not only a spiritual space, but also an economic space where members are prepared for upward mobility through active involvement in the neoliberal market. By so doing, some PCC members are able to negotiate the material conditions of inequality. Indeed, scholars such as Taru (2020) and Gukurume (2020) have also shown how Pentecostalism has become an important space through which people manage and navigate uncertainty and precarity in post-2000 Zimbabwe. This was also echoed by Smith (2001: 602) who noted that Pentecostalism is extremely popular among youth in Nigeria, in part because it provides a social and moral compass with which to navigate the Nigerian political economy of scarcity and inequality.

Some of my interlocutors believed that God blessed people differently, not only because of how much they sacrificed at church, but also because of the nature and size of their businesses they are operating. As such, for these participants prosperity discourses were marked by a very specific socioeconomic differentiation. This finding resonates strongly with Haynes' (2012) argument that salvation and prosperity in Copperbelt Pentecostalism were not always indexed by uniform wealth accumulation, but by economic and spiritual differentiation and relations of inequality.

Conclusion

In the foregoing discussion, I showed the ways in which Pentecostal practices and rituals interacted with socioeconomic inequality. Practices such as entrepreneurship and financial literacy, as well as philanthropy and charity activities, all helped to address inequalities. However, other Pentecostal practices and rituals, such as seeding and partnering, often exacerbated socioeconomic inequality. Similarly, although many of my interlocutors believed in prosperity, many of them acknowledge that God's blessings cannot be uniformly distributed to all born-again Christians. I argued in the chapter that although Pentecostalism offers a scathing critique of forces that (re) produce inequalities by for instance attacking patron-clientism, it sometimes accentuates the very same practices it purports to denigrate. Indeed, this argument was also echoed by other scholars who asserted that Pentecostalism has also produced its own inequalities and embodies the very materialism that motivates so much discontent.

The 'Let Our Voice Be Heard' (LOVBH) movement among Ethiopian Muslims

Realized, aborted or suspended?

Mukerrem Miftah

Introduction

In the years 2010–15, the 'Let Our Voice Be Heard' (LOVBH) movement spearheaded Ethiopian Muslims' demands for religious freedom and social changes in Ethiopia. This chapter examines the relative efficacy of what has been identified as the 'Let Our Voice Be Heard' movement in Ethiopia. Although specifically articulated demands, readily identifiable actors and certain consequences characterized the movement, hardly has any scholarly contribution examined the movement in toto, and most importantly, whether it has succeeded in achieving its initial aspirations. It also attempts to frame the LOVBH movement in the context of the historically grounded Ethiopian Muslims' movement. Drawing from interviews, various reports and web sources, the chapter documents the movement in terms of the factors that gave rise to it, explains the demands that framed and facilitated the movement, and inquires into the conditions in which the movement currently finds itself. It concludes by asking if the movement has ultimately succeeded in achieving its initially articulated demands and the challenges it has faced. Overall, the chapter illustrates how religious actors can mobilize internally to challenge felt and perceived inequalities in society.

Background

Until 1974, Orthodox Christianity had been the source of statecraft and identity marker of the Ethiopian state and society. For centuries, the Ethiopian Orthodox Tewahido Church (EOTC) largely shaped Ethiopia's local, regional and global engagements (Tibebe 2010). Locally, religious and related books, including the holy bible, *Fetha Nagast* and *Kebra Nagast*, were instrumental in constructing Ethiopia as a Christian empire (Tamrat 1968; Tibebe 2010; Chrisna 2012). Even the constitutional order set in motion under the last Ethiopian King Haile Selassie I played a similar role. For instance, the 1955 constitution clearly defines Ethiopia as a Christian empire and its leaders as Orthodox Christians. It recognized the EOTC as 'the established church of the empire and is, as such, supported by the state' (Article 126). In fact, almost all Ethiopian Monarchs considered themselves to be 'the guardians of the national church' (Tibebe 2010: 13). The same provision made it clear that the emperor had to profess Orthodox Christianity. Interestingly, it was not any other version of Orthodox Christianity that the constitution endorsed and promised to protect but it was the 'the doctrines of St. Mark' (Ibid). In short, the Monarchical rule effectively 'cultivated' the notion that views Ethiopia 'as a Christian, Amharigna-speaking nation – that is, an extension of Abyssinia' (Markakis 1989: 119). Regionally and globally, the Ethiopian empire projected itself as a Christian nation and state aiming to forge alliances with other likeminded nations and garner support for its causes (Hussien 1992; Mukerrem 2015). At times, this projection was presented by negation, and as such, Ethiopia had been portrayed as 'an Island of Christianity in a sea of Islam' (Haile Selassie I, a speech to the United States Congress) and Muslims in-and-around Ethiopia as 'historically fixed potential or actual enemies' (Seiffudin 1997: 129; Mukerrem 2015; Chrisna 2021: 7).

Although Christianity and Islam found their way(s) into Ethiopia in equally earlier periods of their inceptions, their reception and synchronization are by no means similar. While Christianity, particularly the EOTC, shaped and provided all the necessary spiritual, moral, legal, and most importantly, cultural and national identity for what came to be Abyssinia and/or Ethiopia, the same thing cannot be said of Islam in Ethiopia. The devolution of essentially a Christian political and elite structure and culture that had been snowballing through centuries of experimentations and global networks apparently conditioned, in some meaningful ways, the way Islam and Muslims found their places in the country. This constitutes one dimension of what I called elsewhere, the 'Muslims in Ethiopia complex' (Mukerrem 2015).

The 'Muslims in Ethiopia complex' (MIC) entails 'a state of imagination, portrayal, and execution of the task of disentangling Islam and Muslims from Abyssinia and/or Ethiopia and the resulting intended sociocultural, economic, and political consequences' (Mukerrem 2015: 74). It expresses itself in three fundamental ways. In the sphere of politics, the MIC 'functioned as policy and praxis of many of the ruling elites throughout Abyssinian and/or Ethiopian history. It was used and applied by many of the kings and state elites in their hand-to-hand and ideological combat against Islam and Muslims' (Mukerrem 2015: 79). In the sphere of education and research, MIC represents a variant of knowledge production under 'Ethiopian Studies', involving Ethiopian and foreign academics, that claim to study Ethiopia's history, culture and society. Here, MIC is a discourse by academics that have 'created, in their discourses and narratives, an over essentialized, homogenous, and "thousands years old" intact culture and society that has disentangled, partly or completely, aspects of an equally important body of history, culture, and society' (Mukerrem 2015: 73). In the sphere of social psychology, MIC signifies 'the actual socioeconomic and political condition of Muslims and the associated low self-perception and alienation' facilitated and sustained by the politics and education of estrangement (Mukerrem 2015: 81). This is the social psychology of being 'Muslims in Ethiopia'. Yet, it should be noted that the three spheres of the MIC are not necessarily mutually exclusive but interact in a number of ways and possibly involving other aspects as well.

Now, the (LOVBH) movement must be understood in light of these circumstances. The LOVBH movement, aka *dimtsachin Yissema* (Amharic version), is a social movement that has precisely revolted against and resisted what it perceived as an imminent threat to Islam and Muslims of Ethiopia. It is a collective and organized force directed against what I have described above as the MIC, particularly the dimensions of policies and politics of the Ethiopian state. Accordingly, in the following sections, this chapter provides a brief snapshot of the LOVBH movement and asks if the movement has achieved its goals. The chapter primarily draws from published articles, books, web sources, personal observations and unstructured interviews with relevant insiders from the LOVBH movement. The primary data have been collected based on interviews with some leading figures of the Ethiopian Muslims' Solution Finding Committee (EMSFC) who led the LOVBH movement and other vocal activists of the movement. Research participants were accessed through snowball sampling strategy and their responses were analysed thematically. In terms of organization, the upcoming discussion first provides the context and the proceeding parts discuss the relative efficacy of the movement; the challenge it has faced; and, if there is any, the possible future of the movement in Ethiopia.

Contextualizing the LOVBH movement:
Actors, aspirations and strategies

Having introduced the overall theme, this section seeks to summarize issues relating to some of the key actors, aspirations and strategies of the LOVBH movement.

Framing the LOVBH movement

Before discussing the nature and characteristic features of the LOVBH movement, there is need for an overarching frame of reference with a relatively nuanced and intelligibly meaningful foundation. A review of pertinent literature on the LOVBH movement reveals that there is a general tendency to spatiotemporally and substantively confine the movement and reduce it to a particular reaction to incidental and/or accidental phenomenon induced from inside and/or outside Ethiopia. Temporally, some approached the movement as a recent phenomenon, mainly developed out of the early-twentieth-century Ethiopia, initially spearheaded by some distinct Muslims of foreign exposure that eventually culminated in the three major questions that framed the LOVBH movement in the twenty-first century. Among others, the works of the Norwegian Terje Østebø (2013; 2014) and others such as Jon Abbink (see, for example, 2014) are relevant. Substantively, this perspective tends to reduce the movement to be a social movement that grew out of intra- and interreligious dynamics in Ethiopia. In terms of intrareligious dynamics, the movement has been approached as the Wahabi's reaction to Ahbash intervention (see Abdurahman 2020). In terms of interreligious dynamics, Hagai Erlich had always believed in the theologically grounded aversion of Islam and Muslims against Christianity, and what he called 'Christian Ethiopia' (2007; 2009; 2010; Mukerrem 2015). In terms of the nature of the movement, there is a tendency to approach the LOVBH movement as a reactionary movement against the backdrop of the regional and global war on terrorism in the world in general and the Horn of Africa in particular. To be fair, it should be made clear that although either of the above three features arguably and typically characterize the works under this perspective, many of them, in some proportion, engaged these and other dimensions but to a less degree and limited attention.

Now, the important question, then, that will ultimately condition the way one decides to approach the LOVBH movement, is whether the movement 'was' and/ or 'is' part and parcel of the larger Ethiopian Muslims' movement and struggle (among other things, of recognition, participation and ownership), which is relatively as old as the Ethiopian state itself, or as a temporally confined and substantively reactionary movement that took place in the years between 2010 and 2015. The present contribution furthers the view that the LOVBH movement is an extension and manifestation, rather than culmination, of Ethiopian Muslims' deep-rooted quest for recognition, participation and ownership in all spheres of life in Ethiopia.

The LOVBH movement

Since late 2010, a growing sense of uneasiness had been characterizing Ethiopia's religious landscape. Either due to local, regional or global developments or the combination of these three, the Ethiopian government, the now defunct TPLF (Tigray People's Liberation Front)-led EPRDF (Ethiopian People's Revolutionary Democratic Front), regime started to manifestly interfere with the religious affairs of Islam and Muslims in Ethiopia. What exactly informed and triggered the regime's decision to 'contain' Islam and Muslims is largely unclear (Østebø 2013; Mukerrem 2015). There have been, however, some efforts to account for it. By way of summary, some three factors have been generally considered. For one thing, from the perspective of the state, the growing revivalist actions and practices of Muslims in the post-1990s Ethiopia might have signalled a trajectory of negative consequence, including political Islam, extremism and terrorism. The second relates to the collective ventures of the USA's project of the Global War on Terrorism (GWOT) and the TPLF-led EPRDF regime in the Horn of Africa. The regime was a USA-commissioned agent in the fight against political Islam, extremism and terrorism in the Horn of Africa. The third possible explanation concerns, in the eyes of state actors, the growing level of interreligious intolerance and violence, especially between Orthodox Christians and Muslims in some parts of Ethiopia. Yet, we know exactly what the state claimed was its initial justification for its decisions and actions. On April 2012, the late Prime Minister Meles Zenawi told Ethiopia's House of People's Representatives that 'we are observing tell-tale signs of extremism. We should nip this scourge in the bud ... [contain the] peddling ideologies of intolerance' (Reuters, 11 May 2012).

Regardless of the actual factors that underpinned the regime's change of heart, the actions of the state were not warmly welcomed among urban Ethiopian Muslims, and in the course of the movement, Muslims throughout the country. However, what led to the emergence of the LOVBH movement as a protest ought to be appraised as a conglomerate of different instances, experiences and narratives of historically accumulated grievances but with a relatively similar outcome. In other words, what ignited the protest may have well been the regime's move to force the Ethiopia Islamic Affairs Supreme Council (EIASC) in the dismissal of several teachers at the Awoliya College in Addis Ababa. It may have been sparked by the government's decision to 'train' members of EIASC on secularism and tolerance (Abbink 2014). Or, what many believed to be the regime's blatant support for 'Al-Ahbash' and forcing religious leaders as mosques Imams and members of EIASC to go through Ahbash, 'tolerant Islam' induction (Østebø 2013; Abbink 2014; Mukerrem 2015). Supporting this last point, the US State Department also documented that 'the Ministry of Federal Affairs, working with the EIASC and other civil society groups, sponsored workshops and training of religious leaders, elders, and influential community members in what it said was an attempt to address *the potential for sectarian violence*' (Italics mine, IRFR, 2015).

In the years between 2011 and 2015, the LOVBH protest clearly articulated its modus operandi and remained relatively committed to its initial aspirations throughout the period of the protest. The protest was held regularly on Fridays, immediately after the Friday prayer in-and-around mosques, first, in Addis Ababa, and later, as the protest expanded and evolved, in the different parts of Ethiopia. Anchored around three specific questions (but with far-reaching ramifications and consequences), the protest started to gain momentum in terms of effectively and efficiently channelling protesters' anger with the TPLF-led EPRDF regime in its dealing with Islam and Muslims. For instance, there was a mass demonstration on 20 April 2012 in Addis Ababa that questioned the state's claim for a neutral and secular position and its meddling in the affairs of Muslim leaders of EIASC. In the subsequent demonstrations and protests, the most commonly voiced slogans included '*mengest bemuslimoch guday talqa aygba*' (Amharic, government shall not interfere in the affairs of Muslims); '*muslimoch ande nen aneleyayem*' (we Muslims are united and will not be divided); '*Yemuslimoch mebt yikeber*' (Muslims' rights be respected) (Mukerrem 2015: 13); 'We Need Freedom!', 'Hear our Voices!' and 'A Government That Refuses to Take Criticism, Will Not Last long!' (International Religious Freedom Report-IRFR, 2016).

These concerns were meticulously articulated by the Ethiopian Muslims Solution Finding Committee (EMSFC), which came into being at Awoliya College in 2012. This gave the protest and demonstration that was initially led by some influential Muslim activists and religious preachers (*da'eyah*), the chance to organize, and eventually transmuted the movement into a well-organized religious-based social movement. In the subsequent protests and demonstrations, three recurrently voiced demands came to the fore: (1) The EPRDF regime cannot and shall not elect and appoint religious leaders and personnel for EIASC and must not interfere with its operation. Muslims must elect their own religious leaders. (2) The government must adhere to the notion of secularism enshrined in Ethiopia's constitution and cease imposing Al-Ahbash teachings on Ethiopian Muslims. (3) Ethiopia's government must refrain from interfering with the operation and functioning of Awoliya College. An independent Board composed of independent representatives would take the role in the administration of Awoliya College. In other words, the administration and operation of Awoliya College was supposed to be left to Muslim civilians and that the state would not play any role whatsoever unless something unconstitutional or illegal happened.

Through time, the movement was able to effectively utilize social media platforms to get across its messages in the weekly protest in terms of the issues to be raised and the form of protest, including the adoption of specific slogans, banners, certain hand gestures and others. The US Department of State's IRFR (2016) noted that "protestors showed red cards, crossed their arms above the head and carried placards that read 'We Need Freedom!', 'Hear Our Voices!' and 'A Government That Refuses to Take Criticism, Will Not Last long!'" Apart from the internet, weekly magazines like *Yemuslimoch Guday* (Muslims' Affair) played significant roles. Other secular content providers such as the weekly magazine *Feteh* (Justice) also helped cement the idea that the state's actions were largely unjustified and regularly reported on Muslims' protests (Human Rights Watch Report-HRWR 2012, 2013). However, the government's response was rather the opposite and started intensifying its constitutional meddling with the EIASC. Through what it called a 'legitimate' election, the government assigned two individuals as leaders of EIASC who were, in the eyes of the protest organizers, very close to the state and not to the Muslim community. They were Kiyar Mohamed Aman, who was made the new chair of EIASC, and Kedir Mahmoud Aman, his deputy. The former was a secretary at the Ethiopian Embassy in Riyadh while the latter was a close affiliate of the Tigray People's Liberation Front (TPLF) (Abbink 2014: 355).

As the LOVBH movement expanded in terms of its organizational complexity and geographical coverage, both locally in Ethiopia and abroad, the mounting pressure on the TPLF-led EPRDF regime had been predictably unbearable and thus needed a response of some sort. Consequently, the regime moved its actions from a soft rhetorically and discursively tailored polemical and political approach to a visibly harsh and violent means to curb the growing Muslims' discontent. This included shooting and imprisoning demonstrators and protesters at Ethiopia's various mosques and religious ceremonies (such as '*Eid al-Fitr*', a holy day celebrated at the end of the month of fasting-*Ramadan*) in Addis Ababa's Stadium. Protesters were increasingly hunted, from their houses and mosques, and thrown into Addis Ababa's notorious jails in their hundreds. As Human Rights Watch (HRW) (2012, 2013) observed, 'the security forces responded to protests by the Muslim community in Oromia and Addis Ababa, the capital, with arbitrary arrests, detentions, and beatings'. The same report documented,

> On several occasions in July, federal police used excessive force, including beatings, to disperse largely Muslim protesters opposing the government's interference with the country's Supreme Council of Islamic Affairs. On July 13, police forcibly entered the Awalia mosque in Addis Ababa, smashing windows and firing tear gas inside the mosque. On July 21, they forcibly broke up a sit-in at the mosque. From July 19 to 21, dozens of people were rounded up and 17 prominent leaders were held without charge for over a week. Many of the detainees complained of mistreatment in detention.
>
> (HRW 2012, 2013)

The regime continued its 'excessive' use of force on the protests, arbitrarily detaining and beating protesters, including '29 prominent activists and leaders who were arrested in July 2012 and charged in October 2012 under the Anti-Terrorism Proclamation' (HRW 2014). In February 2013, the regime unsuccessfully doctored a 'documentary' called 'Jihadawi Harakat' (Jihad Movement) and was aired through the state-run Ethiopian Television (ETV) (Mukerrem 2015). This haplessly produced documentary 'included footage of at least five of the defendants filmed in pretrial detention. The program equated the Muslim protest movement with Islamist extremist groups, casting the protest leaders as terrorists' (HRW, 2014). The video included prominent Ethiopian Muslim figures who were also members of the Muslims Solution Finding Committee. Among others, one can see shackled individuals as Abubekir Ahmed, Kamil Shemsu, Nuri Turki and Yasin Nuru providing false testimonies of extremism and Islamic state aspirations in Ethiopia. Interestingly, almost for months after the airing of the documentary, a research was carried out to investigate the audience reception of the documentary. Contrary to the regime's expected propaganda-outcome, the study found out that research participants viewed the documentary as 'less credible and subjects in the documentary film do not represent the overall Muslim society. The audience also found the theme irrelevant to the socio-religious context of the country' (Nigussie 2013: 3).

Elsewhere, I approached the purpose of this documentary as a 'degradation ceremony' (Harold Garfinkle) through which the TPLF-led government intended to undermine the credibility of Ethiopian Muslims' representative committee of the DY [LOVBH] movement and justify its horrendous and erratic actions (Mukerrem 2020: 3–4). Nevertheless, on 3 August 2015, the Ethiopia Federal High Court found a group of eighteen Muslims, known as the 'Arbitration Committee Members' (*aka*, MSFC) who were identified with the 2012 protests, guilty of terrorism under the ATP. On 3 August, the Federal High Court sentenced them to imprisonment ranging from seven to twenty-two years (IRFR, 2016). Overall, throughout the regime's harsh interventions and treatment of Ethiopian Muslims since 2011, the pretext for its decisions and actions against the LOVBH movement was drawn from the regime's restrictive and politically state-serving 'Anti-Terrorism Proclamation' which was adopted in 2009, and its incessant claims for the alleged links of Muslim protesters to the *Al-qa'ida* and *Al-Shabaab* terrorist groups.

Despite the regime's unsubstantiated accusations and allegations, any first-hand observation of the protests of the LOVBH movement in the years between 2010 and 2015 would unequivocally testify that they were thoroughly peaceful and disciplined. In addition to my own personal-direct observation, such foreign researchers and observers as Østebø and Abbink made similar remarks. For instance, unlike the views of Meles Zenawi's administration, Østebø characterized the protests as 'peaceful', 'calm' and 'disciplined' (2014: 172). Abdurahman observed, 'The protest was considered one of the well-disciplined public demonstrations in the history of Ethiopia'. On his part, Jon Abbink concluded, 'The public demonstrations were peaceful' (2014: 354). The State Department report appraised the protest movement as 'peaceful' (IRFR, 2013).

Interrogating the LOVBH movement: Succeeded, failed or suspended?

Some five leading members from the MSFC and other three vocal activists of the LOVBH movement were asked three general questions. The first was about how they assess the relative efficacy of the LOVBH movement and whether it has succeeded in achieving its goals. Many of the respondents agree that the LOVBH movement has achieved its stated goals. According to them, the three major objectives of the movement, which included the suspension of state interference, on the one hand, in the constitution and operation of EIASC and

Awoliya, and on the other, the imposition of Al-Ahbash, were successfully met. However, two of the respondents, from both MSFC and activists, held different views. A leading figure from the MSFC pointed out that the objectives of the LOVBH movement were not solely confined to the above three and asserted,

> The goals of the movement were four. The first was to stop the regime's intervention. The second was to elevate the social psychology of Ethiopian Muslims. The third was to enable the Ethiopian Muslim community internalize the culture of defending and protecting their rights. Finally, the fourth was to enable the Muslim community protect its identity.

This testimony is very important for at least two relevant reasons. For one thing, it makes it clear that the LOVBH movement was not necessarily an incidental movement; rather, it was a social movement that raised and addressed old questions via contemporary vernaculars. Second, like any type of social movement, its aspirations and goals may or may not necessarily, partly or completely, be congruent with the manifestly communicated expectations. Certainly, what the respondent spelled out patently addressed both the three expressions of state-led manipulation of religion and what was explained above under MIC. Though faint but present in the above response are the sociopolitical issues and historical questions of the Ethiopian Muslims.

Responding to the same question, a leading and vocal activist of the LOVBH movement denies that the movement has succeeded in achieving its manifestly stated goals. He explained,

> Manifestly speaking, I cannot say that the movement was entirely successful. Of the three questions, at least the issue of Awoliya has been properly solved, and to some extent, the issue of Al-Ahbash as well. However, the issue with EIASC has not yet been resolved. The place of EIASC in the LOVBH movement has been very fundamental and of vital importance but remain unaddressed. Measured, therefore, by its stated objectives, it has not succeeded.

Although the issue associated with EIASC constituted an integral element and significantly fuelled the actual protest movement, it remains as a serious cause of concern for Ethiopian Muslims. We know that although almost all members of the EMSFC and many activists were released from prison, some efforts were made to elect some provisional facilitators (a committee of nine members) for the expected properly constituted and functioning EIASC, and the transitional government's initially proactive move to help facilitate intrareligious dialogue, achieving a properly constituted and functioning EIASC, remains a challenge. Drawing on my personal observation, almost ten years since the beginning of the protest, EIASC could not stand as an organization that at least garnered the legitimacy it needed in the eyes of the majority of Ethiopian Muslims, the very reason that initially ignited and sustained the protest movement.

It is interesting to observe that research participants held different opinions when it comes to the existing conditions of EIASC. Even though all participants from the MSFC underscored that the LOVBH movement succeeded in attaining its initially spelled-out three objectives, the way they see the overall conditions of EIASC is worth discussing. Two participants from the MSFC and another one activist contend that as one integral part of the LOVBH movement, state interference in the matters of EIASC was successfully contained and stopped. Furthermore, they argued, EIASC was legally recognized as the single Ethiopian Muslims representing institution in Ethiopia under the PM Abiy-led administration. It is true that

> EIASC had been, though the only symbolic representative institution of Muslims' religious affairs in Ethiopia for generations, functioning as another nongovernmental or charity organization and often serving the subsequent governments' interests. This has, however, been changed on Thursday, 11 June 2020. In an unprecedented move in Ethiopian history, a joint meeting that brought Ethiopia's Council of Federation and the House of Peoples Representatives, a decision has been passed approving the draft proclamations set to legalize EIASC with one vote against.
>
> (Mukerrem 2020: 5–6)

I should mention that it was interesting to note (watch live on TV) that the only person who resisted the proclamation to legalize EIASC in Ethiopia's House of Federation was a party member of the TPLF, which had been EPRDF's core for about three decades, and which had been, in the eyes of many Muslim protesters, the main instigator that caused all the troubles.

Research participants argue, as the new political order was more 'friendly' and keen to work with, partly because Muslims' protest movement had already, in some ways, served as a catalyst to the broader national movement that overthrew the TPLF-led EPRDF regime, Muslims in mitigating the wrongdoings of the previous regime. Furthermore, one of the activists interviewed said, 'The state even went to the extent of offering to issue separate certificates to members of the Muslim community who, in their own ways, were unable to forge unity and make an all-inclusive EIASC possible.'

From the above testimonies, one important theme that emerges is whether the issue of EIASC should be treated as marking the LOVBH movement's honeymoon periods. For many of the respondents, the issue of EIASC was a chapter effectively closed alongside with the last regime. For others, since EIASC is not yet properly constituted and received the necessary acceptance from the majority of Muslims, it will likely continue as a challenge in the context of the broader Muslims' quest for recognition, participation and ownership in Ethiopia if not necessarily in the context of LOVBH movement. Accordingly, almost all respondents, including one activist, from the MSFC viewed the issue of EIASC as an internal challenge rather than an external one from the state and this may or may not be solved any time soon. This will be detailed in the next heading under the 'Challenges' of the LOVBH.

Except for the aforementioned points of contention, all the research participants, activists as well as members of the MSFC shared the view that the LOVBH movement succeeded in many domains, intended or not. That is, viewing the LOVBH movement as part and parcel of the larger Ethiopian Muslims' movement, many things positive were achieved. A thematic analysis reveals three major categories: intrareligious, interreligious and extra-religious outcomes. First, in the sphere of extra-religious outcomes, the LOVBH movement has redefined the nature of state-society relations, particularly between the Ethiopian Muslims and the Ethiopian government. Owing to the effectiveness of the LOVBH movement, respondents claim, the TPLF-led EPRDF regime failed to malign Ethiopian Muslims and it has shown to the world that a protest movement can be disciplined, peaceful and successful at the same time. As a result, the regime was successfully prevented from escalating and causing serious harms and damages to the Ethiopian Muslim community.

Second, in the sphere of intrareligious outcomes, the LOVBH movement as part of the larger Ethiopian Muslims' movement was able to empower the Ethiopian Muslim community in asking and finding solutions to problems threatening its rights. In terms of social psychology, the LOVBH movement made many Muslim Ethiopians active citizens and nurtured a sense of ownership. Besides, unlike the views of some observers and elites of the previous regime, the LOVBH movement was not an elite-centric movement that they could just simply silence and squash by cutting its heads. On the contrary, being mass-based social movement, despite all odds, the protest movement continued mounting even more pressure on the regime. Furthermore, the LOVBH movement proved that, in the face of a collective threat, Ethiopian Muslims could stand together, struggle thoroughly and achieve their meaningful and legal aspirations. Third, in the sphere of interreligious outcomes, the movement facilitated conditions that made non-Muslims and Ethiopian Muslim sceptics to stop and question their positions and ideas about Ethiopian Muslims and their demands. Despite these and other intended and unintended consequences of the LOVBH movement, it was not without challenges.

The LOVBH movement and its challenges

The second general question concerns if the LOVBH movement had faced any challenges. The reactions of the respondents can be divided into two. On the one hand, there were those challenges that had been faced during the planning and implementation of protests and demonstration, and on the other, there have been challenges since the TPLF-led EPRDF regime was overthrown from power in Ethiopia. In the context of the former, research participants include logistical, human resource-related, financial and state-doctored (accusations) challenges that had negatively affected the LOVBH movement. One prominent respondent from the EMSFC explained,

> There were financial constraints, the difficulty of coordinating local and overseas teams and their actions. For instance, as anyone can imagine, to work with about 200 mosque-based teams locally, publishing thousands of pamphlets, planning the *sadaqah* (religious feast programs) and others were very difficult if not impossible as all these activities were successfully carried out.

Another respondent from the EMSFC observed that following the discharge of some members of the EMSFC from prison, there were few instances of misdeeds and misconducts. Furthermore, there were growing instances of mistrust and lack of consensus. This, according to him, went to the extent that 'some acted as if it was their voice was to be only heard, not the views of others in directing the LOVBH movement. This had left lasting negative consequences.' Apart from these, the LOVBH movement had to effectively manage and address the TPLF-led regime's consistent attempt to doctor enmity between Ethiopian Muslims and Orthodox Christians. A respondent from the EMSFC pointed out that, quite contrary to the ill-intentioned moves of the regime, interreligious interactions were more positive and encouraging. At times, some members of the Orthodox faith were actually supporting the protests.

There have also been fears that since the regime was intensifying its crackdown on Muslims, leaders of the LOVBH movement had to size-down activities, an activist explained. This was, he explained, partly because out of the fear of state's increasingly pursued mass arrests and killings of Muslim protests. He observed that there was also growing dissatisfaction with the LOVBH movement. As the years go by, the nature, scope and strategies of the LOVBH movement were relatively becoming the same and redundant and to expect different outcomes was another major challenge.

The challenges that have faced the LOVBH in the aftermath of the overthrow of the TPLF-led EPRDF regime are two in nature, according to research participants. The first concerns problems closely associated with some members of the EMSFC and other Ethiopian Muslim religious leaders. A respondent from the EMSFC elaborated,

> Although the LOVBH movement had largely succeeded in the first level of the movement, it could not move beyond that. Many were unable to propose what needs to be done next, when, where, and how. Unfortunately, the condition has prematurely aborted the possible transition to another level.

The other major challenge shared among all the research participants was the growing discordance among religious scholars. This has a lot to do with the ongoing incongruence between what came to be called the 'Sufi' and 'Salafi' discordance in virtually all matters that concern the constitution and operation of the EIASC. In a research report published in 2020, I argued for the possible state-level intervention in religious affairs, even after the TPLF-led EPRDF regime was overthrown (Mukerrem 2020). There have been signs of state-led attempts to 'upgrade' religion in Ethiopia's newly constituted public sphere under Prime Minister Abiy Ahmed. Among others, the state may have well been behind in 'enclaving' parts of the Muslim community which it viewed as intolerant 'Wahabi' and 'Salafi' groups while 'befriending' others whom it considered tolerant 'Sufi' groups. Measured by consequences, therefore, the government at the time of writing's position cannot be viewed as fundamentally different from the previous regime.

The future of the LOVBH movement

In response to the third question that asked whether the LOVBH movement has any future whatsoever, research participants' views were two in nature. The first is the view that since most of the LOVBH movement's concerns were addressed, the 'next phase' is to move from internal obsession to national socioeconomic and sociopolitical issues. A prominent figure from the EMSFC explained, 'The focus is now national participation in the social, economic and political participation in the country. In the sphere of the economy, the recent interest-free banking is one good forward step in this direction.' He thinks that there are expectations from the Muslim community for national-level participation in the different spheres of life in Ethiopia.

The second view of the future of the LOVBH movement is that since the LOVBH movement was unable to make a meaningful and strategic transition, the future may appear to be gloomy for the movement. Another prominent figure from the LOVBH movement said, there have been instances of mistrust among the former members of EMSFC and less interest in discussing and charting out ways to revive and transition the movement into another level. Quite similar to this is the view of a vocal activist for the LOVBH movement. He also thinks,

> The movement does not necessarily have any future, and as it stands, the movement appears dormant and no one can definitely claim the direction and possible future of the LOVBH movement. I think, the movement is at best in the state of dormancy, and for many others, it looks rather like a concluded chapter. It's unlikely that it can rekindle again.

Regardless of the two possible scenarios for the possible future trajectory of the LOVBH movement, there is one cautionary pessimism that surrounds the spillover effects of the ongoing rhetorical conflict in the contexts of EIASC. One of the activists interviewed explained that the increasingly worrying divisive rhetoric and disunity among Ethiopian Muslim religious leaders and scholars is directly putting the unity of the Muslim community in far greater danger. According to him, such kind of experience was 'unique and never even witnessed when the TPLF-led EPRDF regime was ruling the country harshly. The danger of community-level division is happening and it makes me worry a lot.' Far more even worse is, he added, 'some of the religious preachers are now advocating for a divided EIASC since unity is becoming a scarce commodity'. He thinks, two EIASC(s) mean two prayer arrangements in two different mosques, two religious-based burial arrangements, two contending religious actors and forces, and many other things. He continued, this is, however, very unfortunate as Ethiopian Muslims, unlike many deeply divided Muslim-majority countries along the lines of Shi'a and Sunni, never had such an experience before. He thinks, if the ultimate outcome of any institution and/or movement is social division, it has to be stopped and rejected. Muslims can preserve their collective unity without the necessary presence and functioning of EIASC. Mosques can play many roles.

A concluding remark

The chapter explored the existing conditions, challenges and possible future of the LOVBH movement. One important aspect of the discussion has been finding out whether the LOVBH moment was a detached and temporally recent phenomenon. Although there appears to be some indications that the LOVBH movement could not move beyond what it had initially set out to accomplish, the data from the primary research confirms the idea that the movement was part and parcel of the larger historical Muslims' movement in Ethiopia. In fact, respondents who appraised the LOVBH movement in terms of success and failure make mention of 'transition' going in the right or wrong direction. The former being the LOVBH movement succeeding in the three initial questions and now the focus of the movement, the Muslims' historical movement, has assumed national character. In the context of the latter, respondents think the LOVBH movement has either failed, is in a state of dormancy or aborted, but the normative frame of reference remains the larger historical Ethiopian Muslims' movement.

When it comes to the relative efficacy of the LOVBH movement, some of the research participants doubted that the movement has succeeded in toto. Certainly, there is a credible concern that the EIASC remains a major challenge for the Ethiopian Muslim community. Although the issue of whether the EIASC was under state encroachment under the previous regime in terms of its operation and constitution or the imposition of Al-Ahbash through it is a moot one, a relatively well-functioning and representative EIASC remains a challenge. This credibly casts a shadow of doubt on the success of the LOVBH movement. There have also been challenges that, both during actual protest movement period and after the TPLF-led EPRDF regime was ousted from power, negatively affected the LOVBH movement. Regardless of the source of the problem, some of the challenges continue affecting the Muslim community. Among others, the concern that religious elite-centred ambiguities and discordance from within may, as pessimistically articulated in the primary data, translate into a source of conflict among Muslim lay believers.

Finally, although none of the respondents alluded to the possible role of Ethiopia's transitional as well as elected government of Abiy Ahmed in the problematic conditions of the EIASC and intrareligious dynamics, it may not necessarily be a far-fetched position to maintain a sceptical view of the state. As Bryan Turner (2007) argues, it has always been the prerogative of the modern state to engage religion in some ways. In an earlier contribution, the present author observed that state-religion interaction has moved from 'containment' or 'enclaving' under the TPLF-led EPRDF regime to 'upgrading' religions under the present administration. The point, however, is the same: the state, in some ways, continues to engage religion and this may hamper the proper functioning of institutions affiliated with the latter.

Notes

Chapter 1

1 Hausa and Fulani are two distinct groups, with the Fulani being historically a dominant minority and Hausa a dominant majority (Osaghae 1998). The two are compounded and often referred to together as Hausa-Fulani because of the high level of integration between them and their intertwining histories and religion in the Nigerian context.

2 Government responded to this particular concern by also sponsoring some Christians to Israel every year for religious pilgrimage.

Chapter 2

1 The Islamic religion is often said to promote the subservience of women. We share Akbar Ahmed's position here of the need to pay attention to contexts. For him, 'there is a clear correlation between the treatment of women and Muslim self-perception, which bears upon the position of women in Islam. When Muslim society is confident and in a state of balance, it treats women with fairness and respect. When Muslim society is threatened and feels vulnerable it treats women with indifference and even harshness' (Ahmed 2003: 115–16).

Chapter 4

1 The Hausa people are one of the major ethnic groups in West Africa. They live mainly between the Niger River and Lake Chad with significant populations in Nigeria and Niger and smaller ones in other countries such as Ghana, Cameroon, Sudan, Gabon, the Ivory Coast, Chad, Senegal and Togo-speaking Hausa, a language of the Chadic group and the dominant lingua franca in West Africa. They have a majority Muslim population.

2 For literature on Hausa women, see Coles, Catherine and Beverly Mack, eds. 1991. *Hausa Women in the Twentieth Century*. Madison: University of Wisconsin

Press; Callaway, Barbara and Lucy Creevy. 1994. *The Heritage of Islam: Women, Religion, and Politics in West Africa*. Boulder: Lynne Rienner; Callaway, Barbara. 1987. *Muslim Hausa Women in Nigeria*. Syracuse: Syracuse University Press; Callaway, J. Barbara. 1984. 'Ambiguous Consequences of the Socialisation and Seclusion of Hausa Women,' *The Journal of Modern African Studies* 22(3), 429–50.

3 See, for instance, the Global Gender Gap Report 2021 by the World Economic Forum. http://www3.weforum.org/docs/WEF_GGGR_2021.pdf and the Global Gender Gap Index by World Bank.

4 SLS has written on various topics such as Muslim women and Shari'a, women and political leadership, Muslim family law, punishments under Islamic law (hudud), democracy and religious discrimination. Some of these works were published as newspaper articles, while others were presented at national and international seminars and conferences. See www.gamji.com/sanusi.htm for some of his works. The citations in this chapter are derived from these sources.

5 For intersectionality in Feminist Theory, see Carastathis (2014) and Crenshaw (1991).

Chapter 6

1 The Parliament of Tanzania Reports, 2005–17.
2 The Parliament of Tanzania, 2017.
3 Ministry of Health, Community Development, Gender, Elderly and Children 11 May 2017.
4 PO –RALG, April 2017.

Chapter 7

1 Zwane, B. 2018. Gender links for Equality News Services. http://genderlinks.org.za/news/swaziland-only-14-women-in-secondary-elections-race/
2 Nyawo, S. and Mkhonta, P. (2016) have conducted a study on *Reflections on Women's Political Participation and Representation in the Post Constitutional Era (2005–2015)*.
3 Human Rights Education and Monitoring Center (EMC). 2014. Women and Political Representation Handbook on Increasing Women's Political Participation in Georgia, Tbilisi.

Chapter 8

1   One of the researchers has a sister who is a nurse in the area. She studied how the male leaders got the medicines from the sister in charge at the local clinic. Likewise, the women would also come to take contraceptive pills in private, and the sister in charge did not alert any of the men or women. The conclusion of this is that members do not live up to their claims of the power of healing water since they secretly resort to Western medicine. Also, this shows the deficiency of the claims of healing water to modern diseases.

2   *Interview, Munyori*, (title) Mukubva sect, conducted in Chavhanga, Mukubva sub-group, 4 August 2012. He said that he did not want his name to appear in the chapter since the questions one of the authors asked him were very sensitive. He also said the names of the men and women who had been caught by the prophets at *gedhe romweya* should not be publicized. *Munyori*, however, highlighted that the *gedhe romweya* is very important in weeding out the unscrupulous and the unholy.

Chapter 10

1   One of the authors of this chapter (Chisale) is directing a project titled *Gender-Based Violence among Women and Girls with Disabilities in Relation to Sustainable Development Goals in South Africa*.

Chapter 11

1   It should be noted, however, that in this study we include those between twenty-seven and thirty-five as part of the cohort, as the majority were still quite young when the new democratic dispensation was inaugurated.

2   It should be noted that the study focused on the town of Stellenbosch and not the entire Stellenbosch municipality, which includes other smaller towns.

3   The notion of race is not to be understood in an essentialist manner in this study. Hammet points out that race identity remains fluid, with both the 'reification or erasure of racial identities' continuing to take place among population groups and social and political structures in South Africa (Hammett 2010: 247–8). The notion of race identification remains contested and complex in South Africa (Boesak et al. 2015: 157–70). In reality there is no racial category that could adequately contain the complexity of human identities (Hammett 2010: 247). The three dominant descriptors are 'so-called Coloured', Black and white. At times, race is identified

and described in relation to a community of reference. For example, in relation to family and friends a person may self-identify as coloured, while in a political setting the same persons may self-identify as Black so as not to be excluded from the political solidarity of redressing the racial legacies of apartheid (Adhikari 2005: 98–130; Hammett 2010: 247–60; Goldin 2014: 156–80). The Broad-Based Black Economic Empowerment Act 53 of 2003 as Amended by Act No 46 of 2013 in South Africa uses the term 'Black people' as a generic term to refer to 'Africans, Coloureds and Indians'. The Black Consciousness movement in South Africa employed the term Black inclusively in order to raise consciousness around Black experience and Black identity, but also to subvert the essentialist and divisive intentions of Apartheid era race classifications.

4 This denotes a 'phenotypically varied social group of highly diverse social and geographical origins' whose heritage includes slaves from African and Asian origin, the indigenous Khoi and San populations and various European settlers. The term itself was a creation of the Apartheid state and so, as noted in the previous footnote, itself remains contested.

5 This is a software data analysis tool for qualitative data analysis.

6 Cf. Gebrekidan and Onishi (2019) for a discussion on the land grabs, which took place in 2018 on one of the farms close to Kayamandi.

Chapter 13

1 During apartheid, South Africa was divided according to race and the colour of skin. The four main racial categories include Black, white, coloured and Indian. Access to economic opportunities depended on the race of an individual, with white people at the forefront of such opportunities.

2 The statistics were taken from the annual Statistics South Africa for 2019.

References

Introduction

Agbiji, Obaji M. and Ignatius Swart. 2015. 'Religion and Social Transformation in Africa.' *Scriptura* 114, 1–20.

Ajide, Kazeem B. et al. 2019. Ethnic Diversity and Inequality in Sub-Saharan Africa: Do Institutions Reduce the Noise? African Governance and Development Institute Research Department WP/19/018.

Alcorta, Ludovico et al. 2018. 'Inequality and Ethnic Conflict in Sub-Saharan Africa.' *Social Forces* 97(2), 769–92.

Alesina, Alberto et al. 2020. 'Religion and Educational Mobility in Africa.' National Bureau of Economic Research Working Paper 28270. https://www.nber.org/papers/w28270, accessed 22 April 2022.

Alesina, Alberto et al. 2021. 'Intergenerational Mobility in Africa.' *Econometrica* 89(1), 1–35.

Álvarez, María J. 2016. 'An Interview with Göran Therborn.' *Revista de Estudios Sociales* 57, 118–21.

Appau, Samuelson and Matthew G. Mabefam. 2020. 'Prosperity for the Poor: Religion, Poverty and Development in Sub-Saharan Africa,' in Sefa Awaworyi Churchill, ed., *Moving from the Millennium to the Sustainable Development Goals: Lessons and Recommendations*. Singapore: Palgrave Macmillan, 243–65.

Basedau, Matthias. 2017. 'The Rise of Religious Armed Conflicts in Sub-Saharan Africa: No Simple Answers,' *GIGA Focus Africa*, April 2017.

Basedau, Matthias and Johanna Schaefer-Kehnert. 2019. 'Religious Discrimination and Religious Armed Conflict in Sub-Saharan Africa: An Obvious Relationship?' *Religion, State and Society* 47(1), 30–47. DOI: 10.1080/09637494.2018.1531617

Beyers, Jaco. 2014. 'The Effect of Religion on Poverty.' *HTS Teologiese Studies/Theological Studies* 70(1), Art. #2614, 8 pages. http://dx.doi.org/10.4102/hts.v70i1.2614

Bourdillon, Michael F. C. 1990. *Religion and Society: A Text for Africa*. Gweru: Mambo Press.

Brackney, William H. and Reuben Das. Eds. 2019. *Poverty and the Poor in the World's Religious Traditions: Religious Responses to the Problem of Poverty*. San Francisco: ABC-CLIO, LLC.

Burton, Bonnie. 2020. 'NASA Set to Launch New $23 Million Space Toilet to the ISS Friday Night,' October 20. https://www.cnet.com/news/nasa-set-to-launch-new-23-million-space-toilet-to-the-iss-friday-night/, accessed 4 October 2020.

Chancel, Lucas et al. 2019. 'How Large Are African Inequalities? Towards Distributional National Accounts in Africa, 1990–2017,' WID.world WORKING PAPER N° 2019/13.

Chitando, Ezra. 2009. *Troubled but Not Destroyed: African Theology in Dialogue with HIV and AIDS*. Geneva: World Council of Churches.

Chitando, Ezra and Adriaan Van Klinken. Eds. 2016. *Christianity and Controversies over Homosexuality in Africa*. London: Routledge.

Chitando, Ezra, Masiiwa R. Gunda and Lovemore Togarasei. Eds. 2020. *Religion and Development in Africa*. Bamberg: University of Bamberg Press.

Christiansen, Christian O. and Steven L. B. Jensen. Eds. 2019. *Histories of Global Inequalities: New Perspectives*. Cham: Palgrave Macmillan.

Cohn-Sherbok, Dan. Ed. 1992. *World Religions and Human Liberation*. Maryknoll, NY: Orbis Books.

Comstock, W. Richard. 1984. 'Toward Open Definitions of Religion.' *Journal of the American Academy of Religion* 52(3), 499–517.

Cox, James L. 1994. 'Religious Studies by the Religious: A Discussion of the Relationship between Theology and the Science of Religion.' *Journal for the Study of Religion* 7(2), 3–31.

Darity, William and Jessica G. Nembhard. 2000. 'Racial and Ethnic Inequality: The International Record.' *American Economic Review* 90(2), 308–11.

De La Torre, Miguel A. Ed. 2008. *The Hope for Liberation in World Religions*. Waco, TX: Baylor University Press.

Dickie, June. 2018. 'African Youth Engage with Psalms of Lament to Find Their Own Voice of Lament.' *Journal of Theology for Southern Africa* 160, 4–20.

Grusky, David B. and Szonja Szelényi. Eds. 2018. *The Inequality Reader: Contemporary and Foundational Readings in Race, Class, and Gender*. New York: Routledge.

The Guardian. 20 May 2020. 'Black Americans Dying of Covid-19 at Three Times the Rate of White People.' https://www.theguardian.com/world/2020/may/20/black-americans-death-rate-covid-19-coronavirus, accessed 29 May 2020.

The Guardian. 25 May 2020. 'Six in 10 UK Health Workers Killed by Covid-19 Are BAME,' https://www.theguardian.com/world/2020/may/25/six-in-10-uk-health-workers-killed-by-covid-19-are-bame, accessed 29 May 2020.

Islam, S. Nazrul and John Winkel. 2017. 'Climate Change and Social Inequality,' DESA Working Paper No. 152; ST/ESA/2017/DWP/152.

Jelen, Ted G. Ed. 2002. *Sacred Markets, Sacred Canopies: Essays on Religious Markets and Religious Pluralism*. Lanham: Rowman & Littlefield.

Johnston, David C. Ed. 2014. *Divided: The Perils of Our Growing Inequality*. New York: The New Press.

Jordan, Jason. 2016. 'Religion and Inequality: The Lasting Impact of Religious Traditions and Institutions on Welfare State Development.' *European Political Science Review* 8(1), 25–48.

Kabue, Samuel, James Amanze and Christina Landman. Eds. 2016. *Disability in Africa: Resource Book for Theology and Religious Studies*. Nairobi: Acton.

Keister, Lisa A. and David Eagle. 2014. 'Religion and Inequality: The Role of Status Attainment and Social Balance Processes.' *Social Thought & Research* 33, 141–71.

Keister, Lisa A. and Darren E. Sherkat. 2014. *Religion and Inequality in America: Research and Theory on Religion's Role in Stratification.* Cambridge: Cambridge University Press.

Kim, Dai-Won, Yung-Suk Yu and M. Kabir Hassan. 2020. 'The Influence of Religion and Social Inequality on Financial Inclusion.' *The Singapore Economic Review* 65(1), 193–216.

Klingorová, Kamila and T. Tomáš Havlíček. 2015. 'Religion and Gender Inequality: The Status of Women in the Societies of World Religions.' *Moravian Geographical Reports* 23(2), 2–11.

Llewellyn, Dawn and Sonya Sharma. 2016. *Religion, Equalities, and Inequalities.* London: Routledge.

Manglos-Weber, Nicolette D. 2017. 'Identity, Inequality, and Legitimacy: Religious Differences in Primary School Completion in Sub-Saharan Africa.' *Journal for the Scientific Study of Religion* 56(2), 302–22.

Mapuranga, Tapiwa P. Ed. 2018. *Powered by Faith: Pentecostal Businesswomen in Harare.* Eugene, OR: Resource Publications.

Massey, James. 1995. *Dalits in India: Religion as a Source of Bondage or Liberation with Special Reference of Christians.* Delhi: Manohar.

Messer, Donald E. 2010. *Names, Not Just Numbers: Facing AIDS and Global Hunger.* Golden, CO: Speaker's Corner Book.

McCleary, Rachel M. and Robert J. Barrow. 2018. *The Wealth of Religions: The Political Economy of Believing and Belonging.* Princeton: Princeton University Press.

Mosher, Lucinda. Ed. 2021. *A World of Inequalities: Christian and Muslim Perspectives: A Record of the Seventeenth Building Bridges Seminar.* Washington, DC: Georgetown University Press.

Mukharjee, Shantanu et al. 2017. 'Inequality, Gender and Human Development in Africa,' in Ayadole Adusola et al., eds., *Income Inequality Trends in Sub-Saharan Africa: Divergence, Determinants and Consequences.* New York: UNDP, 245–66.

Murrell, Nathaniel S., William D. Spencer and Adrian A. McFarlane. Eds. 1998. *Chanting Down Babylon: A Rastafari Reader.* Philadelphia: Temple University Press.

Navarro, Jose and Vegard Skirbekk. 2018. 'Income Inequality and Religion Globally 1970–2050.' *Scripta Instituti Donneriani Aboensis* 28, 175–99. DOI: 10.30674/scripta.70072

Nel, Philip. 2021. 'Why Africans Tolerate Income Inequality.' *The Journal of Modern African Studies* 59(3), 343–65. DOI: https://doi.org/10.1017/S0022278X21000161

Oduyoye, Mercy A. 2019. *Re-membering Me: The Memoirs of Mercy Amba Oduyoye.* Ibadan: Sefer.

Offutt, Stephen et al. 2016. 'Religion, Poverty, and Development.' *Journal for the Scientific Study of Religion* 55(2), 207–15.

Ogbonnaya, Joseph. 2012. 'Religion and Sustainable Development in Africa: The Case of Nigeria.' *International Journal of African Catholicism* 3(2), 1–22.

Öhlmann, Phillip, Wilhelm Gräb and Marie-Luise Frost. Eds. 2020. *African Initiated Christianity and the Decolonisation of Development: Sustainable Development in Pentecostal and Independent Churches.* London: Routledge.

Oloruntoba, Samuel O. and Toyin Falola. Eds. 2018. *The Palgrave Handbook of African Politics, Governance and Development.* New York: Palgrave Macmillan.

Orobator, Agbonkhianmeghe E. 2018. *Religion and Faith in Africa: Confessions of an Animist.* Maryknoll, NY: Orbis Books.

Oxfam. 2019. 'Public Good or Private Wealth?' Oxford: Oxfam GB.

Perry, Brea, Brian Aronson and Bernice A. Pescosolido. 2021. Pandemic Precarity: COVID-19 Is Exposing and Exacerbating Inequalities in the American Heartland. *Proceedings of the National Academy of Sciences.* https://doi.org/10.1073/pnas.2020685118

Paris, Peter J., Ed. 2009. *Religion and Poverty: Pan-African Perspectives.* Durham, NC: Duke University Press.

Pew Forum on Religion & Public Life. 2010. *Tolerance and Tension: Islam and Christianity in Sub-Saharan Africa.* Washington, DC: The Pew Research Center.

Peterson, E. Wesley F. 2017. 'Is Economic Inequality Really a Problem? Review of the Arguments.' *Social Sciences* 6(147), 1–25.

Pinilla-Roncancio, Mónica. 2015. 'Disability and Poverty: Two Related Conditions. A Review of the Literature.' *Revista de la Facultad de Medicina* 63(Supl. 1), 113–23.

Rajkumar, Peniel. 2010. *Dalit Theology and Dalit Liberation Problems, Paradigms and Possibilities.* Farnham: Ashgate.

Ramutsindela, Maano and David Mickler. Eds. 2020. *Africa and the Sustainable Development Goals.* Cham: Springer Nature.

Religions. 2018. Special Issue. 'Growing Apart: Religious Reflection on the Rise of Economic Inequality.' 8:4.

Schweiger, Gottfried. 2019. 'Religion and Poverty.' *Palgrave Communication* 5(59). https://doi.org/10.1057/s41599-019-0272-3

Sharma, Arvind and Katherine K. Young. Eds. 2007. *Fundamentalism and Women in World Religions.* New York: T & T Clark.

Sibanda, Fortune. 2017. 'Praying for Rain? A Rastafari Perspective from Zimbabwe.' *The Ecumenical Review* 69(3), 411–24.

Smart, Ninian. 1996. *Dimensions of the Sacred: An Anatomy of the World's Beliefs.* New York: HarperCollins.

Smith, Brian K. 1987. 'Exorcising the Transcendent: Strategies for Defining Hinduism and Religion.' *History of Religions* 27(1), 32–55.

Smith, Christian and Robert Faris. 2005. 'Socioeconomic Inequality in the American Religious System: An Update and Assessment.' *Journal for the Scientific Study of Religion* 44(1), 95–104.

Soares, Judith. 2008. 'Religion and Poverty in the Caribbean.' *Peace Review: A Journal of Social Science* 20(2), 226–34.

Social Inclusion. 2018. 'Complex Religion: Intersections of Religion and Inequality.' 6(2).

Soudien, Craig et al. 2019. 'South Africa 2018: The State of the Discussion on Poverty and Inequality,' in Craig Soudien et al., eds., *Poverty & Inequality: Diagnosis, Prognosis, Responses. State of the Nation*. Cape Town: HSRC Press, 1–28.

South African Journal of Economics. 2019. Special issue. 'Inequalities in the Least Developed Countries – Some Lessons from Africa.' 87(2), 85–252.

Stark, Rodney, Laurence Iannaccone and Roger Finke. 1996. 'Linkages between Economics and Religion.' *American Economic Review* 86(2), 433–7.

Tarusarira, Joram. 2017. 'African Religion, Climate Change, and Knowledge Systems.' *The Ecumenical Review* 69(3), 398–410.

Tarusarira, Joram and Ezra Chitando. Eds. 2020. *Themes in Religion and Human Security in Africa*. London: Routledge.

Therbon, Göran. 2013. *The Killing Fields of Inequality*. Cambridge: Polity Press.

Togarasei, Lovemore, David Bishau and Ezra Chitando. Eds. 2020. *Religion and Social Marginalisation in Zimbabwe*. Bamberg: University of Bamberg Press.

Togarasei, Lovemore and Joachim Kügler. Eds. 2014. *The Bible and Children in Africa*. Bamberg: University of Bamberg Press.

Tomalin, Emma. 2018. 'Religions, Poverty Reduction and Global Development Institutions.' *Palgrave Communications* 4(132). https://doi.org/10.1057/s41599-018-0167-8

Tomalin, Emma. Ed. 2015. *The Routledge Handbook of Religions and Development*. London: Routledge.

Tsikata, Dzodzi. 2015. 'Understanding and Addressing Inequalities in the Context of Structural Transformation in Africa: A Synthesis of Seven Country Studies.' *Development* 58(2–3), 206–29.

UN 2020. World Social Report 2020. *Inequality in a Rapidly Changing World*. New York: United Nations, Department of Economic and Social Affairs.

UNAIDS 2020. 'UNAIDS Calls for Increase in Health Spending and Social Protection as an Essential Part of the Economic Response to COVID-19.' https://www. unaids.org/en/resources/presscentre/pressreleaseandstatementarchive/2020/ april/20200417_economic-response-to-covid19press statement, accessed 29 May 2020.

van Kersbergen, Kees and Phillip Manow. Eds. 2009. *Religion, Class Coalitions, and Welfare States*. New York: Cambridge University Press.

Ward, Kate and Kenneth Himes. Eds. 2019. *Growing Apart: Religious Reflection on the Rise of Economic Inequality*. Basel: MDPI.

Wilde, Melissa, Patricia Tevington and Wensong Shen. 2018. 'Religious Inequality in America.' *Social Inclusion* 6(2), 107–26.

Wood, Hannelie J. 2019. 'Gender Inequality: The Problem of Harmful, Patriarchal, Traditional and Cultural Gender Practices in the Church.' *HTS Teologiese Studies/ Theological Studies* 75(1), a5177. https://doi.org/10.4102/hts.v75i1.5177

World Inequality Report. 2018. Paris: World Inequality Lab.

Chapter 1

Adenrele, Adetoro Rasheed. 2012. 'Boko Haram Insurgency in Nigeria as a Symptom of Poverty and Political Alienation.' *IOSR Journal of Humanities and Social Science* 3(5), 21–6.

Aghedo, Iro and Surulola James Eke. 2013. 'From Alms to Arms: The Almajiri Phenomenon and Internal Security in Northern Nigeria.' *The Korean Journal of Policy Studies* 28(3), 97–123.

Ajayi, A. I. 1990. '"Boko Haram" and Terrorism in Nigeria: Exploratory and Explanatory Notes.' *Defense & Security Analysis* 29(3), 253–62.

Akinade, Akintunde E. 2002. 'The Precarious Agenda: Christian-Muslim Relations in Contemporary Nigeria.' *Public Lecture*, 118–27.

Akpoilih, Roland Avura and Adesoji Oladapo Farayibi. 2012. 'Economic Growth and Inequality in Nigeria: Magnitudes and Challenges.' MPRA Paper 74156. https://mpra.ub.uni-muenchen.de/74156

Archibong, Belinda. 2018. 'Historical Origins of Persistent Inequality in Nigeria.' *Oxford Development Studies* 46(3), 325–47.

Bienen, Henry. 1986. 'Religion, Legitimacy, and Conflict in Nigeria.' *The Annals of the American Academy of Political and Social Science* 483(1), 50–60.

Binniyat, Luka and Sam Eyoboka. 2013. 'Nigerian Christians Are Treated as Second Class Citizens – Oritsejafor.' *Vanguard News* (blog). July 27. https://www.vanguardngr.com/2013/07/nigerian-christians-are-treated-as-second-class-citizens-oritsejafor/

Clarke, Peter. 1988. 'Islamic Reform in Contemporary Nigeria: Methods and Aims.' *Third World Quarterly* 10(2), 519–38.

Conference of Nigerian Muslim Organizations. 2005. 'USA/Africa Dialogue, No 691: Marginalizing Nigerian Muslims?' https://www.laits.utexas.edu/africa/ads/691.html

Cook, David. 2018. *The Boko Haram Reader: From Nigerian Preachers to the Islamic State*. Oxford: Oxford University Press.

Dudley, Billy J. 2013. *Parties and Politics in Northern Nigeria*. London: Routledge.

Ebhomienlen, Thomas O. and Emmanuel I. Ukpebor. 2013. 'Religion and Politics in Nigeria: A Comparative Study of the Nigeria Supreme Council for Islamic Affairs and the Christian Association of Nigeria.' *International Journal of Science and Research* 2(9), 166–70.

Emmanual, Jonah C. and Vahyala A. Tari. 2015. 'The Myth and Reality of Middle Belt Geo-politics in Nigeria: A Discourse.' *Journal of Culture, Society and Development* 10, 1–9.

Fani-Kayode, Femi. 2016. 'Are Christians Second Class Citizens in Nigeria?' *Vanguard News* (blog). 7 August 2016. https://www.vanguardngr.com/2016/08/christians-second-class-citizens-nigeria/

Garuba, Harry. 2001. 'Language and Identity in Nigeria.' *Shifting African Identities* 2, 7–20.

Hallum, Christian and Kwesi W. Obeng. 2019. 'The West Africa Inequality Crisis: How West African Governments Are Failing to Reduce Inequality, and What Should Be Done about It.' Oxfam Briefing Paper. Oxford: Oxfam International.

Hoechner, Hannah. 2014. 'Traditional Quranic Students (Almajirai) in Nigeria: Fair Game for Unfair Accusations?' in Marc-Antoine Pérouse de Montclos, ed., *Boko Haram: Islamism, Politics, Security and the State in Nigeria*. Leiden: Africa Studies Centre, 63–84.

Ibrahim, Jibrin. 1989. 'The Politics of Religion in Nigeria: The Parameters of the 1987 Crisis in Kaduna State.' *Review of African Political Economy* 16(45–46), 65–82.

John, Sokfa F. 2018. 'Genocide, Oppression, Ambivalence: Online Narratives of Identity and Religion in Postcolonial Nigeria.' *Open Library of Humanities* 4(2). https://doi.org/10.16995/olh.284

Jordan, Jason. 2016. 'Religion and Inequality: The Lasting Impact of Religious Traditions and Institutions on Welfare State Development.' *European Political Science Review: EPSR* 8(1), 25–48 DOI:10.1017/S1755773914000381.

Kane, Ousmane. 2003. *Muslim Modernity in Postcolonial Nigeria: A Study of the Society for the Removal of Innovation and Reinstatement of Tradition*. Leiden: Brill.

Kazah-Toure, Toure. 1999. 'The Political Economy of Ethnic Conflicts and Governance in Southern Kaduna, Nigeria: [De]Constructing a Contested Terrain.' *Africa Development* 24(1), 109–44.

Keister, L. A. and Eagle, D. 2014. 'Religion and Inequality: The Role of Status Attainment and Social Balance Processes.' *Social Thought & Research* 33, 141–71.

Kukah, Matthew Hassan. 1993. *Religion, Politics and Power in Northern Nigeria*. Ibadan: Spectrum Books.

Kukah, Matthew Hassan and Kathleen McGarvey. 2013. 'Christian-Muslim Dialogue in Nigeria: Social, Political, and Theological Dimensions,' in Akintunde E. Akinade, ed., *Fractured Spectrum: Perspectives on Christian-Muslim Encounters in Nigeria*. New York: Peter Lang, 12–29.

Kuznar, Lawrence A. 2019. 'Nigeria Inequality Report.' nsiteam.com: NSI.

Lergo, Tunga. 2011. 'Deconstructing Ethnic Politics: The Emergence of a Fourth Force in Nigerian Political Discourse.' *International Journal of Humanities and Social Science* 1(15), 87–94.

Loimeier, Roman. 2011. *Islamic Reform and Political Change in Northern Nigeria*. Evanston, IL: Northwestern University Press.

Lugard, Lord Frederick J. D. 2013. *The Dual Mandate in British Tropical Africa*. London: Routledge.

Malachy, Chukwuemeka Eze. 2013. 'Boko Haram Insurgency: A Northern Agenda for Regime Change and Islamization in Nigeria, 2007–2013.' *Global Journal of Human-Social Science Research* 13(5), 1–13.

Mayah, Emmanuel, Chiara Mariotti, Evelyn Mere and Celestin Okwudili Odo. 2017. *Inequality in Nigeria: Exploring the Drivers*. Oxfam International.

Miles, William F. S. 2003. 'Shari'a as de-Africanization: Evidence from Hausaland.' *Africa Today* 50(1), 51–75.

Mustapha, Abdul Raufu. 2006. *Ethnic Structure, Inequality and Governance of the Public Sector in Nigeria*. Switzerland: United Nations Research Institute for Social Development Geneva.

Mustapha, Abdul Raufu. 2007. 'Institutionalizing Ethnic Representation: How Effective Is the Federal Character Commission in Nigeria.' *CRISE Working Paper* 43.

Mustapha, Abdul Raufu. 2014. *Sects & Social Disorder: Muslim Identities & Conflict in Northern Nigeria*. Woodbridge: Boydell & Brewer Ltd.

National Population Commission. 2014. 'Nigeria Demographic and Health Survey 2013.' Maryland.

Ngbea, Gabriel and Hilary Chukwuka Achunike. 2014. 'Poverty in Northern Nigeria.' *Asian Journal of Humanities and Social Studies* 2(2), 266–72.

Ochonu, Moses E. 2014. *Colonialism by Proxy: Hausa Imperial Agents and Middle Belt Consciousness in Nigeria*. Bloomington, IN: Indiana University Press.

Onapajo, Hakeem. 2012. 'Politics for God: Religion, Politics and Conflict in Democratic Nigeria.' *The Journal of Pan African Studies* 4(9), 42–66.

Osaghae, Eghosa E. 1998. 'Managing Multiple Minority Problems in a Divided Society: The Nigerian Experience.' *The Journal of Modern African Studies* 36(1), 1–24.

Osaghae, Eghosa E. and Rotimi T. Suberu. 2005. *A History of Identities, Violence and Stability in Nigeria*. Vol. 6. Oxford: Centre for Research on Inequality, Human Security and Ethnicity, University of Oxford.

Pals, Daniel L. 2006. *Eight Theories of Religion*. Oxford: Oxford University Press.

Taiye, Adamolekun. 2013. 'A Historical Perspective in the Christian-Muslim Relations in Nigeria since 1914.' *Journal of Arts and Humanities* 2(5), 59–66.

Ukiwo, Ukoha. 2005. 'The Study of Ethnicity in Nigeria.' *Oxford Development Studies* 33(1), 7–23.

Umukoro, Nathaniel. 2014. 'Democracy and Inequality in Nigeria.' *Journal of Developing Societies* 30(1), 1–24. https://doi.org/10.1177/0169796X13516340

Usman, Lantana M. 2008. 'Assessing the Universal Basic Education Primary and Koranic Schools' Synergy for Almajiri Street Boys in Nigeria.' *International Journal of Educational Management* 22(1), 62–73.

Vaughan, Olufemi. 2016. *Religion and the Making of Nigeria*. Durham, NC: Duke University Press.

Weimann, Gunnar J. 2010. *Islamic Criminal Law in Northern Nigeria: Politics, Religion, Judicial Practice*. Amsterdam: Amsterdam University Press.

Weber, Max. 2002. *The Protestant Ethic and the Spirit of Capitalism and Other Writings*. London: Penguin.

Wilde, Melissa and Lindsay Glassman. 2016. 'How Complex Religion Can Improve Our Understanding of American Politics.' *Annual Review of Sociology* 42, 407–25.

Wilde, Melissa J. and Patricia Tevington. 2015. 'Complex Religion: Toward a Better Understanding of the Ways in Which Religion Intersects with Inequality.' *Emerging Trends in the Social and Behavioral Sciences: An Interdisciplinary, Searchable, and Linkable Resource*, 1–14. https://doi.org/10.1002/9781118900772.etrds0440.

Chapter 2

Adam, Yussuf. 2006. *Escapar aos dentes do crocodilo e cair da boca do leopardo: trajectória de Moçambique pós colonial, 1975–1990.* Maputo: Promédia.

Ahmed, Akbar S. 2003. *Islam under Siege: Living Dangerously in a Post-Honor World.* New Delhi: Vistar Publications.

Bonate, Liazzat J. K. 2005. 'Dispute over Islamic Funeral Rites in Mozambique: "A Demolidora dos Prazeres" by Shaykh Aminuddin Mohamad.' *Social Sciences & Missions* 17, 41–59.

Bonate Liazzat, J. K. 2013. 'Muslims Memories of the Liberation War in Cabo Delgado,' *Kronos: Southern African Histories – Aquilo que o Povo Precisa Saber* (Special Issue – The Liberation Script in Mozambican History), 39, 230–56.

Bonate, Liazzat J. K. 2019. 'Muslim Female Political Leadership in Precolonial Northern Mozambique: The Letters by Nunu Fatima Binti Zakaria of Mogincua,' in Veira Pawliková-Vilhanová and Martina Buková, eds., *AD FONTES: Reflections on Sources of Africa's Pasts, Their Preservation, Publication and/or Digitisation.* Brussels: Union Académique Internationale and Bratislava: Slovak Academic Press, 81–105.

Cabrita, João. 2000. *The Tortuous Road to Democracy.* New York: Palgrave.

Casimiro, Isabel and Andrade, Ximena. 2009. 'Critical Feminism in Mozambique Situated in the Context of our Experience as Women, Academics and Activists,' in Ampofo, Akosua Adomako and Signe Arnfred eds., *African Feminist Politics of Knowledge: Tensions, Challenges, Possibilities.* Uppsala: Nordiska Afrikainstitutet, 137–56.

Cau, Boaventuram, Arusyak Sevoyan and Victor Agadjanian. 2013. 'Religious Affiliation and under-Five Mortality in Mozambique.' *Journal of Biosocial Science* 45(3), 415–29.

Centro de Estudos Africanos. 1998. *O mineiro moçambicano: um estudo sobre a exportação da mão-de-obra em Inhambane.* Maputo: Centro de Estudos Africanos.

Dias de Andrade, Inacio. 2016. '"Tem um espírito que vive dentro dessa pele": feitiçaria e desenvolvimento em Tete, Moçambique.' Campinas: Universidade Estadual de Campinas., PhD Thesis.

Gardín, Carlos and Finn Tarp. 2019. 'Gender Inequality in Employment in Mozambique.' *South African Journal of Economics* 87(2), 110–38.

Grupos Dinamizadores. 1975. *Circular de Grupos Dinamizadores.* Maputo: Centro de Estudos Africanos (CEA), Referência 97/CPN/95, CEA, pasta 13.

Guebuza, A. 1975. 'Combate Popular organizado contra estandartes do imperialismo.' In *Notícias*, 17 October.

Hedges, David et al. 1993. *História de Moçambique Vol. 3: Moçambique no auge do colonialismo, 1930-1961.* Maputo: Departamento de História/Imprensa Universitária.

Heyen-Dubé, Thomas and Richard Rands. 2021. 'Evolving Doctrine and Modus Operandi: Violent Extremism in Cabo Delgado.' *Small Wars & Insurgencies* 33(3), 437–66. DOI: 10.1080/09592318.2021.1936956.

Igreja, Victo and Béatrice Dias Lambranca. 2009. 'The Thursdays as They Live: Christian Religious Transformation and Gender Relations in Postwar Gorongosa, Central Mozambique.' *Journal of Religion in Africa* 39(3), 262–94.

Junod, Henri A. 1996. *Usos e costumes dos Bantu*. Vol. 2. Maputo: AHM.

Kotany, S. Ed. 2003. *Espírito Corpo – DVD*. Maputo: Coopimagem.

Liesegang, Gerhard. 1990. 'Achegas para o estudo das biografias de autores de fontes narrativas e outros documentos da história de Moçambique, II, III: três autores sobre Inhambane – a vida e obra de Joaquim de Santa Rita (1806–1870), Aron S. Mukhombo (ca. 1885–1940) e Elias S. Mucambe (1906–1969).' *Arquivo*, Maputo, Número 8, Outubro: 61–142.

Machele, Júlio. 2019. 'Religion and Development in Mozambique,' in M. Christian Green ed., *Law, Religion and Human Flourishing in Africa*. Stellenbosch: AFRICAN SUN MeDIA, 325–42.

Maia, Carlos Chadreque Penicela da. 2012. 'Understanding Poverty and Inequality in Mozambique: The Role of Education and Labour Market Status.' Stellenbosch: Faculty of Economic and Management Sciences at Stellenbosch University, PhD Thesis.

Matine, Manuel Henriques. 2005. 'A integração de famílias autóctones no Colonato de Limpopo em Moçambique, 1959–1977.' Niterói-Rio de Janeiro: Universidade Federal Fulminense/Instituto de Ciências Humanas e Filosofia (Dissertação de mestrado).

Meneses, Maria Paula. 2009. 'Poderes, direitos e cidadania: O "retorno" das autoridades tradicionais em Moçambique.' *Revista Crítica de Ciências Sociais* 87, 26.

MHN, *Gabriel Makavi, 1897–1982: Dossier MZ-0451*. http://www.mozambiquehistory. net/gabriel_makavi.php, accessed 15 May 2020.

Mindoso, André Vitorino. 2017. *Os Assimilados de Moçambique: da situação colonial à experiência socialista*. Curitiba: Universidade Federal do Paraná Sector de Ciências Humanas.

Morier-Genoud, E. 2002. *O Islão em Moçambique após a independência: História de um poder em ascensão*. Paris: Karthala. (Revised version of L'Afrique politique 2002. Islam d'Afrique. Entre le local et le global Paris: Karthala, 2002).

Mudenge, Stan I. Gorerazvo. 1976. 'The Dominicans at Zumbo: an Aspect of Missionary History in the Zambezi Valley, c. 1726–1836.' *Mohlomi, Journal of Southern African Historical Studies* I, 32–63.

Myers, David G. 2007. 'Religion and Human Flourishing,' in M. Eid and R. J. Laarsen eds., *The Science of Subjective Well-being*. New York: Guilford Press, 323–43.

Pfeiffer, James. 2002. 'African Independent Churches in Mozambique: Healing the Afflictions of Inequality.' *Medical Anthropology Quarterly* 16(2), 176–99.

Pfeiffer, James, Kenneth Gimbel-Sherr and Orvalho Joaquim Augusto. 2007. 'The Holy Spirit in the Household: Pentecostalism, Gender and Neoliberalism in Mozambique.' *American Anthropologist* 109(4), 688–700.

Raimundo, Inês. 2009. 'Mobilidade da população, pobreza e feitiçaria no meio rural de Moçambique.' *Economia, Política e Desenvolvimento* 1(1), 13–39.

RPM. 1975. *Constituição da República Popular de Moçambique*. Maputo: Imprensa Nacional.

Rita-Ferreira, António. nd. *Moçambique Post 25 de Abril: Causas do Êxodo da População de Origem Europeia e Asiática*. Lisboa: Arquivo Histórico de Moçambique.

Rita-Ferreira, António. 'Etno-história e cultura tradicional do grupo Angoni.' *Memórias do Instituto de Investigação Científica de Moçambique*, Vol. 11, Série C, 1974.

Serra, Carlos (org.) 2000. *História de Moçambique: Parte I: Primeiras sociedades sedentárias e impacto de mercadores, 200/300 – 1885ç Parte II: Agressão imperialista*. Maputo: livraria Universitária.

Shapiro, Martin. 1983. 'Medicine in the Service of Colonialism: Medical Care in the Portuguese Africa.' Los Angeles: University of California, PhD Thesis.

Souza, Sheila Perina de. 2019. 'Educação em Moçambique: a política do assimilado trilhando o caminho de privilegio da língua portuguesa no ensino.' *Crítica Educativa* (Sorocaba/SP), 5(1), 77–91, jan./jun.

Thoele, Alexandre. 2005. 'Uma família quase moçambicana,' in *SwissInfo*, 05. Julho. https: swissinfo.ch/por/uma-família-quase-moçambicana–II-/4560382, accessed 15 May 2020.

VaticaNews. 2019. 'A Igreja Católica em Moçambique: a história da evangelização de Moçambique está intimamente ligada à colonização portuguesa.' https://www.vaticannews.va/pt/igreja/news/2019-09/papa-francisco-viagem-mocambique-igreja-dados-estatisticos.html, accessed 15 May 2020.

Vletter, Fion De. 2007. 'Migration and Development in Mozambique: Poverty, Inequality and Survival.' *Development Southern Africa* 24(1), 137–53.

Von Sicard, S. 2008. 'Islam in Mozambique: Some Historical and Cultural Perspectives.' *Journal of Muslim Minority Affairs* 28(3), 473–90. DOI: 10.1080/13602000802548201

Zimba, Benigna 2005. "Achivanjila I' and the Making of the Niassa Slave Routes,' in B. Zimba, E. Alpers and A. Isaacman eds., *Slave Routes and Oral Tradition in Southeastern Africa*. Maputo: Filsom Entertainment, Lda, 219–51.

Chapter 3

Adedibu, B. A. 2013. 'Reverse Mission or Migrant Sanctuaries? Migration, Symbolic Mapping, and Missionary Challenges of Britain's Black Majority Churches.' *Pneuma* 35(3), 405–23.

Adogame, A. 2013. *The African Christian Diaspora: New Currents and Emerging Trends in World Christianity*. London: Bloomsbury.

Appiah, B. O. 2015. 'Negotiating the Integration Strategies and the Transnational Statuses of Ghanaian-led Pentecostal Churches in Britain.' University of Birmingham, UK, Doctoral Thesis.

Awolalu, J. O. S. 1976. 'What Is African Traditional Religion?' *Studies in Comparative Religion* 10, 1–10.

Bettendorf, L. and E. Dijkgraaf. 2010. 'Religion and Income: Heterogeneity between Countries,' *Journal of Economic Behavior and Organization* 74 (1–2), 12–29.

Braunstein, R. 2017. *Prophets and Patriots: Faith in Democracy across the Political Divide*. Oakland: University of California Press.

Brenner, R. and N. M. Kiefer. 1981. 'The Economics of the Diaspora: Discrimination and Occupational Structure.' *Economic Development Culture Change* 29(3), 517–34.

Burgess, R. 2008. 'Freedom from the Past and Faith for the Future: Nigerian Pentecostal Theology in Global Perspective.' *PentecoStudies* 7(2), 29–63.

Burgess, R. 2009. 'African Pentecostal Spirituality and Civic Engagement: The Case of the Redeemed Christian Church of God in Britain.' *Journal of Beliefs and Values* 33(3), 225–73.

Curtis, E. E. IV. 2014. *The Call of Bilal: Islam in the African Diaspora*. Chapel Hill: The University of North Carolina Press.

Engelke, M. E. 2007. *A Problem of Presence: Beyond Scripture in an African Church*. Berkeley: University of California Press.

Hondius, D. 2014. *Blackness in Western Europe. Racial Patterns of Paternalism and Exclusion*. New Brunswick: Transaction.

Keister, L. A. and David E. 2014. 'Religion and Inequality: The Role of Status Attainment and Social Balance Processes.' *Social Thought and Research* 33, 141–71.

Knott, K. 2010. 'Geography, Space and the Sacred,' in J. R. Hinnells ed., *The Routledge Companion to the Study of Religion*. Abingdon and New York: Routledge, 476–91.

Machoko, C. G. 2013. 'Religion and Interconnection with Zimbabwe: A Case Study of Zimbabwean Diasporic Canadians.' *Journal of Black Studies* 45(5), 472–95.

Marx, K. 1978. 'The Marx-Engels Reader 1978,' in Tucker, R. C. ed., 2nd edn. New York: W. W. Norton and Company, 16–65.

Oduro, T. 2006. 'Theological Education and Training: Challenges of African Independent Churches in Ghana.' *Journal of African Instituted Church Theology* 2, 1–15.

Olupona, J. K. and R. Gemignani 2007. 'Introduction,' in K. J. Olupona and R. Gemignani eds., *African Immigrant Religions in America*. New York: New York University Press, 1–35.

Pasura, D. 2014. *African Transnational Diasporas: Fractured Communities and Plural Identities of Zimbabweans in Britain*. London: Palgrave.

Pasura, D. and M. B. Erdal. Eds. 2016. *Migration, Transnationalism and Catholicism: Global Perspectives*. London: Palgrave.

Piketty, T. 2014. 'Capital in the Twenty-first Century: A Multidimensional Approach to the History of Capital and Social Classes.' *The British Journal of Sociology* 65(4), 736–47.

Sande, N. forthcoming. 'Deconstructing Theological and Political Voices: The case of Zimbabweans in the Diaspora.'

Sande, N. and H. M. Samushonga. 2020. 'African Pentecostal Ecclesiastical Practices and Cultural Adaption in a Changing World.' *Journal of the European Pentecostal Theological Association* 40(1), 17–23.

Sande, N. and D. Manyanga. 2020. 'Youth Identity Crisis in Diaspora: Christian Youth Identity Crisis in the Diaspora: Christian Zimbabweans in the United Kingdom.' *Alternation* Special Edition 33, 57–75.

Small, S. 2018. 'Theorizing Visibility and Vulnerability in Black Europe and the African Diaspora.' *Journal of Ethnic and Racial Studies* 41(6), 1182–97.

Ter Haar, G. 1998. *Halfway to Paradise: African Christians in Europe*. Cardiff: Cardiff Academic Press.

Tettey, W. J. 2007. 'Transnationalism, Religion and the African Diaspora in Canada: An Examination of Ghanaians and Ghanaian Churches,' in J. K. Olupona and R. Gemignani eds., *African Immigrant Religions in America*. New York: New York University Press, 321–64.

United Nations. 2019. *The Sustainable Development Goals Report 2019*. New York: United Nations.

United Nations. 2020. 'Inequality in a Rapid Changing World.' Department of Economics and Social Affairs World Social Report. New York: United Nations.

World Bank Record High Remittances Sent Globally in. 2018. https://www.worldbank.org/en/news/press-release/2019/04/08/record-high-remittances-sent-globally-in-2018

World Bank Remittance Report. 2012. https://www.worldbank.org/en/news/press-release/2012/11/20/developing-countries-to-receive-over-400-billion-remittances-2012-world-bank-report, accessed 20 June 2022.

World Inequality Report. 2018. Paris: World Inequality Lab.

Chapter 4

Abu-Lughod, Lila. 2002. 'Do Muslim Women Need Saving?' *American Anthropologist* 104(3), 783–90. URL: https://www.jstor.org/stable/3567256

Ahmed, Leila. 1992. *Women and Gender in Islam: Historical Roots of a Modern Debate*. New Haven, CT: Yale University Press.

al-Ahmad, Yusuf Abd Allah. 2008. *Sawt al-Marʾa: Bahth Fiqhi*. KSA: Muʾassasa al-Dar al-Sunniya, Zahran.

al-Falah, Musaʿid ibn Qasim. 1993. *Aḥkam al-ʿAwra wa al-Nazr*. Riyadh: Maktaba al Maʿrifa li al-Nashr wa al-Tawziʿ.

al-Hajjaj, Muslim al-ḥāfiẓ Abu al-Husayn Muslim ibn al-Naysaburi. 2010. *Sahih Muslim*. Tahqiq Fuʾad ʿAbd-al-Baqi. Istanbul: al-Maktaba al-Islamiyya.

al-Qurtubi, Abu Abdullah Muhammad ibn Ahmad. 1964. *Al-Jamiʿ li aḥkam al-Qurʾan*. Cairo: Dar al Misriyya.

Al-sabuni, Muhammad ʿAli. 1981. *Rawaiʿ al-Bayan Tafsir Ayat al-Ahkam min al-Qurʾan*. Dimashq: Maktabatu al–Ghazali.

Badran, Margot. 2002. 'Feminism and the Qur'an,' in Jane Dammen McAuliffe ed., *Encyclopaedia of the Qur'an*. Leiden: Brill, 199–203.

Badran, Margot. 2005. 'Between Secular and Islamic Feminism/s: Reflections on the Middle East and beyond.' *Journal of Middle Eastern Women's Studies* 1(1), 6–28.

Badran, Margot. 2008. 'Between Muslim Women and the Muslim Woman.' *Journal of Feminist Studies in Religion* 24(1), 101–6.

Badran, Margot. 2009. *Feminism in Islam: Secular and Religious Convergences*. Oxford: Oneworld.

Badran, Margot. 2011. 'Introduction: Gender and Islam in Africa – Rights, Sexuality, and Law,' in Margot Badran ed., *Gender and Islam in Africa: Rights, Sexuality, and Law*. Stanford, CA: Stanford University Press, 1–14.

Badran, Margot. 2013. 'Political Islam and Gender,' in John Esposito and Emad El-Din Shahin eds., *The Oxford Handbook of Islam and Politics*. Oxford: Oxford University Press, 112–28.

Barkow, Jarome H. 1972. 'Hausa Women and Islam.' *Canadian Journal of African Studies* 6(2), Special Issue: *The Roles of African Women: Past, Present, and Future*, 317–28.

Barlas, Asma. 2001. 'Muslim Women and Sexual Oppression: Reading Liberations from the Qur'an.' *Macalester International* 10.

Barlas, Asma. 2002. *Believing Women in Islam: Unread Patriarchal Interpretations of the Qur'an*. Austin: University of Texas Press.

Ben Amara, Ramzi. 2011. 'The Izala Movement in Nigeria: Its Split, Relationship to Sufis and Perception of Shari'a Re-implementation.' PhD dissertation, accessed 5 June 2018. https://epub.uni-bayreuth.de/101/1/BenAmaraDiss.pdf

Ben Amara, Ramzi. 2012. 'Shaykh Isma'ila Idris (1937–2000), the Founder of the *Izala* Movement in Nigeria.' *Annual Review of Islam in Africa* 11, 74–8.

Borts, Barbara. 2021. 'The Voice in Women: Subjected and Rejected.' *European Judaism*, 22, 54(1), 105–15.

Boyd, Jean. 1984. 'The Role of Women Scholars in the Sokoto Caliphate.' *Seminar Paper*. Department of Islamic Studies, Bayero University, 10, Article 15.

Boyd, Jean. 2001. 'Distance Learning from Purdah in Nineteenth-century Northern Nigeria: The Work of Asma'u Fodiyo.' *Journal of African Cultural Studies* 14(1), 7–22.

Boyd, Jean and Murray Last. 1984. 'The Role of Women as "Agents Religieux" in Sokoto.' *Canadian Journal of African Studies* 19(2), 283–300.

Bukhārī, Muḥammad ibn Ismā'īl, and Muhammad Muhsin. Khan. 1997. *Ṣaḥīḥ Al-Bukhārī : the Translation of the Meanings of Sahih Al-Bukhari: Arabic-English*. Riyadh-Saudi Arabia: Darussalam Pub. & Distr.

Callaway, J. Barbara. 1984. 'Ambiguous Consequences of the Socialisation and Seclusion of Hausa Women.' *The Journal of Modern African Studies* 22(3), 429–50.

Callaway, Barbara. 1987. *Muslim Hausa Women in Nigeria*. Syracuse: Syracuse University Press.

Callaway, Barbara and Lucy Creevy. 1994. *The Heritage of Islam: Women, Religion, and Politics in West Africa*. Boulder, CO: Lyne Reinner.

Carastathis, Anna. 2014. 'The Concept of Intersectionality in Feminist Theory.' *Philosophy Compass* 9(5), 304–14.

Charrad, Mounira. 2009. 'Kinship, Islam or Oil: Culprits of Gender Inequality?' *Politics & Gender* 5(4), 546–53.

Coles, Catherine and Beverly Mack, Eds. 1991. *Hausa Women in the Twentieth Century*. Madison: University of Wisconsin Press.

Connell, Raewyn. 2002. *Gender*. Cambridge: Polity.

Connell, Raewyn. 2009. *Gender in World Perspective*. Cambridge: Polity Press.

Crenshaw, Kimberly. 1991. 'Mapping the Margins: Intersectionality, Identity Politics, and Violence against Women of Color.' *Stanford Law Review* 43(6), 1241–99.

Edwin, Shirin. 2016. *Privately Empowered: Expressing Feminism in Islam in Northern Nigerian Fiction*. Evanston, IL: Northwestern University Press.

Frede, Britta. 2020. 'Female Muslim Scholars in Africa,' in Fallou Ngom et al. eds., *The Palgrave Handbook of Islam in Africa* Cham: Palgrave Macmillan, 221–32.

General academic reading for the session: Spierings, Niels, Jeroen Smits and Mieke Verloo. 2009. 'On the Compatibility of Islam and Gender Equality: Effects of Modernization, State Islamization, and Democracy on Women's Labour Market Participation in 45 Muslim Countries.' *Social Indicators Research* 90(3), 503–22. https://core.ac.uk/download/pdf/81737867.pdf

Ibn Kathir, al-Hafiz ʿImad al-Din Abu al-Fidaʾ Ismaʿil al-Qarshi. nd. *Tafsir al-Qurʾan al-ʿAzim*. Sami ibn. Muhammad Salami ed. Cairo: Dar al-Tayyiba li-l-Nashr wa-l-Tawziʿ. Maktaba al-Shamila, accessed 7 September 2017.

Kandiyoti, Deniz. 1991. 'Introduction,' in Deniz Kandiyoti ed., *Women, Islam and the State*. London: Palgrave MacMillan, 1–21.

Kandiyoti, Deniz, Nadia Al-ali and Kathryn Spellman Poots. Eds. 2019. *Gender, Governance, and Islam*. Edinburgh: Edinburgh University Press.

Krawietz, Birgit. 2018. 'Body, in Law,' in Kate Fleet, Gudrun Kramer, Denis Matringe, John Nawas and Everett Rowson eds., *Encyclopedia of Islam*. THREE, Brillonline, accessed 13 February 2019.

Larzreg, Marnia. 1990. 'Gender and Politics in Algeria: Unraveling the Religious Paradigm.' *Signs* 15(4), 755–80.

Mernissi, Fatima. 1992. *The Veil and the Male Elite: A Feminist Interpretation of Women's Rights in Islam*. Translated by Mary Jo Lakeland. New York: Basic Books.

Mernissi, Fatima. 1997. *Forgotten Queens of Islam*. Minneapolis: University of Minnesota Press.

Moghadam, Valentine. 2005. 'Women's Economic Participation in the Middle East: What Difference Has the Neoliberal Policy Turn Made?' *Journal of Middle East Women's Studies* 1(1), 110–46.

Muazu, Rahina. 2012. 'The Recited Qur'an and the Female Voices: Ethnography of the Women Reciters in Jos, Nigeria.' London: Institute for the Study of Muslim Civilizations, Aga Khan University, MA Thesis.

Muazu, Rahina. 2014. 'Nigerian Muslim Women and the Interpretation of Religion: Right, Freedom and Access,' in Kingsley U. A. Owete (Hrgs.) *Freedom, Self-Determination and Growth in Africa*. Africa–Berlin Conference Proceeding. Berlin, 316–36.

Muazu, Rahina. 2019. 'Qur'an Recitation and the Nudity of the Female Voice in Nigeria.' Berlin, Germany: Berlin Graduate School Muslim Cultures, and Societies, Freie Universität.

Mukhtar, Fatima Batul. 2007. *The Shehu's Daughter: Story of Nana Asma'u*. Kano: Government Printing Press, Kano.

Nīsābūrī, Niẓām al-Dīn al-Ḥasan ibn Muḥammad. 1903. Jāmiʿ al-bayān fī tafsīr al-Qurʾañ Miṣr: al-Maṭbaʿah al-Maymanīyah.

Omar, Sadiya. 2014. 'Yantarun Nana Asma'u [anfodiyo Tasarinsu Da Taskace Waɗoɗinsu. Lagos: Zeetma.

Rahma, Majid A. 2006. *Mace Mutum*. Kano: Iyaruwa Publishers.

Ross, Michael L. 2012. *The Oil Curse: How Petroleum Wealth Shapes the Development of Nations*. Princeton: Princeton University Press.

Spierings, Niels. 2014. 'The Influence of Patriarchal Norms, Institutions, and Household Composition on Women's Employment in Twenty-eight Muslim-majority.' *Feminist Economics* 20(4), 87–112.

Wadud, Amina. 1996. 'Towards a Qur'anic Hermeneutics of Social Justice: Race, Class, and Gender.' *Journal of Law and Religion* 12(1), 37–50.

Wadud, Amina. 1999. *Qur'an and Woman: Rereading the Sacred Text from a Woman's Perspective*. Oxford: Oxford University Press.

Chapter 5

Anderson, A. 2002. 'The Newer Pentecostal and Charismatic Churches: The Shape of Future Christianity in Africa?' *PNEUMA: The Journal of the Society for Pentecostal Studies* 24(2), 167–84.

Antonakis, J., M. Fenley and S. Liechti 2012. 'Learning Charisma.' *Harvard Business Review*. June 2012. https://hbr.org/2012/06/learning-charisma-2

Beguy, D., J. Mumah and L. Gottschalk. 2014. 'Unintended Pregnancies among Young Women Living in Urban Slums: Evidence from a Prospective Study in Nairobi City, Kenya.' *PLoS ONE* 9(7), e101034. DOI: 10. 1371/journal.pone.0101034

Bourdieu, P. 1986. 'The Forms of Capital,' in John Richardson ed., *Handbook of Theory and Research for the Sociology of Education*. New York: Greenwood Press, 241–58.

Bourdieu, P. 1991. 'Genesis and Structure of the Religious Field.' *Comparative Social Research* 13, 1–44.

Bourdieu, P. 1998. *Practical Reason: On the Theory of Action*. Stanford: Stanford University Press.

Corten, A. and R. Marshall-Fratani. Eds. 2001. *Between Babel and Pentecost: Transnational Pentecostalism in Africa and Latin America*. London: C. Hurst & Co. Publishers.

Cox, H. 1995. *Fire from Heaven: The Rise of Pentecostal Spirituality and the Reshaping of Religion in the Twenty-first Century*. Reading, MA: Addison-Wesley.

Collins, R. 2014. Napoleon as CEO: A Career of Emotional Energy, 3 January 2014. http://sociological-eye.blogspot.ch, accessed 15 January 2017.

Echtler, M. and A. Ukah. 2016. *Bourdieu in Africa: Exploring the Dynamics of Religious Fields*. Leiden: Brill.

Ellis, S. and G. ter Haar. 1998. 'Religion and Politics in Sub-Saharan Africa.' *Journal of Modern African Studies* 36(2), 175–201.

Eni, E. 1987. *Delivered from the Powers of Darkness*. Ibadan: Scripture Union.

Fabian, J. 1971. *Jamaa: A Charismatic Movement in Katanga*. Evanston: Northwestern University Press.

Jentges, E. 2014. 'Political Charisma as Performance and Projection.' Paper prepared for the ECPR Joint Session in Salamanca/ Spain, 10 April–14 April 2014.

Kalu, O. 2008. *African Pentecostalism: An Introduction*. Oxford: Oxford University Press.

Maseno, L. 2015. 'Christianity in East Africa,' in Elias Kifon Bongmba ed., *The Routledge Companion to Christianity in Africa*. New York: Routledge, 108–21.

Maseno, L. 2017. '"The Glory Is Here!" Faith Brands and Rituals of Self-Affirmation for Social Responsibility in Kenya.' *Alternation Special Edition* 19, 252–67.

Migwi, J. 2016. 'The Place of Women in Selected African Pentecostal Churches in Limuru Sub-County Kiambu County, Kenya.' Kenyatta University Repository, Unpublished MA Thesis.

Mwaura, P. 2002. '"A stick plucked out of the fire": The Story of Rev. Margaret Wanjiru of Jesus Is Alive Ministries,' in I.A. Phiri et al., eds., *Her-Stories: Hidden Histories of Women of Faith in Africa*. Pietermaritzburg: Cluster Publications, 202–24.

Oduyoye, M. A. 1992. 'Women and Ritual in Africa,' in M. R. Kanyoro and M. A. Oduyoye, eds., *The Will to Arise: Women, Tradition and the Church in Africa*. Maryknoll, NY: Orbis Books, 9–24.

Parsitau, D. 2011. '"Arise O ye daughters of faith". Women, Pentecostalism and Public Culture in Kenya,' in H. Englund ed., *Christianity and Public Culture in Africa*. Cambridge: Cambridge Centre of African Studies, 131–8.

Parsitau, D. 2014. 'The Civic and Public Roles of Neo-Pentecostal Churches in Kenya (1970-2010).' Kenyatta University, Unpublished PhD Thesis.

Parsitau, D. and N. P. Mwaura. 2010. 'God in the City: Pentecostalism as an Urban Phenomenon in Kenya.' *Studia Historiae Ecclesiaticae Journal of the Church History Society of Southern Africa, University of Pretoria* 36(2), 95–112.

Riesebrodt, M. 1999. 'Charisma in Max Weber's Sociology of Religion.' *Religion* 29(1), 1–14.

Salomonsen, J. 2003. 'Love of Same, Love of Other.' *Studia Theologica: Scandinavian Journal of Theology* 17(2), 103–23.

Schweitzer, A. 1984. *The Age of Charisma*. Chicago: Nelson Hall.

Turner, S. 2003. 'Charisma Reconsidered.' *Journal of Classical Sociology* 3(1), 5–26.

Weber, M. 1978. *Economy and Society: An Outline of Interpretive Sociology*. Berkeley, CA: University of California Press.

Chapter 6

Beckford, J. 1996. 'Postmodernity, High Modernity and New Modernity: Three Concepts in Search of Religion,' in Kieran Flanagan and Peter C. Jupp, eds., *Postmodernity, Sociology, and Religion*. London: Macmillan, 30–47.

Beckford, J. 2000. 'Start Together and Finish Together: Shifts in the Premises and Paradigms Underlying the Scientific Study of Religion.' *Journal for the Scientific Study of Religion* 39(4), 481–95.

Chabal, P. 2009. *Africa: The Politics of Smiling and Suffering*. Scottsville, South Africa: University of KwaZulu-Natal Press.

Chaudhuri, S. 2013. 'A Life Course Model of Human Rights Realization: Female Empowerment, and Gender Inequality in India.' *World Development* 52, 55–70.

Giorgi, A. 2016. 'Gender, Religion, and Political Agency: Mapping the Field.' *Revista Crítica de Ciências Sociais* 110, 51–72.

Hopkins, P. 2009. 'Men, Women, Positionalities and Emotion: Doing Feminist Geographies of Religion.' *ACME: An International Journal for Critical Geographers* 8(1), 1–17.

Inglehart, R. and Norris, P. 2003. *Rising Tide: Gender Equality and Cultural Change around the World*. Cambridge: Cambridge University Press.

King, U. Ed. 1995. *Religion and Gender*. Oxford: Basil Blackwell.

Klingorová, K. and T. Havlíček. 2015. 'Religion and Gender Inequality: The Status of Women in the Societies of World Religions.' *Moravian Geographical Report* 23(2), 2–11.

Makulilo, A. B. 2019. 'Who Should Slaughter Animals and Poultry? Rethinking the Tensions between Muslims and Christians in Tanzania,' in Ezra Chitando and Joram Tarusarira, eds., *Religion and Human Security in Africa*. London: Routledge, 128–38.

Mernissi, F. 1991. *Women and Islam: An Historical and Theological Enquiry*. Oxford: Blackwell.

Mesaki, S. 2011. 'Religion and the State in Tanzania.' *Cross-Cultural Communication* 7(2), 249–59.

Moghadam, V. M. 1991. 'The Reproduction of Gender Inequality in Muslim Societies: A Case Study of Iran in the 1980s.' *World Development* 19(10), 1335–49.

Mukandala, R. 2006. 'Introduction,' in R. Mukandala, S. Yahya-Othman, S. S. Mushi and L. Ndumbaro, eds., *Justice, Rights and Worship: Religion and Politics in Tanzania*. Dar es Salaam: REDET, University of Dar es Salaam, 1–17.

Ndaluka, T. 2012. '"We Are Ill-treated": A Critical Discourse Analysis of Muslims' Social Differentiation Claims in Tanzania,' in T. Ndaluka and F. Wijsen, eds., *Religion and State in Tanzanian Revisited: Reflection from 50 Years of Independence*. Berlin: LIT, 81–94.

Page, S-J and A. Kam-Tuck Yip. 2017. 'Gender Equality and Religion: A Multi-Faith Exploration of Young Adults' Narratives.' *European Journal of Women's Studies* 24(3), 249–65.

Peach, C. 2006. 'Islam, Ethnicity and South Asian Religions in the London 2001 Census.' *Transactions of the Institute of British Geographers* 31(3), 353–70.

Renzetti, C. M. and D. J. Curran. 1999. *Women, Men, and Society*. Boston: Allyn and Bacon.

Russell, L. M. Ed. 1985. *Feminist Interpretation of the Bible*. Oxford: Blackwell.

Seguino, S. 2011. 'Help or Hindrance? Religion's Impact on Gender Inequality in Attitudes and Outcomes.' *World Development* 39(8), 1308–21.

Stump, R. 2008. *The Geography of Religion: Faith, Place, and Space*. Maryland: Rowman and Littlefield Publishers.

Young, K. 1987. 'Introduction,' in A. Sharma ed., *Women in World Religions*. Albany, NY: State University of New York Press, 1–36.

Chapter 7

Asamoah-Gyadu, J. K. 2007. 'Broken Calabashes and Covenants of Fruitfulness: Cursing Barrenness in Contemporary African Christianity.' *Journal of Religion in Africa* 37(4), 437–60.

Bartkowski, J. P. and L. M. Hempel. 2009. 'Sex and Gender Traditionalism among Conservative Protestants: Does the Difference Make a Difference?' *Journal for the Scientific Study of Religion* 48(4), 805–16.

Bem, S. L. 1993. *The Lenses of Gender: Transforming the Debate on Sexual Inequality*. New Haven, CT: Yale University Press.

Carli, L. L. and A. H. Eagly. 2001. 'Gender, Hierarchy, and Leadership: An Introduction.' *Journal of Social Issues* 57(4), 629–36.

Clifford, A. M. 2001. *Introducing Feminist Theology*. Maryknoll, NY: Orbis Books.

Connell, R. W. 2005. *Masculinities*. 2nd edn. Berkeley, CA: University of California Press.

Constitution of the Kingdom of Swaziland, Act No.1 of. 2005.

Daly, J. 2001. 'Gender Equality Rights versus Traditional Practices: Struggles for Control and Change in Swaziland.' *Development Southern Africa* 18(1), (online). http://econpapers.repec.org/article/tafdeveza/v-3a18-2ay%202001-3ai-3a1

Eagly, A. H. and Karau, S. J. 2002. 'Role Congruity Theory of Prejudice toward Female Leaders.' *Psychological Review* 109(3), 573–98.

Eagly, A. H., W. Wood and A. B. Diekman. 2000. 'Social Role Theory of Sex Differences and Similarities: A Current Appraisal,' in T. Eckes and H. M. Trautner, eds., *The Developmental Social Psychology of Gender*. Mahwah, NJ: Erlbaum, 123–74.

Elshtain, J. 1982. 'On Beautiful Souls, Just Warriors and Feminist Consciousness.' *Women Studies International Forum* 5, 341–8.

Ford, L. E. 2002. *Women and Politics: The Pursuit of Equality*. Boston: Houghton Mifflin Co.

Giddens, S. A. 2005. *Sociology*. 4th edn. Cambridge: Polity Press.

Human Rights Education and Monitoring Center (EMC). 2014. 'Women and Political Representation Handbook on Increasing Women's Political Participation in Georgia, Tbilisi.'

Kabeer, N. 1996. *Mainstreaming Gender in Social Protection for the Informal Economy*, ed. T. Johnson. London: Commonwealth Secretariat.

Matei, M. G. 2013. 'Ideology and Construction of Feminine Identity.' *Bulletin of the Transilvania, University of Brasov. Series IV: Philology and Cultural Studies* 6(55) No.2, 23–8.

National Elections in the Kingdom of Swaziland, Preliminary Statement.

Niemanis, N. 2001. *Gender Mainstreaming in Practice: A Handbook*. New York: United Nations Developmental Programme.

Ntawubona, J. 2013. 'Women's Political Participation in Uganda: A Case Study of Mbarara Municipality,' in M. Prah, ed., *Insights into Gender Equity, Equality and Power Relations in Sub-Saharan Africa*. Addis Ababa: Fountain Publishers, 43–60.

Nyawo, S. 2014. '"*Sowungumuntfukenyalo*" – "You Are Now a Real Person": A Feminist Analysis of How Women's Identities and Personhood Are Constructed by Societal Perceptions on Fertility in the Swazi Patriarchal Family.' University of KwaZulu-Natal, Pietermaritzburg, PhD Thesis.

Nyawo, S. and P. Mkhonta. 2016. 'Reflections on Women's Political Participation and Representation in the Post Constitutional Era (2005–2015).' *UNISWA Research Journal* 15, 1–13.

Nyawo, S. and N. Nsibande. 2014. 'Beyond Parity: Gender in the Context of Educational Leadership in Swaziland.' *UNISWA Research Journal* Special Volume 27, 45–58.

Prah, M. 2013. *Insights into Gender Equity, Equality and Power Relations in Sub-Saharan Africa*. OSSREA, Addis Ababa: Fountain Publishers.

Preliminary Statement of the SADC LA Elections Observer Mission, 22 September 2013.

Railey, M. 1989. *Transforming Feminism*. Kansas City, MO: Sheed and Word.

Rakoczy, S. 2004. *In Her Name: Women Doing Theology*. Pietermaritzburg: Cluster Publications.

Report of the African Union Election Observer Mission (AUEOM). The 20th September 2013.

Report of the Commonwealth Elections Observer Mission.

Report of the Election and Boundaries Commission. 2008. Judicial Service Commission, Mbabane, Eswatini.

Report of the Elections and Boundaries Commission: Conduct of Elections in Swaziland. 2008. Judicial Service Commission, Mbabane, Eswatini.

Rinehart, S. and J. Perkins. 1989. 'The Intersection of Gender Politics and Religious Beliefs.' *Political Behaviour* 11(1), 33–56.

Senath, R. E. 2013. *Gender, Governance and Participatory Development in Uganda: Lessons for the Local Government*, ed. M. Prah. OSSREA, Addis Ababa: Fountain Publishers.

Shvedova, N. 2005. 'Obstacles to Women's Political Participation in Parliament,' in J. Ballington and A. Karam, eds., *Women in Parliament, Beyond Numbers*. Stockhlolm: International Institute for Democracy and Electoral Assistance (IDEA), 34–38.

Times of Swaziland. 2013. 22 October.

Uchem, R. N. 2004. 'Overcoming Women's Subordination: An Igbo African and Christian Perspective. Envisioning an Inclusive Theology with Reference to Women.' SNAAP Press, PhD Dissertation. http://www.dissertation.com, accessed 26 June 2014.

White, S. 1997. 'Men, Masculinities, and the Politics of.' *Gender and Development* 5(2), 14–22.

WLSA. 1998. *Family in Transition: The Experience of Swaziland. Women and Law in Southern Africa Research Trust*. Manzini: Ruswanda Publishing Bureau.

WLSA. 2001. *Multiple Jeopardy: Domestic Violence and Women's Search for Justice in Swaziland*. Mbabane: Women and Law.

Zwane, B. 2018. Gender Links for Equality News Services. http://genderlinks.org.za/news/swaziland-only-14-women-in-secondary-elections-race/

Chapter 8

Barrett, David. 1968. *Schism and Renewal in Africa: An Analysis of Six Thousand Contemporary Religious Movements*. Nairobi: Oxford University Press.

Bourdillon, Michael F. C. 1976. *The Shona Peoples: An Ethnography of Contemporary Shona, with Special Reference to Their Religion*. Gweru: Mambo Press.

Chitando, Ezra. 2007. *Living with Hope: African Churches and HIV/AIDS*. Geneva: WCC Publications,

Daneel, Marthinus. L. 1971. *Old and New in Southern Shona Independent Churches: Volume 1: Background and Rise of the Major Movements*. The Hague: Morton.

Feierman, Steven et al. Ed. 1992. *The Social Basis of Healing and Health in Africa*. Los Angeles: University of California Press.

Flint, Adrian. 2011. *HIV/AIDS in Sub-Saharan Africa. Politics, AIDS and Globalization*. New York: Palgrave MacMillan.

Hastings, Adrian. 1979. *History of African Christianity 1950–1975*. Cambridge: Cambridge University Press.

Igo, Robert. 2009. *A Window into Hope: An Invitation to Faith in the Context of HIV/AIDS*. Geneva: WCC Publications.

Josephine, K. et al. 2001. *Churches and the HIV/AIDS Pandemic: Analysis of the Situation in 10 West/Central Countries*. Geneva: WCC Publications.

Jules-Rosette, Bennetta. 1975. *African Apostles: Ritual and Conversion in the Church of John Marange.* London: Cornell University Press.

Jules-Rosette, Bennetta. Ed. 1979. *The New Religions of Africa.* Norwood, NJ: Ablex Publishing Corporation.

Makoni, Betty. 2012. 'Johane Marange Sect Satanic: GNC,' www.theZimbabwean.co.uk

Marange, Johane. 1973. *Humbowo Hutsva wewaPostori (New Testament of the Apostles).* Salisbury: JMAC.

Maxwell, David. 2006. *African Gifts of the Spirit: Pentecostalism & the Rise of Zimbabwean Transnational Religious Movement.* Harare: Weaver Press.

Moswane, Perpetoa C. N. 2013. 'The Role of Churches in HIV Prevention among Young Adults in Polokwane Municipality, Limpopo Province.' Pretoria: UNISA, MA Thesis.

Mukonyora, Isabel. 2007. *Wandering in a Gendered Wilderness: Suffering and Healing in an African Initiated Church.* New York: Peter Lang.

Murphree, Marshall W. 1969. *Christianity and the Shona.* London: The Athlone Press.

Murphree, Marshall W. 1971. 'Religious Interdependency among the Budya Vapositori,' in D.B. Barrett, ed., *African Initiatives in Religion.* Nairobi: East Africa Publishing House.

Musevenzi, J. 2017. 'The African Independent Apostolic Church's Doctrine under Threat: The Emerging Power of Faith-based Organisations' Interventions and the Johanne Marange Apostolic Church in Zimbabwe.' *Journal for the Study of Religion* 30(2), 178–206.

Mwaura, Philomena N. 2008. 'Stigmatization and Discrimination of HIV/AIDS women in Kenya: A Violation of Human Rights and Its Theological Implications.' *Exchange* 37(1), 35–51.

Phiri, Isabel. A. and Sarojini Nadar. Eds. 2006. *African Women, Religion, and Health: Essays in Honor of Mercy Amba Ewudziwa Oduyoye.* New York: Obis Books.

Pillay, Miranda N. 2003. 'Church Discourse on HIV/AIDS: A Responsible Response to a Disaster?' *Scriptura* 82, 108–21.

Sibanda, Maureen. 2011. *Married too Soon: Child Marriages in Zimbabwe.* Research and Advocacy. Harare: Research and Advocacy Unit (RAU).

Ucheaga, Dorothy N. and Kari A. Hartwig. 2010. 'Religious Leaders' Response to AIDS in Nigeria.' *Global Public Health* 5(6), 611–25.

National Archives of Zimbabwe (NAZ) Files

Native Commissioner's Report, *Report of Wankie*, 22 October 1918.

Native Commissioner's Report, Umtali District, 31 December 1932, *Native Commissioner's Annual Report, Umtali, 1929, File S235/506*

NAZ S1542/12

Interviews with (pseudonymns):

Mrs. Dupwa conducted at Ministry of Health and Child Welfare, Harare, 20 January 2011.

Mbuya Phiri, conducted at her home in Chavhanga, 22 December 2011.

A. Samaringa, a Johane Marange Member in Honde Valley, Samanga area, conducted on 8 January 2012.

M. Marekwa, conducted at Murara, Honde Valley, 8 January 2012.

B. Madzitire, conducted at his home in Chavhanga, Honde Valley, 16 January 2012.

J. Masamvu, conducted at Hauna Passover, 17 January 2012.

Mrs. Makoni, conducted at St Columbus Mission School, 1 August 2012.

M. Chigweshe, conducted at Hauna, 18 August 2012.

H. Chimuswe, conducted at Chavhanga, 20 September 2012.

K. Kuchocha, conducted at Chavhanga, 22 September 2012.

M. Dodzo, conducted at Chavhanga, 24 September 2012.

E. Dodzo, 26 September 2012.

R. Dodzo, 26 September 2012.

P. Marira, conducted at Hauna, 11 August 2016.

Chapter 9

Adams, Maurianne, Lee Anne Bell and Pat Griffin. 2007. *Teaching for Diversity and Social Justice*. London: Routledge.

Alava, Henni. 2017. 'Homosexuality, the Holy Family and a Failed Mass Wedding in Catholic Northern Uganda.' *Critical African Studies* 9(1), 32–51.

Albuquerque, Grayce Alencar et al. 2016. 'Access to Health Services by Lesbian, Gay, Bisexual, and Transgender Persons: Systematic Literature Review.' *BMC International Health and Human Rights* 16(2).

Badgett, Lee, Sheila Nezhad, Kees Waaldijk and Yana van der Meulen Rodgers. 2014.*The Relationship between LGBT Inclusion and Economic Development: An Analysis of Emerging Economies*. Los Angeles, CA: The Williams Institute, UCLA School of Law.

Gloppen, Siri and Lise Rakner. 2020. 'LGBT Rights in Africa,' in *Research Handbook on Gender, Sexuality and the Law*. Cheltenham: Edward Elgar Publishing, 194–209

Malamba, Manuel. 2012.'The Controversy of Homosexuality: A Critical Look at the Issues That Make Legalizing Homosexuality in Malawi Difficult.' Universitetet i Tromsø, Master's Thesis.

Mawerenga, Jones Hamburu. 2018. *The Homosexuality Debate in Malawi*. No. 28. Mzuzu: Mzuni Press.

McCormack, Mark. 2013. *The Declining Significance of Homophobia*. Oxford: Oxford University Press.

Meyer, Doug. 2015. *Violence against Queer People: Race, Class, Gender, and the Persistence of Anti-LGBT Discrimination*. New Brunswick: Rutgers University Press.

Msosa, Allan. 2019. *Under Wraps: A Survey of Public Attitudes to Homosexuality and Gender Non-conformity in Malawi*. Johannesburg: Other Foundation.

Reddy, Vasu, Theo Sandfort and Laetitia Rispel. 2009. *From Social Silence to Social Science: Same-Sex Sexuality, HIV & AIDS and Gender in South Africa: Conference Proceedings*. Cape Town: HSRC Press.

Tuck, Ryan C. 2012. 'Parting the Red Sea: The Religious Case for LGBT Equality.' Retrieved from http://ssrn.com/abstract=2101854, 15 December 2020.

Van Klinken, Adriaan and Ezra Chitando. 2016. 'Introduction: Christianity and the Politics of Homosexuality in Africa,' in A. Van Klinken and E. Chitando, eds., *Christianity and Controversies over Homosexuality in Contemporary Africa*. London: Routledge, 1–18.

Warner, Michael. 1991. 'Introduction: Fear of a Queer Planet.' *Social text* 29, 3–17.

Newspaper Articles

Bee, Sacramento. 2012. 'Malawi Unlikely to Axe anti-Gay Laws.' *Associated Press*, 28 September, 3.

Chilunga, Z. 2014. 'Kill the Gays! Penalty Proposed by Muslim Association of Malawi.' *Nyasa Times*, 17 February, 2.

Chirombo, Richard. 2012. 'Reiterating Malawi Council of Churches' Position on Homosexuality.' *Zachimalawi*, 3 January, 3.

Chunga, Sam. 2016. 'Bishops Warn APM over Homosexuality Laws.' *The Nation*, 10 January, 1.

Gwede, Wanga. 2016a. 'Malawi Catholic Bishop Rejects K 50 000 Cash Hand-out from State House: Talk Tough on Gays.' *Nyasa Times*, 10 January, 1.

Gwede, Wanga. 2016b. 'God Not Giving Malawi Sufficient Rains because of Sexual Immorality- Clergy.' *Nyasa Times*, 11 January, 1.

Khamula, Owen. 2015. 'PAC Tells Government to Serve Malawians Not Donors, Reject Gays.' *Nyasa Times*, 26 December, 1.

Moyo, Judith. 2016. 'Malawi Court Dismisses Anti-Gay Law Moratorium.' *Nyasa Times*, 12 May, 1.

Muheya, Green. 2016. 'CEDEP Faults Malawi Churches on Demo "for Life and family."' *Nyasa Times*, 5 December, 1.

Nkawihe, Maurice. 2016. 'Kill Gays in Malawi, Demands Msonda: Devil Has No Rights.' *Nyasa Times*, 3 January, 1.

'Malawi Catholic Bishops Clash with Rights Campaigners over Homosexuality.' 2013. *Nyasa Times*, 4 March, 1.

'Malawi Catholic MPs Urged to Reject Gays, Defend Family in Parliament.' 2015. *Nyasa Times*, 31 January, 1.

Phimbi, Elijah. 2017. 'Rights Defenders Angered by "Kill the Gays" Penalty Proposed by the Muslim Association of Malawi.' *Nyasa Times*, 9 September, 1.

Sangala, Tom. 2017. 'Church Firm on Stance against Abortion.' *The Times Group*, 10 December, 1.

Online Sources

https://www.hrw.org/news/2020/02/03/tanzania-obstructions-lgbt-health-rights, accessed 11 August 2020.

https://www.hrw.org/report/2018/10/26/let-posterity-judge/violence-and-discrimination-against-lgbt-people-malawi, accessed 11 August 2020.

Chapter 10

Ackermann, D. M. 2008. 'Found Wanting and Left Untried? – Confessions of a Ragbag Theologian,' in M. Pillay, S. Nadar and C. le Bruyns, eds., *Ragbag Theologies: Essays in Honour of Denise M Ackermann a Feminist Theologian of Praxis*. Stellenbosch: Sun Press, 265–82.

Agbo, B. N. 2017. 'Inculturation of Liturgical Music in the Roman Catholic Church of Igbo land: A Compositional Study.' *Journal of Global Catholicism* 1(2), 6–27.

Amanze, J. N. 2014. 'Disability Discourse: Imago Dei, Teaching Theology from a Disability Perspective,' in H. Kroesbergen ed., *Christian Identity and Justice in a Globalized World from a Southern African Perspective*. Wellington, South Africa: Christian Literature Fund, 257–69.

Bate, S. C. 1998. 'Inculturation in South Africa.' *Grace and Truth* 15(3), 26–43.

Bengtsson, S. 2014. 'On the Borderline – Representations of Disability in the Old Testament.' *Scandinavian Journal of Disability Research* 16(3), 280–92.

Bennett, J. M. 2012. 'Women, Disabled,' in J. Swinton and B. Brock, eds., *Disability in the Christian Tradition: A Reader*. Grand Rapids: Eerdmans, 427–66.

Bunning, K., J. K. Gona, C. R. Newton and S. Hartley. 2017. 'The Perception of Disability by Community Groups: Stories of Local Understanding, Beliefs and Challenges in a Rural Part of Kenya.' *PLoS ONE* 12, 1–20.

Chirongoma, S., D. L. Manda and Z. Myeni. 2008. 'Ubuntu and Women's Health Agency in Contemporary South Africa,' in S. De Gruchy, N. Koopman and S. Strijbos, eds., *From Our Side: Emerging Perspectives on Development and Ethics*. Pretoria: UNISA Press, 189–207.

Chisale, S. S. 2018a. '"Disabled Motherhood in an African Community": Towards an African Women Theology of Disability.' *die Skriflig* 52(1), a2375:1–9.

Chisale, S. S. 2018b. 'Ubuntu as Care: Deconstructing the Gendered Ubuntu.' *Verbum et Ecclesia* 39(1), a1790:1–8.

Chitando, E. 2015. "'Do Not Tell the Person Carrying that s/he stinks": Reflections in Ubuntu and Masculinities in the Context of Sexual and Gender-based Violence and HIV,' in E. Mouton, G. Kapuma, L. Hansen and T. Togom, eds., *Living with Dignity: African Perspectives on Gender Equality*. Stellenbosch: Sun Press, 269–83.

Dreyer, Y. 2011. 'Women's Spirituality and Feminist Theology: A Hermeneutic of Suspicion Applied to "Patriarchal marriage".' *HTS Teologiese Studies/Theological Studies* 67(3), Art. #1104, 1–5.

Dube, M. W. 2000. *Postcolonial Feminist Interpretations of the Bible*. St Louis: Chalice Press.

Du Toit, L. 2011. 'Old Wives' Tales and Philosophical Delusions: The Problem of Women and African Philosophy,' in G. Walmsley ed., *African Philosophy and the Future of Africa*. Washington, DC: The Council For Research in Values and Philosophy, 111–28.

Eiesland, N. L. 1994. *The Disabled God: Towards a Liberatory Theology of Disability*. Nashville: Abingdon Press.

Eiesland, N. L. 2004. *Encountering the Disabled God*. Viewed online on 10 April 2016. https://www.biblesociety.org.uk/uploads/content/bible_in_transmission/files/2004_spring/BiT_Spring_2004_Eiesland.pdf

Freeman, D. 2002. 'A Feminist Theology of Disability.' *Feminist Theology*, 10(29), 71–85.

Gutierrez, G. 1973. *A Theology of Liberation*. London: SCM.

Helander, E. 1993. *Prejudice and Dignity: An Introduction to Community-based Rehabilitation*. New York: United Nations Development Programme.

Henderson, G. and W. Bryan. 2011. *Psychosocial Aspects of Disability*. Springfield, IL: Charles C. Thomas.

Kamaara, E. and Wangila, M. N. 2009. 'Contextual Theology and Gender Reconstructions in Kenya.' *Theologies and Cultures* 6(2), 110–33.

Kamga, S. D. 2011. *The Rights of Women with Disabilities in Africa: Does the Protocol on the Rights of Women in Africa Offer Any Hope?* Barbara Fayne Waxman Fiduccia Papers on Women and Girls with Disabilities, Center for Women Policy Studies, viewed online 22 December 2016. http://proadiph.org/IMG/pdf/bfwfp_therightsofwomenwithdisabilitiesinafrica_doestheprotocolontherightsofwomeninafric.pdf

Kanyoro, M. R. A. 2001. 'Engendered Communal Theology: African Women's Contribution to Theology in the Twenty-first Century.' *Feminist Theology* 9(27), 36–56.

Kanyoro, M. R. A. 2002. *Introducing Feminist Cultural Hermeneutics: An African Perspective*. Cleveland, OH: The Pilgrim Press.

Kruger, J., S. Lifshitz and L. Baloyi. 2007. 'Healing Practices in Communities,' in N. Duncan, B. Bowman, A. Naidoo, J. Pillay and V. Roos, eds., *Community Psychology: Analysis, Context and Action*. Cape Town: UCT Press, 323–44.

Louw, D. 2010. 'Power Sharing and the Challenge of Ubuntu Ethics. Power Sharing and African Democracy: Interdisciplinary Perspective,' in C. W. Du Toit, ed., *Research Institute for Theology and Religion*. Pretoria: University of South Africa, 121–37.

Mangena, F. 2009. 'The Search for an African Feminist Ethic: A Zimbabwean Perspective.' *Journal of International Women's Studies* 11(2), 18–30.

Manyonganise, M. 2015. 'Oppressive and Liberative: A Zimbabwean Woman's Reflections on Ubuntu.' *Verbum et Ecclesia* 36(2), Art.#1438:1–7.

Masenya (ngwan'a Mphahlele), M. 2003. 'Trapped between Two "Canons": African-South African Christian Women in the HIV/AIDS Era,' in I. A. Phiri, B. Haddad and M. Masenya (ngwan'a Mphahlele), eds., *African Women, HIV/AIDS and Faith Communities*. Pietermaritzburg: Cluster Publications, 113–27.

Mbiti, J. S. 1969. *African Religions and Philosophy*. New York: Doubleday.

McClure, J. 2007. *Preaching Words*. Louisville, KY: Westminster John Knox Press.

Ndlovu, H. L. 2016. 'African Beliefs Concerning People with Disabilities: Implications for Theological Education.' *Journal of Disability & Religion* 20(1–2), 29–39.

Ndlovu, L. 2013. '"Neglected Objects or Valued Human Beings": The Ndebele People's Perception of the Disadvantaged as Expressed in the Proverb.' *European Journal of Humanities and Social Sciences* 20(1), 991–1006.

Ngubane-Mokiwa, S. and S. S. Chisale 2019. 'Male Rape or Consensual Sex: Hidden Hegemonic Masculinities by Zulu Speaking Men with Disabilities.' *Ubuntu: Journal of Conflict and Social Transformation* 8(2), 107–24.

Njoroge, N. 1997, 'The Missing Voice: African Women Doing Theology.' *Journal of Theology for Southern Africa* 99, 77–83.

Nussbaum, B. 2003. '*Ubuntu*: Reflections of a South African on Our Common Humanity.' *Perspectives* 4(4), 21–6.

Nyangweso, M. 2018. *Disability in Africa: A Cultural/Religious Perspective*. http://www.researchgate.net/publication/325642373, accessed 29 December 2019.

Lintvelt, M. 2015. 'Disability and Gender: Twofold Discrimination,' in E. Mouton, G. Kapuma, L. Hansen and T. Togom, eds., *Living with Dignity: African Perspectives on Gender Equality*. Stellenbosch: Sun Press, 285–305.

Oduyoye, M. A. 2001. *Introducing African Women's Theology*. London: Sheffield Academic Press.

Oladipo, O. 1998. 'Metaphysics, Religion, and Yoruba Traditional Thought,' in P. H. Coetzee and A. P. J. Roux, eds., *The African Philosophy Reader*. New York: Routledge, 200–8.

Phiri, I. A. 2004. 'African Women's Theologies in the New Millennium.' *Agenda: Empowering Women for Gender Equality* 61, 16–24.

Phiri, I. A. and S. Nadar. 2010. 'African Women Theologies,' in D. B. Stinton, ed., *African Theology on the Way: Current Conversations*. SPCK: London, 90–100.

Reynolds, T. E. 2008. *Vulnerable Communion: A Theology of Disability and Hospitality*. Grand Rapids, MI: Brazos Press.

Swinton, J. 2011. 'Who Is the God We Worship? Theologies of Disability; Challenges and New Possibilities.' *International Journal of Practical Theology* 14(2), 273–307.

Wilhelm, D. 1994. 'About the Hostile Land in Me.' *Journal of Feminist Studies in Religion* 10(2), 104–8.

Chapter 11

Adhikari, M. 2005. *Not White Enough, Not Black Enough: Racial Identity in the South African Coloured Community*. Athens, OH: Ohio University Press.

Babbie, E. and J. Mouton 2010. *The Practice of Social Research*. Cape Town: Oxford University Press.

Baker, A. 2019. 'What South Africa Can Teach Us as Worldwide Economic Inequality Grows.' *Time. South Africa*. 1–11.

Benhabib, S. 2004. *The Rights of Others: Aliens, Residents, and Citizens*. Cambridge: Cambridge University Press.

Benhabib, S. 2013. *Dignity in Adversity: Human Rights in Troubled Times*. Hoboken: John Wiley & Sons.

Boesak, A. A. 2016. *Kairos, Crisis, and Global Apartheid: The Challenge to Prophetic Resistance*. New York: Palgrave Macmillan.

Boesak, A., E. J. Fitchue, L. G. Fitchue, W. E. Fluker, F. E. Harris, N. Koopman, A. Mingo, R. Nel, et al. 2015. *Contesting Post-racialism: Conflicted Churches in the United States and South Africa*, eds., R. D. Smith, W. Ackah, A. G. Reddie and R. S. Tshaka. Jackson: University Press of Mississippi.

Bornman, E. 1999. 'Self-image and Ethnic Identification in South Africa.' *The Journal of Social Psychology* 139(4), 411–25.

Bornman, E. 2011. 'Patterns of Intergroup Attitudes in South Africa after 1994.' *International Journal of Intercultural Relations* 35(6), 729–48.

Bowers du Toit, N. F. and G. Nkomo. 2014. 'The Ongoing Challenge of Restorative Justice in South Africa: How and Why Wealthy Suburban Congregations Are Responding to Poverty and Inequality.' *HTS Theological Studies* 70(2), 1–8.

Brewer, M. B. and R. M. Kramer. 1985. 'The Psychology of Intergroup Attitudes and Behavior.' *Annual Review of Psychology* 36(1), 219–43.

Bryman, A. 2008. *Social Research Methods*. Oxford: Oxford University Press.

Byrne, M. 2007. *Trauma and Forgiveness: Lessons from South Africa and East Timor*. Alexandria, NSW: Australian Catholic Social Justice Council.

Chapman, A. and B. Spong. 2003. *Religion & Reconciliation in South Africa*. West Conshohocken, PA: Templeton Foundation Press.

Cloete, A. 2015. 'Youth Unemployment in South Africa. A Theological Reflection through the Lens of Human Dignity.' *Missionalia* 43(3), 513–25.

Costandius, E., I. Nell, N. Alexander, M. McKay, M. Blackie, R. Malgas and E. Setati. 2018. '#FeesMustFall and Decolonising the Curriculum: Stellenbosch University Students' and Lecturers' Reactions.' *South African Journal of Higher Education* 32(2), 65–85.

Cubizolles, S. 2011. 'Marketing Identity and Place: The Case of the Stellenbosch Kayamandi Economic Corridor before the 2010 World Cup in South Africa.' *Journal of Sport & Tourism* 16(1), 33–53.

Daye, R. 2012. *Political Forgiveness: Lessons from South Africa*. Eugene: Wipf & Stock Publishers.

Duncan, N. 2003. '"Race" Talk: Discourses on "Race" and Racial Difference.' *International Journal of Intercultural Relations* 27(2), 135–56.

Ebr-Vally, R. 2001. 'Diversity in Imagined Umma,' in A. Zegeye, ed., *Social Identities in the New South* Africa, *vol. 1.* Cape Town: Maroelana Kwela Books, 269–300.

Elkington, R. 2011. *Transformation: Race, Prejudice and Forgiveness in the New South Africa.* New York: Lulu.com.

Forster, D. A. 2018. *Translation and the Politics of Forgiveness in South Africa? What Black Christians Believe and White Christians Don't Understand.* In Stellenbosch: Stellenbosch University Society for Ricoeur Studies, Stellenbosch University, 1–13.

Forster, D. A. 2019a. *The (Im)possibility of Forgiveness: An Empirical Intercultural Bible Reading of Matthew 18.15-35.* Eugene, OR: Wipf and Stock Publishers.

Forster, D. A. 2019b. 'A Social Imagination of Forgiveness.' *Journal of Empirical Theology* 1(32), 70–88.

Gebrekidan, S. and N. Onishi. 2019. 'In South Africa's Fabled Wine Country, White and Black Battle Over Land.' *The New York Times.* 9 March [Online]. https://www.nytimes.com/2019/03/09/world/africa/stellenbosch-south-africa.html, accessed 15 April 2020.

General Household Survey 2013. 2014. (Statistical Information 1). Pretoria, South Africa: Statistics South Africa [Online]. http://www.statssa.gov.za/publications/P0318/P03182013.pdf, accessed 11 June 2015.

Gobodo-Madikizela, P. and C. Van der Merwe. 2009. *Memory, Narrative and Forgiveness: Perspectives on the Unfinished Journeys of the Past.* Newcastle upon Tyne: Scholars Publishing.

Goldin, I. 2014. 'The Reconstitution of Coloured Identity in the Western Cape,' in S. Marks and S. Trapido, eds., *The Politics of Race, Class and Nationalism in Twentieth Century South Africa.* New York: Routledge, 156–81.

Graham, L. and Mlatsheni, C. 2015. 'Youth Unemployment in South Africa: Understanding the Challenge and Working on Solutions,' in A. De Lannoy, S. Swartz, L. Lake and C. Smith, eds., *South African Child Gauge.* Rondebosch: UCT, 51–9.

Grassow, L. and C. Le Bruyns. 2017. 'Embodying Human Rights in #FeesMustFall? Contributions from an Indecent Theology.' *HTS Theological Studies* 73(3), 1–9.

Hammett, D. 2010. 'Ongoing Contestations: The Use of Racial Signifiers in Post-apartheid South Africa.' *Social Identities* 16(2), 247–60.

Hendrich, G. 2006. 'Die dinamika van Blank en Bruin verhoudinge op Stellenbosch (1920–1945).' Stellenbosch: University of Stellenbosch (Doctoral Dissertation).

Hendriks, J. and J. Erasmus. 2005. 'Religion in South Africa: 2001 Population Census Data.' *Journal of Theology for Southern Africa* 121, 88–111.

Hofmeyr, J. H. and R. Govender. 2015. *SA Reconciliation Barometer 2015: National Reconciliation, Race Relations, and Social Inclusion. Cape Town: Institute for Justice and Reconciliation* [Online]. http://www.ijr.org.za/uploads/IJR_SARB_2015_WEB_002.pdf

Jansen, J. 2015. *Leading for Change: Race, Intimacy and Leadership on Divided University Campuses*. London: Routledge.

John, S. F., C. J. Kaunda and N. C. Madlala. 2015. 'Contesting the "Born Free" Identity: A Postcolonial Perspective on Mzansi Stories.' *Alternation* 14, 106–25.

Jurgens, L. 2018. 'Africa in Fact: Culture.' *The Journal of Good Governance Africa* 47.

Krige, M.U. 1998. 'Determinants of Undernutrition in One to Two Year Old Children Residing in Historically Black and Coloured Areas in Stellenbosch.' Stellenbosch: Stellenbosch University (Doctoral Dissertation).

Kotzé, H. 2016. 'Shared Values in South Africa? A Selection of Value Orientations in the Field of Personal Ethics.' *Scriptura* 75, 437–48.

Kotzé, H. and C. Garcia-Rivero. 2017. 'Institutions, Crises, and Political Confidence in Seven Contemporary Democracies. An Elite–Mass Analysis.' *Journal of Public Affairs* 17(1–2), 1–17.

Kotze, J. S. and G. Prevost. 2015. Born Free – An Assessment of Political Identity Formation and Party Support of South Africa's First Post-apartheid Generation. *Africa Insight* 44(4), 142–68.

Krog, A. 2010. *Country of My Skull*. New York: Random House.

Lee, J. 2018. 'Hope Has Two Daughters: The Intersections of Faith and Activism for Christian Fallists in South Africa.' Virginia, Eastern Mennonite University (Masters Dissertation).

Lewis, J. 2003. 'Design Issues,' in J. Ritchie and J. Lewis, J., eds., *Qualitative Research Practice: A Guide for Social Science Students and Researchers*. London: SAGE Publications, 45–76.

Lugo, L. and A. Cooperman. 2010. *Tolerance and Tension: Islam and Christianity in Sub-Saharan Africa*. Washington, DC: Pew Research Center, 1–147.

Malila, V. 2013. 'Born Free without a Cause? Young and Mediated.' *Rhodes Journalism Review* 33, 4–7.

Manamela, B. 2015. 'Reflections on Youth,' in A. De Lannoy, S. Swartz, L. Lake and C. Smith, eds., *South African Child Gauge*. Rondebosch, Cape Town: Children's Institute, University of Cape Town, 8.

Mandela, N. 1995. *Long Walk to Freedom: The Autobiography of Nelson Mandela*. 1st Paperback edn. Boston, MA: Little, Brown and Company.

Mandela, N. 2012. *Notes to the Future: Words of Wisdom*. New York: Simon and Schuster.

Mattes, R. 2012. 'The "Born Frees": The Prospects for Generational Change in Post-Apartheid South Africa.' *Australian Journal of Political Science* 47(1), 133–53.

Mawuko-Yevugah, L. C. and P. Ugor. 2015. *African Youth Cultures in a Globalized World: Challenges, Agency and Resistance*. New York: Ashgate Publishing.

Meiring, R. 2017. 'A Case Study of Women's Households, Sanitation and Care in Zwelitsha, an Informal Settlement Section in Stellenbosch Municipality.' Stellenbosch: Stellenbosch University (Doctoral Dissertation).

Mtshiselwa, N. 2015. 'The Emergence of the Black Methodist Consultation and Its Possible Prophetic Voice in Post-apartheid South Africa: Original Research.' *HTS: Theological Studies* 71(3), 1–9.

Nwadeyi, L. 2019. *Our #storiesmatter - Lovelyn Nwadeyi*. Stellenbosch University [Online]. https://www.youtube.com/watch?v=KKO7CsOa03o, accessed 16 January 2020.

Robertson, C. A. and C. A. Du Plessis. 2015. 'Leadership Development for Technical and Vocational Education and Training College Leaders in South Africa: A Post-graduate Curriculum Framework.' Stellenbosch: Stellenbosch University (Doctoral Dissertation).

Robyn, J. B. 1998. 'n Ondersoek na en kategorisering van huiswinkels en die standaardvoorwaardes vir huiswinkels wat binne die munisipale gebied van Stellenbosch geld.' Stellenbosch: Stellenbosch University (Doctoral Dissertation).

Schoeman, W. J. 2017. 'South African Religious Demography: The 2013 General Household Survey.' *HTS Teologiese Studies/Theological Studies* 73(2), 1–7.

Simmons, C. 2008. 'A Profile of the Fatal Injury Mortalities and Suicides among Children and Youth in the Stellenbosch District.' Stellenbosch: Stellenbosch University (Doctoral Dissertation).

Smith, G. T. 2017. 'Inter-generationality and Spiritual Formation in Christian Community.' *Journal of Spiritual Formation and Soul Care* 10(2), 182–93.

Snape, D. and L. Spencer. 2003. 'The Foundations of Qualitative Research,' in J. Ritchie and J. Lewis, eds., *Qualitative Research Practice: A Guide for Social Science Students and Researchers*. London: SAGE Publications, 1–23.

Streaty Wimberly, A. E. and E. L. Parker. Eds. 2002. *In Search of Wisdom: Faith Formation in the Black Church*. Nashville: Abingdon Press.

Swilling, M., B. Sebitosi and R. Loots. Eds. 2012. *Sustainable Stellenbosch:Opening Dialogues*. Stellenbosch: African Sun Media.

Thesnaar, C. 2008. 'Restorative Justice as a Key for Healing Communities.' *Religion and Theology* 15(1), 53–73.

Thesnaar, C. 2013. 'Reformed Churches Struggle for Justice: Lessons learnt from Their Submissions before the TRC.' *NGTT Is Now Stellenbosch Theological Journal* (STJ) 54(3–4), 1–13.

Tutu, D. 2012. *No Future without Forgiveness*. New York: Random House.

Villa-Vicencio, C. and F. du Toit. 2006. *Truth & Reconciliation in South Africa: 10 Years on*. Cape Town: New Africa Books.

Vosloo, R. 2012. 'Memory, History, and Justice: In Search of Conceptual Clarity' [Online]. http://scholar.sun.ac.za/handle/10019.1/85275, accessed 25 August 2015.

Vosloo, R. 2015. 'Between the Prose of Justice and the Poetics of Love? Reading Ricœur on Mutual Recognition in the Light of Harmful Strategies of "Othering."' *Études Ricoeuriennes/Ricoeur Studies* 6(2), 105–17.

Waal, C. S. V. der. 2014. *Winelands, Wealth and Work: Transformations in the Dwars River Valley, Stellenbosch*. Pietermaritzburg: University of KwaZulu-Natal Press.

Weber, S. 2015. 'A Reflection on the Youth Culture within the Reformed Church,' in N. Nel and Z. Van Der Westhuizen, eds., *Skokkend Positief: Insigte vanuit nuwe navorsing oor aktiewe Afrikaanse kerkjeug*. Bybel–Media.

Weber, S. 2017. 'Decolonising Youth Ministry Models? Challenges and Opportunities in Africa.' *HTS Teologiese Studies/Theological Studies* 73(4), a4796. https://doi.org/10.4102/hts.v73i4.4796

Weber, S. 2020. 'The Necessity of Intergenerational Dialogue on Social Justice within the South African church (unpublished).'

Winter, S. and L. T. Burchert. 2015. *Value Change in Post-apartheid South Africa. South Africa*: Konrad-Adenauer-Stiftung e.V. [Online]. http://www.kas.de/wf/doc/kas_41566-1522-2-30.pdf?150609093459

Yin, R. K. 2009. *Case Study Research: Design and Methods*. 4th edition. Los Angeles: Sage.

Chapter 12

Agi, S. P. I. 2008. 'Religion and the Consolidation of Democracy in Nigeria,' in O. E. Uya, ed., *Civil Society and the Consolidation of Democracy in Nigeria*. Ibadan: Daybis, 123–38.

Amanze, J. N. 1994. *Botswana Handbook of Churches: A Handbook of Churches, Ecumenical Organisations, Theological Institutions and Other World Religions in Botswana*. Gaborone: Pula Press.

Botswana Public Officers Pension Fund (BPOPF). 2017. FAQ's. Gaborone: BPOPF. http://www.bpopf.co.bw/faq-s, accessed 9 November 2018.

Butler, R. N. 1980. 'Ageism: A Foreword.' *Journal of Social Issues* 36(2), 8–11.

Casson, Mark C., Marina Della Giusta and Uma S. Kambhampati. 1983. 'Formal and Informal Institutions and Development.' *World Development* 38(2), 137–41.

Clausen, F., E. Sandberg, B. Ingstad and P. Hjortdahl. 2000. 'Morbidity and Health Care Utilisation among Elderly People in Mmankgodi Village, Botswana,' *Journal of Epidemiology and Community Health* 54(1), 58–63.

Clinebell, H. J. 1984. *Basic Types of Pastoral Care and Counseling: Resources for the Ministry of Healing and Growth*. Nashville: Abingdon Press.

Cook, J. 2011. 'The Socioeconomic Contribution of Older People in the UK.' *Working Older People* 15(4), 141–6.

Davis, B. 2003. *Choosing a Poverty Mapping Method*. Rome, Italy: FAO.

Endfield, G. H. and D. J. Nash. 2007. 'A Good Site for Health: Missionaries and the Pathological Geography of Central Southern Africa.' *Singapore Journal of Tropical Geography* 28, 142–57.

Fombad, C. M. 2004. 'The Constitutional Protection against Discrimination in Botswana.' *International and Comparative Law Quarterly* 53(1), 139–70.

Gillett, R. W. 2005. *The New Globalization: Reclaiming the Lost Ground of Our Christian Social Tradition*. Cleveland: The Pilgrim Press.

Gunn, T. J. 2003. 'The Complexity of Religion and the Definition of "Religion" in International Law.' *Harvard Human Rights Journal* 16, 189–215.

Jennings, M. 2002. 'This Mysterious and Intangible Enemy: Health and Disease amongst the Early UMCA Missionaries 1860–1918.' *Social History of Medicine*, 15(1), 65–87.

Johnson-Hill, J. 2008. *Ethics of Global Village: Moral Insights of Post 9–11 USA*. Grand Rapids: Pole Bridge.

Jones, L. 2005. *Encyclopedia of Religion*. Vol. 1. Detroit: Macmillan Reference USA, 325–7. Gale Virtual Reference Library.

Help Age International. 2006. Ageways. Issue 67 on *older citizens monitoring*, June.

Humanitarian Action Report. 2006, UNICEF.

Kalu, O. U. 2010. 'Harsh Flutes: The Religious Dimension of the Legitimacy Crisis in Nigeria, 1993–1998,' in W. Kalu, N. Wariboko and T. Falola, eds., *Religions in Africa: Conflicts, Politics and Social Ethics: The Collected Essays of Ogbu Uke Kalu*, Vol. 3. Trenton, NJ: Africa World Press, 31–64.

Lartey, E. Y. 2003. *In Living Color: An Intercultural Approach to Pastoral Care and Counseling*. London: Jessica Kingsley Publishers.

Lartey, E. Y. 2006. *Practical Theology in an Intercultural World*. Werrington, Peterborough: Epsworth.

Lee, C. et al. 2005. 'Cohort Profile: The Australian Longitudinal Study on Women's Health.' *International Journal of Epidemiology* 34(5), 987–91. DOI: http://dx.doi.org/10.1093/ije/dyi098 PMID: 15894591

Lindbeck, G. A. 1984. *Nature of Doctrine*. Louisville, KY: Westminster John Knox Press.

Little, D. 1993. 'Religion – Catalyst or Impediment to International Law? The Case of Hugo Grotius.' *Proceedings of the Annual Meeting (American Society of International Law)*, 87, 322–7. Retrieved 25 April 2020, from www.jstor.org/stable/25658740.

Madigele, T. 2019. 'Pastoral Care to the Elderly Caretakers of AIDS Orphans: An Integrated Pastoral Theological Approach.' University of Botswana (Unpublished Doctoral Thesis).

Maluleke, T. S. 2010. 'A Postcolonial South African Church: Problems and Promises,' in D. B. Stinton, ed., *African Theology on the Way: Current Conversations*. London: SPCK, 150–60.

Maruapula, S. and K. Chapman-Novakofski. 2007. 'Health and Dietary Patterns of the Elderly in Botswana.' *Journal of Nutrition Education and Behavior* 39(6), 311–19.

Matshalaga, N. 2004. *Grandmothers and Orphan Care in Zimbabwe*. Harare, Zimbabwe: SAFAIDS.

Mbiti, J. S. 1999. *African Religions and Philosophy*. 2nd edn. Oxford: Heinemann.

Msomi, V. V. 2008. *Ubuntu Contextual African Pastoral Care and Counselling*. Pretoria: CB Powell Bible Centre, Unisa.

Mudavanhu, D. 2008. 'The Psychosocial Impact on Rural Grandmothers Caring for Their Grandchildren Orphaned by HIV/AIDS.' University of South Africa, South Africa (Masters Dissertation. Pretoria).

Nkomazana, F. 1998. 'Livingstone's Ideas of Christianity, Commerce and Civilization.' *Pula: Botswana Journal of African Studies* 12(1 & 2), 44–57.

Nkomazana, F. and S. Setume 2015. 'Missionary Colonial Mentality and the Expansion of Christianity in Bechuanaland Protectorate, 1800 to 1900.' *Journal for the Study of Religion*, 29(2), 29–55.

Ogunbado, A. F. 2012. 'Impacts of Colonialism on Religions: An Experience of South-western Nigeria.' *Journal of Humanities and Social Science* 5(6), 51–7.

Onen, B. L. et al. 2019. 'Ageing, Frailty and Resilience in Botswana: Rapid Ageing, Rapid Change. Findings from a National Working Group Meeting and Literature Review.' *BMC Proceedings* 13, 8. https://doi.org/10.1186/s12919-019-0171-z

Patton, J. 1993. *Pastoral Care in Context*. Louisville, KT: West Minster John Knox Press.

Patton, J., 2005. *Pastoral Care in Context: An Introduction to Pastoral Care*. West Minster John Knox Press.

Pears, A. 2010. *Doing Contextual Theology*. Abingdon: Routledge.

Plecher, H. 2020. Youth Unemployment Rate in Botswana in 2019. http://www.statistica.com>International>Botswana, accessed 9 November 2020.

Prill, T. 2019. Ambassadors of Christ or Agents of Colonialism?: Protestant Missionaries in Africa and Their Critics. *The Scottish Bulletin of Evangelical Theology*, 37(1), 81–99.

Public Holidays Act (Cap 03:07) and Government Notice 506 of 2007. In 2008, the following Christian days will be observed as public holidays: Good Friday 21 March; Easter Monday 24 March and Ascension Day 1 May.

Republic of Botswana. 2001. Botswana Population and Housing Census, 2001. Gaborone: Government Printer.

Rogers, M. and M. E. Konieczny. 2018. 'Does Religion Always Help the Poor? Variations in Religion and Social Class in the West and Societies in the Global South.' *Palgrave Communications* 4, 73. https://doi.org/10.1057/s41599-018-0135-3

Ruele, M. 2009. 'Calvinism and the Socio-economic Politics of Botswana Liberal Democracy.' *Studia Historiae Ecclesiastica* 35(2), 185–203.

Ruele, M. 2016. 'Relating the Teachings of the Gospel to Social Justice in Africa: The Case of Botswana.' *Botswana Notes and Records* 48, 240–9.

Shaibu, S. 2013. 'Experiences of Grandmothers Caring for Orphan Grandchildren in Botswana.' *Journal of Nursing Scholarship* 45(4), 363–70.

Shaibu, S. and M. I. Wallhagen. 2002. 'Family Caregiving of the Elderly in Botswana: Boundaries of Culturally Acceptable Options and Resources.' *Journal of Cross-Cultural Gerontology* 17(2), 139–54.

Sundkler, B. and C. Steed 2000. *A History of the Church in Africa*. Cambridge and New York: Cambridge University Press.

Tlou, S. D. 1994. 'The Elderly and Youths' Perceptions of Each Other,' in F. Bruun, Y. Coombes and M. Mugabe, eds., *The Situation of the Elderly in Botswana*. Gaborone: University of Botswana, 43–52.

Togarasei, L. 2005. 'Modern Pentecostalism as an Urban Phenomenon: The Case of the Family of God Church in Zimbabwe.' *Exchange: Journal of Missiological and Ecumenical Studies* 34(4), 349–75.

Togarasei, L. 2011. 'The Pentecostal Gospel of Prosperity in African Contexts of Poverty.' *Exchange* 30, 336–50.

Togarasei, L. 2013. 'African Gospreneurship: Assessing the Possible Contribution of the Gospel of Prosperity to Entrepreneurship in Light of Jesus' Teaching on Earthly Possessions,' in H. Kroesbergen, ed., *Search of Health and Wealth: The Prosperity Gospel in African, Reformed Perspective*. Wellington: CLF, 113–28.

Togarasei, L. 2016. 'The Place and Challenges of Modern Pentecostal Christianity in Botswana.' *Botswana Notes and Records: A Special Issue on Humanities at UB and Botswana's 50 Years of Independence* 48(1), 229–39.

Tsele, M. 2001. 'The Role of the Christian Faith in Development,' in D. Belshaw, R. Calderisi and C. Sandugden, eds., *Faith in Development: Partnership between the World Bank and the Churches of Africa*. Oxford: Regnum, 203–18.

United Nations Population Fund. 2018. Policy Brief: Maximising the Demographic Dividend in Botswana. Gaborone: UNFPA.

Walls, A. F. 1987. 'The Legacy of David Livingstone.' *International Bulletin of Missionary Research* 11(3), 12–29.

The World Bank. FAQs: Global Poverty Line Update: World Bank Group; 2015. http://www.worldbank.org/en/topic/poverty/brief/global-poverty-line-faq, accessed 27 November 2018.

Chapter 13

Anderson, Allan. 1992. *Bazalwane: African Pentecostals in South Africa*. Pretoria: University of South Africa.

Anderson, Allan. 2002. 'The Newer Pentecostal and Charismatic Churches: The Shape of Future Christianity in Africa?' *Pneuma* 24(2), 167–84.

Anderson, Allan. 2005. 'New African Initiated Pentecostalism and Charismatics in South Africa.' *Journal of Religion in Africa* 35(1), 66–92.

Anderson, Allan. 2018. *Spirit-filled World: Religious Dis/continuity in African Pentecostalism*. London: Palgrave Macmillan.

Akanbi, Solomon O. and Jaco Beyers. 2017. 'The Church as a Catalyst for Transformation in the Society.' *HTS Theological Studies* 73(4), 1–8.

Bafford, Douglas. 2019. 'The Prosperity Gospel and an Unprosperous Reality in Post-apartheid South Africa: Conservative Evangelical Responses to Charismatic Christianity.' https://wiser.wits.ac.za/content/prosperity-gospel-and-unprosperous-reality-post-apartheid-south-africa-conservative

Banda, Collium. 2019. 'Redefining Religion? A Critical Christian Reflection on CRL Rights Commission's Proposal to Regulate Religion in South Africa.' *Verbum et Ecclesia* 40(1), 1–11.

Banda, Collium. 2020. 'Mediating God's Relationality? A Trinitarian Perichoretic Critique of the Reliance on Anointed Objects in African Neo-Pentecostalism.' *HTS Teologiese Studies/Theological Studies* 76(1), 1–10

Chitando, Ezra and Kudzai Biri. 2016. 'Walter Magaya's Prophetic Healing and Deliverance (PHD) Ministries and Pentecostalism in Zimbabwe: A Preliminary Study with Particular Reference to Ecumenism.' *Studia Historiae Ecclesiasticae* 42(2), 72–85.

The citizen. 2016. 'Millions Later, Still No Church Building – Bushiri Congregants.' Retrieved 28 November 2016. https://citizen.co.za/news/south-africa/1359237/millions-later-still-no-church-building-bushiri-congregants/

De Witte, Marleen 2018. 'Buy the Future: Charismatic Pentecostalism and African Liberation in a Neoliberal World,' in Adeshina Afolayan et al., eds., *Pentecostalism and Politics in Africa*. Cham: Palgrave Macmillan, 65–85.

Dube, Bekithemba. 2019. 'Conundrum of Religious Mafia and Legislation in South Africa: When Does Religion Become a National Threat? Reference to the Seven Angels Ministry.' *Verbum et Ecclesia* 40(1), 1–8.

Dube, Bekithemba. 2020. '"Go and Prophesy in Your Own Land": Foreign Prophets and Popularism in South Africa. Evoking the Need of Jonathanic Theology for Peaceful Resolution of Difference.' *Religions* 11(1), 42. https://doi.org/10.3390/rel11010042

Du Toit, Nadine F. Bowers and Grace Nkomo. 2014. 'The Ongoing Challenge of Restorative Justice in South Africa: How and Why Wealthy Suburban Congregations Are Responding to Poverty and Inequality.' *HTS Teologiese Studies/Theological Studies* 70(2), 1–8.

EntertainmentSA. 2017. 'Exclusive: Prophet Shepherd Bushiris life and Net Worth.' Retrieved on 17 March 2017. https://www.entertainmentsa.co.za/exclusive-prophet-shepherd-bushiris-life-and-net-worth/

Gabaitse, Rosinah Mmannana. 2015. 'Pentecostal Hermeneutics and the Marginalisation of Women.' *Scriptura* 114(1), 1–12.

Gelb, Stephen. 2003. 'Inequality in South Africa: Nature, Causes and Responses. Johannesburg: Edge Institute.' http://www.tips.org.za/files/Gelb_Inequality_in_SouthAfrica.pdf

IOL. 2017. 'Prophet Shocks with Luxury Car for Daughter.' Retrieved on 17 December 2017. https://www.iol.co.za/pretoria-news/prophet-shocks-with-luxury-car-for-daughter-6-12512430

Kangwa, Jonathan. 2016. 'The Role of the Theology of Retribution in the Growth of Pentecostal-Charismatic Churches in Africa.' *Verbum et Ecclesia* 37(1), 1–9.

Kaunda, Chammah. 2015, 'Towards Pentecopolitanism: New African Pentecostalism and Social Cohesion in South Africa.' *African Journal on Conflict Resolution* 15(3), 111–34.

Kgatle, Mookgo S. 2020. 'New Paradigms of Pneumatological Ecclesiology Brought about by New Prophetic Churches within South African Pentecostalism.' *Verbum et Ecclesia* 41(1), 1–6.

Kgatle, Solomon. 2019. *The Fourth Pentecostal Wave in South Africa: A Critical Engagement.* London: Routledge.

Kusch, Celena. 2016. *Literary Analysis: The Basics.* Abingdon: Routledge.

Lephakga, Tshepo. 2017. 'Colonial Institutionalisation of Poverty among Blacks in South Africa.' *Studia Historiae Ecclesiasticae* 43(2), 1–15.

Masango, Maake J. 2014. 'An Economic System that Crushes the Poor.' *HTS Theological Studies* 70(1), 1–5.

Mashau, Derrick. T. 2013. 'Ministering Effectively in the Context of Pentecostalism in Africa: A Reformed Missional Reflection.' *In die Skriflig* 47(1), 10–17.

Mashau, Thinandavha D. and Mookgo S. Kgatle. 2019. 'Prosperity Gospel and the Culture of Greed in Post-Colonial Africa: Constructing an Alternative African Christian Theology of Ubuntu.' *Verbum et Ecclesia* 40(1), 1–8.

Molobi, Victor. 2016. 'Dealing with Poverty, Health and Maternal Child Survival: The Organisation of African Independent Churches perspective.' *Verbum et Ecclesia* 37(1), 1–8.

Moodley, Kogila and Heribert Adam. 2000. 'Race and Nation in Post-apartheid South Africa.' *Current Sociology* 48(3), 51–69.

Ncube, Mthuli, Abebe Shimeles and Audrey Verdier-Chouchane. 2014. 'South Africa's Quest for Inclusive Development,' in Bruce Currie-Alder et al., eds., *International Development: Ideas, Experiences, Prospects.* Oxford Scholarship Online. DOI:10.1093/acprof:oso/9780199671656.001.0001

Omenyo, Cephas N. and Wonderful Adjei Arthur. 2013. 'The Bible Says! Neo-Prophetic Hermeneutics in Africa.' *Studies in World Christianity* 19(1), 50–70.

Quayesi-Amakye, Joseph. 2015. 'Prophetism in Ghana's New Prophetic Churches.' *Journal of the European Pentecostal Theological Association* 35(2), 162–73.

Rabboni Centre Ministries. 2017. 'Rabboni Centre Ministries/Home/Facebook,' viewed 15 May 2017. https://www.facebook.com/rabboniministries/

Ramantswana, Hulisani. 2019. 'Prophets Praying for, or Preying on People's Faith: A Reflection on Prophetic Ministry in the South African Context.' *die Skriflig/In Luce Verbi* 53(4), 1–8.

Resane, Kelebogile T. 2018. 'Pentecostals and Apartheid: Has the Wheel Turned around since 1994?' *In die Skriflig* 52(1), 1–8.

Revelator. 2017. *The Prophetic Dimension: A Divine Revelation of How to Accurately Prophesy and Operate in the Prophetic Realm of God.* Sandton, South Africa: Global Destiny House.

Statistics South Africa. 2019. 'Inequality Trends in South Africa: A Multidimensional Diagnostic of Inequality,' Report No. 03- 10-19. Retrieved http://www.statssa.gov.za/?p=12744

Timeslive. 2019. 'There Are Prophets and then There Are Profits - Just Ask Pastor Alph Lukau VIP Escort, Fast Cars and Yes, Even a Zuma Connection,' 26 February 2019. https://www.timeslive.co.za/news/south-africa/2019-02-26-there-are-prophets-and-then-there-are-profits-just-ask-alph/

Timeslive. 2019. '"Resurrection Pastor" Raises Fury with Sandton Home Renovations.' https://www.timeslive.co.za/sunday-times/news/2019-03-10-resurrection-pastor-raises-fury-with-sandton-home-renovations/, 10 March 2019.

Tsekpoe, Christian. 2019. 'Contemporary Prophetic and Deliverance Ministry Challenges in Africa.' *Transformation* 36(4), 280–91.

Vengeyi, Obvious. 2013. 'Zimbabwean Pentecostal Prophets,' in Ezra Chitando, Masiiwa Ragies Gunda and Joachim Kügler, eds., *Prophets, Profits and the Bible in Zimbabwe*. Bamberg: University of Bamberg Press, 29–54.

Zimbardo, Philip G. 1999. 'Discontinuity Theory: Cognitive and Social Searches for Rationality and Normality—May Lead to Madness,' in Mark P. Zanna ed., *Advances in Experimental Social Psychology*. Vol. 31 Amsterdam: Elsevier, 345–486.

Chapter 14

Asamoah-Gyadu, K. 2013. *Contemporary Pentecostal Christianity: Interpretations from an African Context*. Eugene, OR: Wipf and Stock Publishers.

Berger, P. 2008. 'You Can Do It! Two Cheers for the Prosperity Gospel.' *Books and Culture* 14(5).

Bayart, J. F. 1993. *The State in Africa: The Politics of the Belly*. London: Longman.

Biri, K. 2012. The Silent Echoing Voice: Aspects of Zimbabwean Pentecostalism and the Quest for Power, Healing and Miracles. http://www.unir.unisa.ac.za/handle/10500/6609, accessed 21 June 2022.

Chabal, P. and J. P. Daloz. 1999. *Africa Works: Disorder as Political Instrument*. Oxford: James Currey, for the International African Institute.

Chitando, E., M. R. Gunda and L. Togarasei. Eds. 2020. *Religion and Development in Africa*. Bamberg: University of Bamberg Press.

Comaroff, J. and J. L. Comaroff. 2000. 'Millennial Capitalism: First Thoughts on the Second Coming.' *Public Culture* 12, 291–343.

Dashwood, H. S. 2002. 'Inequality, Leadership, and the Crisis in Zimbabwe.' *International Journal* 57(2), 209–26.

Geschiere, P. 1997. *The Modernity of Witchcraft: Politics and the Occult in Postcolonial Africa*. Charlottesville, VA: University of Virginia Press.

Gukurume, S. 2015. Livelihood 'Resilience in a Hyperinflationary Environment: Experiences of People Engaging in Money-burning (kubhena mari) Transactions in Harare, Zimbabwe.' *Social Dynamics*, 41(2): 219–34.

Gukurume, S. 2017. 'Singing Positivity: Prosperity Gospel in the Musical Discourse of Popular Youth Hip-Hop Gospel in Zimbabwe.' *Muziki: Journal of Music Research in Africa* 14(2), 36–54.

Gukurume, S. 2018. 'New Pentecostal Churches, Politics and the Everyday Life of University Students at the University of Zimbabwe.' University of Cape Town, South Africa (PhD Thesis).

Gukurume, S. 2020. 'Investing in the Future Generation New Pentecostal Charismatic Churches in Harare, Zimbabwe', in P. Öhlmann, W. Gräb and M. L. Frost, eds., *African Initiated Christianity and the Decolonisation of Development: Sustainable Development in Pentecostal and Independent Churches*. London: Routledge, 267–83.

Gukurume, S. 2022. '"You Are Blessed to Be a Blessing": Pentecostal-Charismatic Churches and the Politics of Redistribution in Harare'. *Religion and Development*, 1(1): 25–43.

Gukurume, S. and J. Taru 2021. '"We Are Soldiers in God's Army": Spiritual Warfare and Adoption of Military trope in Pentecostal Charismatic Churches in Southern Africa'. *Journal of Religion in Africa*, 50: 1–22.

Griera, M. and A. Clot-Garrell. 2015. 'Banal Is Not Trivial: Visibility, Recognition, and Inequalities between Religious Groups in Prison'. *Journal of Contemporary Religion* 30(1), 23–37.

Haynes, N. 2012. 'Pentecostalism and the Morality of Money: Prosperity, Inequality and Religious Sociality on the Zambian Copperbelt'. *Journal of the Royal Anthropological Institute* 18(1), 123–39.

Haynes, N. 2013. 'On the Potential and Problems of Pentecostal Exchange'. *American Anthropologist* 115(1), 85–95.

Kanji, N. and Jazdowka, N. 1993. 'Structural Adjustment and Women in Zimbabwe'. *Review of African Political Economy*, 20 (56), 11–26.

Koehersen, J. 2018. 'Religious Tastes and Styles as Markers of Class Belonging: A Bourdieuian Perspective on Pentecostalism in South America', *Sociology* 52(6), 1237–1253.

Manero, A. 2017. 'Income Inequality within Smallholder Irrigation Schemes in Sub-Saharan Africa'. *International Journal of Water Resources Development*, 33(5), 770–87.

Marshall, R. 1995. '"God Is Not a Democrat": Pentecostalism and Democratisation in Nigeria', in P. Gifford, ed., *The Christian Churches and the Democratisation of Africa*. New York: Brill, 239–60.

Maxwell, D. 1998. 'Delivered from the Spirit of Poverty? Pentecostalism, Prosperity and Modernity in Zimbabwe'. *Journal of Religion in Africa* 28(3), 350–73.

McCauley, J. F. 2012. 'Africa's New Big Man Rule? Pentecostalism and Patronage in Ghana'. *African Affairs* 112(446), 1–21.

Miller, D. E. and T. Yamamori. 2007. Global Pentecostalism: The New Face of Christian Social Engagement. California: University of California Press.

Norris, P. and R. Inglehart. 2004. *Sacred and Secular: Religion and Politics Worldwide*. Cambridge: Cambridge University Press.

Öhlmann, P., W. Gräb and L. Frost. 2020. *African Initiated Christianity and the Decolonisation of Development: Sustainable Development in Pentecostal and Independent Churches*. London: Routledge.

Pfeiffer, J. 2002. 'African Independent Churches in Mozambique: Healing the Afflictions of Inequality'. *Medical Anthropology Quarterly* 16(2), 176–99.

Robbins, J. 2004. 'The Globalisation of Pentecostal and Charismatic Christianity'. *Annual Review of Anthropology* 33, 117–43.

Robbins, J. 2009. 'Pentecostal Networks and the Spirit of Globalization: On the Social Productivity of Ritual Forms.' Social Analysis, 53(1): 55–66.

Schnabel, L. 2020. 'Religion across Axes of Inequality in the United States: Belonging, Behaving, and Believing at the Intersections of Gender, Race, Class, and Sexuality.' *Religions*, 11(296): 1–27.

Smith, D. J. 2001. 'The Arrow of God: Pentecostalism, Inequality and the Supernatural in South Eastern Nigeria.' *Africa* 71(4), 587–613.

Taru, J. and Settler, F. 2015. 'Patterns of Consumption and Materialism among Zimbabwean Christians: A Tale of Two Indigenous Churches.' *Journal for the Study of Religion*, 28(2): 113–37.

Taru, J. 2020. 'Pentecostal Charismatic Christianity and the Management of Precarity in Postcolonial Zimbabwe,' in P. Öhlmann, W. Gräb and L. Frost, eds., *African Initiated Christianity and the Decolonisation of Development: Sustainable Development in Pentecostal and Independent Churches*. London: Routledge, 284–302.

van de Kamp, Linda. 2011. 'Converting the Spirit Spouse: The Violent Transformation of the Pentecostal Female Body in Maputo, Mozambique.' *Ethnos*, 76(4), 510–33.

Van Dijk, R. 2009. 'Social Catapulting and the Spirit of Entrepreneurialism: Migrants, Private Initiative and the Pentecostal Ethic in Botswana,' in G. Huwelmeier, and K. Krause, eds., *Traveling Spirits: Migrants, Markets and Mobilities*. Routledge: New York.

Van Wyk, I. 2015. 'Prosperity and the Work of Luck in the Universal Church of the Kingdom of God, South Africa.' *Critical African Studies* 7(3), 262–79.

Weber, M. 2001[1904]. *The Protestant Ethic and the Spirit of Capitalism*. Oxford: Routledge.

Weber, M. 2001 [1940–5]. *The Protestant Ethic and the Spirit of Capitalism*. translated by Talcott Parsons. London: Routledge.

Chapter 15

Abbink, Jon. 2014. 'Religious Freedom and the Political Order: The Ethiopian "Secular State" and the Containment of Muslim Identity Politics.' *Journal of Eastern African Studies* 28(3), 346–65.

Chrisna, David. 2012. 'Kebra Nagast and Al-Najāshī: The Meaning and Use of Collective Memory in Christian-Muslim Political Discourse In Ethiopia.' *Journal of Interreligious Studies* 33, 5–23.

Erlich, Haggai. 2007. *Saudi Arabia and Ethiopia: Islam, Christianity, and Politics Entwined*. Boulder and London: Lynne Rienner Publishers.

Erlich, Haggai. 2009. 'The Grandchildren of Abraham,' in Svein Ege, Harald Aspen, Birhanu Teferra and Shiferaw Bekele, eds., *Proceedings of the 16th International Conference of Ethiopian Studies*. Trondheim: Norwegian University of Science and Technology, 457–62.

Erlich, Haggai. 2010. *Islam and Christianity in the Horn of Africa: Somali, Ethiopia and Sudan*. London: Lynne Reiner Publishers.

Henok, Nigussie. 2013. 'Audience Reception Analysis on "Jihadawi Harakat" Documentary Film Aamong Addis Ababa Communities.' Addis Ababa University.

Human Rights Watch. 2012, 2013. 'World Human Rights Report: Ethiopia.'

Hussein, Ahmed. 1992. 'The Historiography of Islam in Ethiopia.' *Journal of Islamic Studies* 31, 15–46.

Markakis, John. 1989. 'Nationalities and the State in Ethiopia.' *Ethnicity in World Politics* 11(4), 118–30.

Mukerrem, Miftah. 2015. 'The Muslims in Ethiopia Complex: The Trilogy of Discourse, Policy, and Identity.' *African Studies Quarterly* 16(1), 71–91.

Mukerrem, Miftah. 2020. 'Upgrading Religion in Ethiopia: PM Abiy's Experiment,' Ethiopia Center for Strategic Studies (ECS), Report.

Østebø, Terje. 2013. 'Islam and State Relations in Ethiopia: From Containment to the Production of a "Governmental Islam".' *Journal of American Academy of Religion* 81, 1029–60.

Østebø, Terje. 2014. 'Salafism, State Politics, and the Question of "Extremism" in Ethiopia.' *Comparative Islamic Studies* 8, 165–84.

Seifuddin, Adem. 1997. 'Islam, Christianity and Ethiopia's Foreign Policy.' *Journal of Muslim Minority Affairs* 17(1), 129–39.

Taddesse, Tamrat. 1968. 'Church and State in Ethiopia 1270–1527.' University of London.

Tibebe, Eshete. 2010. 'Evangelical Christians and Indirect Resistance to Religious Persecution in Ethiopia.' *The Review of Faith & International Affairs* 8(1), 13–21.

Turner, Bryan. 2007. 'Managing Religions: State Responses to Religious Diversity.' *Contemporary Islam* 1, 123–37.

The US State Department. 2013, 2016. 'International Religious Freedom Report: Ethiopia.'

Index

Locators followed by "n." indicate endnotes